Joaquín Dicenta:
Spain's Forgotten Dramatist

Juan de la Cuesta
Hispanic Monographs

FOUNDING EDITOR
Tom Lathrop
University of Delaware

EDITOR
Alexander R. Selimov
University of Delaware

EDITORIAL BOARD
Samuel G. Armistead
University of California, Davis

Annette G. Cash
Georgia State University

Alan Deyermond
Queen Mary and Westfield College of the University of London

Daniel Eisenberg
Regents College

John E. Keller
University of Kentucky

Steven D. Kirby
Eastern Michigan University

Joel Rini
University of Virginia

Donna M. Rogers
Middlebury College

Russell P. Sebold
Real Academia Española

Noël Valis
Yale University

Amy Williamsen
University of Arizona

Joaquín Dicenta:
Spain's Forgotten Dramatist

LETICIA MCGRATH
Georgia Southern University

Juan de la Cuesta
Newark, Delaware

On the cover, a 1917 drawing by Tovar, from the Biblioteca Nacional de Madrid.

Cover design by Michael Bolan.

Copyright © 2004 by Juan de la Cuesta—Hispanic Monographs
270 Indian Road
Newark, Delaware 19711
(302) 453-8695
Fax: (302) 453-8601
www.JuandelaCuesta.com

MANUFACTURED IN THE UNITED STATES OF AMERICA

ISBN: 1-58871-062-9

To my husband, Michael J. McGrath.

Acknowledgments

I would like to express my most sincere gratitude to those who have supported me both intellectually and emotionally while researching and preparing this first comprehensive study of one of Spain's most intriguing dramatists.

I am deeply indebted to my dear friend and former professor Dr. Brian J. Dendle for not only being responsible for introducing me to Joaquín Dicenta's work, but also for being an invaluable mentor and role model as I strived to follow in his footsteps. In fact, the title of this book is a direct influence from one of Professor Dendle's books, *Spain's Forgotten Novelist: Armando Palacio Valdes (1853-1938)*. When I politely asked him if I could use his idea for a title, he humbly replied that he was flattered; truth be told, I consider myself privileged to have had the opportunity to work very closely with Professor Dendle over the years as I have greatly benefited from his remarkable knowledge, his quick wit, his sincere humility, and his endearing personality. Through his example I have learned firsthand what a true scholar embodies. I shall never forget the first time we met when he stunned me to silence with the question: "So, do you think Fortunata is in heaven or in hell?" made in reference to my work on a famous novel (*Fortunata y Jacinta*) by one of Professor Dendle's favorite authors, Benito Pérez Galdós.

I would also like to thank Dr. Margaret Jones and Dr. Joseph Jones, both of whom provided many ideas and suggestions during both the research and the writing phases of this endeavor. In addition, Dr. Aníbal Biglieri, Dr. Donald Buck, and Dr. Linda Glaze were very influential in their valuable advice and constructive criticism.

To my many friends who have laughed and cried with me along the way, I fully appreciate your emotional support through the years, especially given the many times you have each laughed at my expense, making me realize how important it is that your friends know your strengths as well as your weaknesses. In no particular order, I wish to thank the following: Candice Trollope, Heather Roberts, Heather Campbell-Speltz, Dr. Maritza Bell-Corrales, Virna Troillo, Wesley Shea Wells, Habib Zanzana, Angie Boggess, Denise Cribb, Tracey Tkachuk, Lory French, Kim Blackwell, Donnie Richards, Vicki Meade, and Virginia and David McGrath. Each of you has made a profound impact on my life.

To my incredible parents, Lionel and Joyce Lawrence, I would like to express how grateful I am that you have always pushed me to do my absolute best, proving to me that dedication and determination are the keys to success and that despite bumps in the road, one can choose to succeed. I pray that I am able to follow your example in order to instill the same confidence in my children as they grow to face exciting challenges in their lives.

And speaking of my children, I cannot forget to thank Matthew (4) and Luke (2) for taking long naps and understanding when "mommy had to work on her ka-weeter (computer)." And of course, in thanking them, I must not neglect to thank their daddy, my husband, the love of my life, Dr. Michael McGrath, to whom I dedicate this book, for his wit, his wisdom, his optimism, his love, his advice, his support, his constant encouragement, and most of all for his unfailing belief in me.

Table of Contents

Preface 11

1
The State of the Spanish Stage in Dicenta's Time 13

2
Life, Works, and Critical Reception of Joaquín Dicenta 24
    Life and Work 24
    Critical Reception 39

3
The Early Plays: 1888-1894 50
    El suicidio de Werther (February 23, 1888) 50
    La mejor ley (January 2, 1889) 55
    Los irresponsables (November 27, 1890) 60
    Honra y vida (April 16, 1891) 66
    Luciano (February 24, 1894) 72
    El duque de Gandía (March 10, 1894) 78
    Conclusions to Chapter Three 84

4
Dicenta's First Social Dramas: *Juan José* and *El señor feudal* 87
    Juan José (October 29, 1895) 87
    El señor feudal (December 2, 1896) 111
    Conclusions to Chapter Four 122

5
The Productive Years: 1898-1907 124
    Curro Vargas (December 10, 1898) 124
    La cortijera (March 2, 1900) 129
    El tío Gervasio (March 21, 1900) 135
    El león de bronce (April 30, 1900) 139
    Raimundo Lulio (May 1902) 144
    Aurora (June 1902) 147
    De tren a tren (November 29, 1902) 157

Pa mí que nieva (December 12, 1904) 161
Juan Francisco (December 22, 1904) 163
La conversión de Mañara (December 2, 1905) 169
El vals de las sombras (March 8, 1906) 172
Amor de artistas (May 14, 1906) 174
Marinera (February 11, 1907) 177
Conclusions to Chapter Five 179

6
Dicenta's Final Contributions: 1907-1916 182
Daniel (March 7, 1907) 182
Lorenza (December 12, 1907) 201
El crimen de ayer (February 18, 1908) 206
Los majos de plante (April 11, 1908) 212
Entre rocas (May 21, 1908) 214
Confesión (September 5, 1908) 215
Los tres maridos burlados (February 5, 1909) 218
Sobrevivirse (January 21, 1913) 221
El lobo (1914) 225
Overall Conclusions to Chapter Six 232

7
Conclusions 235

BIBLIOGRAPHY OF PRIMARY WORKS 243

BIBLIOGRAPHY 245

Preface

JOAQUÍN DICENTA Y BENEDICTO published thirty plays in his lifetime (1863-1917), beginning with *El suicidio de Werther* in 1888 and ending with *El Lobo* in 1913. The success of his most famous play, *Juan José* (1895), was both a blessing and a curse for Dicenta. It certainly brought him the fame that he had longed for, but it also placed upon him the stigma that he would never overcome, that of being Spain's first social dramatist. He was never able to live up to the hype that surrounded the premiere of *Juan José*, and consequently many of his noteworthy dramas were ignored. Dicenta was far more than a social dramatist whose only worthwhile piece is *Juan José*; he entertained audiences for years following that landmark piece. Dicenta enjoyed abundant success during his lifetime as a playwright, and he brought about significant change in the dynamics of the theater in late nineteenth- and early twentieth-century Spain. Dicenta's multifaceted talent has been unduly ignored since his death in 1917, and it is my contention that such a creative and noteworthy dramatist certainly deserves further study, acknowledging not only the plays for which he is most remembered but also his many lesser known dramas, that consistently have been ignored over the last century.

To date, no comprehensive study of the entirety of Dicenta's dramas has ever been published despite the fact that he played such an important role in the development of Spanish drama at the turn of the century. The only study attempted is that by Jaime Mas Ferrer, *Vida, teatro y mito de Joaquín Dicenta*, published in 1978, yet like many critics, Mas Ferrer explores only those dramas that treat the social question, keeping with the common thought that Dicenta's talent is only found in select few dramas that provide a social commentary.

In this study, I explore fully Dicenta's plays in the order of their first performance, illuminating his development as a playwright from his early neo-Romantic plays to his later social dramas, including the many *zarzuelas* that brought him great popularity on the Spanish stage. I present a chronological study including a brief plot summary and a critical analysis of Dicenta's technique and ideology of each play, including comments made by other critics, when available. I elucidate the development of Dicenta's ideology and the presence of recurring themes: art and the artist's world, church, marriage, divorce, free love, family, orphaned and illegitimate children, and the exploitation of the working class by the ruling class, among others. Through this study, it is my goal to demonstrate Dicenta's great talent and versatility not only in those dramas that treat the social question and for which he is most remembered, but also in his other lesser-known pieces that deserve further study.

1
The State of the Spanish Stage in Dicenta's Time

SPAIN HAS LONG BEEN influenced by her northern neighbors and their literary trends and ideas. As realism began to dominate European drama starting in the 1850's, Spain continued to be influenced by foreign thought. Realism, as it came to be known on the stage, represents the dramatist's newfound attempt to approximate reality in every detail, and this new realistic approach to drama led to the subcategories of naturalism and social theater. Common characteristics of realistic drama include the rejection of verse in favor of prose, the use of authentic dialect to represent true speech patterns, detailed stage directions, objective presentation, and the tendency to study life in a more scientific manner than ever before. Naturalism is the extreme form of realism in its attempt to show numerous aspects of human existence without censure and to trace the development of the characters as dictated by rules of heredity and environment. The study of individuals in their environment led to modern social drama. In the broadest sense of the term, social drama takes the sociological approach of focusing on cultural and environmental factors rather than on psychological or personal characteristics. Throughout Europe social drama treated the "social question" and came to define plays that focus their attention on class struggle and human drama rising from unjust social structures.

As realism continued to dominate in France, French dramatists demanded there be more harmony between the action and the setting, calling for realistic staging and costuming. This is also evident on the Spanish stage as the set slowly changed from "flat pasteboards on which a painter could paint the chairs, cupboards, and tables" to the actual inclusion of furniture on the stage (Klein 9). As oil lamps were replaced by gas lighting, which in turn was replaced by electric lighting, dramatists were able to realize new dramatic effects of light and darkness on the stage. The public also appreciated the changes taking effect in the theater. David Thatcher Gies notes: "Women in particular voiced approval of the gas lighting, since it freed them from having to duck drippings from the candles or wipe oil stains from their dresses" ("Glorious" 228). Playwrights enjoyed their newfound control of set design and filled their dramas with explicit instructions, specifying every detail. This is especially true of the Scandinavian dramatists Henrik Ibsen (1828-1906) and August Strindberg (1849-1912). Spanish dramatists also took advantage of this opportunity as is evident in the lengthy descriptions given to the details of the setting by Benito Pérez Galdós, Angel Guimerá, and especially Joaquín Dicenta, who sometimes wrote several pages of instructions to the director. Since plays began to be read as well as performed on a much larger scale in the later half of the nineteenth century, with the advent of realism the reader was able to reconstruct the dramatist's world more accurately with the aid of detailed descriptions of the costuming, setting, and overall appearance of the characters.

Henrik Ibsen is an important influence on the development of Spanish realism as is seen in Echegaray's attempts to model his drama on Ibsen's style, and Dicenta himself became the Spanish Ibsen for his success in staging realistic situations on the stage. Ibsen, who was greatly influenced by Zola's naturalistic theory, insisted that character is largely a product of social factors, and in his social drama, Ibsen attempts to explore the effects society has on individuals. Not long after Mavrikii Eduardovich Prozor's first volume of Ibsen's translations into French were published, several Spanish critics make mention of his work: in December of 1889 Clarín in *Correspondencia de España*, and in May of 1891 Melchor de Palau in *Revista Contemporánea* (Gregersen 51). Barcelona was the first center to embrace fully Ibsen and his ideas on the stage after the production of a Spanish translation of *An Enemy of the People* at the Teatre de Novetats on April 14, 1893. *A Doll's House* soon followed that same year as well as a Catalan translation of *Ghosts*. It is important to mention at this point that part of the influx of foreign influences in Spain is due to the many visiting Italian dramatic troupes who, besides their usual repertoire, interpreted several of Ibsen's plays on the Spanish stage.

Ibsen's drama finally arrived on the stage in Madrid on March 5, 1896 in another Spanish translation of *An Enemy of the People* (Gregersen 73); however, the play was not well received. Apparently the translator, F. F. Villegas, took too many liberties in adapting the Norwegian play to the Spanish stage:

> Aside from reducing the number of acts from five to three by telescoping the first and second into one, and eliminating the fourth, he apparently substituted Spanish names and places for Norwegian ones, did away with some of the characters, and introduced an active love affair between Dr. Stockman's daughter and Captain Horster—a theme which is merely suggested in the original. (Gregersen 75)

The failure of Ibsen's first production in Madrid discouraged any other Spanish translations of his plays from being presented there for another ten years. Ibsen's *Ghosts*, however, proved to be well-known to both Carlos Arniches and, of course, José Echegaray, who wrote *El hijo de Don Juan* (1892), a symbolic play heavily influenced by Ibsen and his style. Carlos Arniches wrote a short farce entitled *Los aparecidos* (1891), which could possibly have been inspired by Ibsen's *Ghosts* (Gregersen 76).

Ibsen's worldwide fame is the result of his reputation as a "radical thinker and controversial dramatist," who shocked his readers and audience members with bold new ideas (Brockett 549). In *A Doll's House* (1879), Ibsen questions the sanctity of marriage just as Dicenta does in many of his controversial dramas. Ibsen had the talent of a photographer, and the strength of his characters, the realism of the scenes, and the immediacy of his themes prove him to be one of the best dramatists of all time. All of the late nineteenth-century Spanish dramatists were affected by Ibsen as is evidenced in the new trend to stage controversial social issues with realistic precision, especially in works by Joaquín Dicenta, Angel Guimerá, and Vicente Medina.

Before Spain had completely grown accustomed to realism on the stage, French realism had already evolved into naturalism with its scientific objectivity and photographic representation of life. The primary spokesman of naturalism was Émile Zola (1840-1902), who argued that all drama should be scientific studies of heredity and environment and that the dramatist should act as a physician whose job is to experiment until the cause or origin of the disease is discovered and cured. Jesús Rubio Jiménez credits the initial arrival of Zola's thought to the Iberian Peninsula to the traveling troupes, who have always been an important factor in the introduction of new ideas to the Spanish stage. As early as 1882, the company of Giovanni Emmanuel produced *Nana*, and one year later, Luis Furtado Coelho's Portuguese company represented *Teresa Raquín* (19). Unfortunately, the few performances of Zola's plays by the foreign companies were not true to the French originals in that they tended to minimize the naturalistic and social elements while adding moralistic themes. For that reason, Zola's influence is more the result of his 1881 essay, "Naturalism in the Theatre," which was not translated into Spanish until its 1892 publication in *La España Moderna* (Rubio Jiménez, *Ideología* 229). Zola's ideas on naturalism inspired Spanish dramatists to embrace wholeheartedly the exclusive use of prose on stage, the simplification of the plot, and the importance of realistic representations of contemporary customs with a social commentary.

The development of realism into "social" theater is due in part to the great success of Gerhart Hauptmann (1862-1946). He is largely responsible for bringing the naturalist style to the stage in Central Europe, and his social drama, *The Weavers*, is the first example of working-class problems explored on the stage. Unlike others before him, Hauptmann appealed to all people, even simple miners, farmers, and weavers, for he often chose to portray their suffering in his plays. His best known work, *The Weavers* (*Die Weber* 1893), presents an incident in the struggle of the Silesian weavers in the 1840's, who, suffering starvation after being cruelly underpaid and eventually laid off by their indifferent employers, destroy their employer's new home and demolish the newly introduced machines upon which they blame their misfortunes. This is a drama of a group rather than an individual, and none of the characters is well developed. Ibsen and others chose to deal with a single person; whereas Hauptmann uses a collective hero of some seventy characters. Hauptmann's attention to the poor working classes and their suffering marks a substantial change of direction for the drama of the time. Unfortunately, unforeseen circumstances kept this landmark play off the Spanish stage:

> Existía el proyecto de estrenar *Los tejedores* de Hauptmann, traducido por Soler de las Casas y precedido de una conferencia de Pitarra, pero la bomba del Liceo y la consiguiente persecución de anarquistas redujeron muchos de estos proyectos a la nada. (Rubio Jiménez, *Ideología* 57)

Although the original play did not make it to the Spanish stage in the nineteenth century, there was an adaptation of *The Weavers* presented in 1894 by the title of *El pan de pobre*, written by González Llana and Francos Rodríguez. H. B. Hall points out its weakness: "This version was highly successful, but the cost was great: a descent into pure melodrama of the brand favoured by the audience at the Teatro de Novedades" (54-55). *The Weavers*, however, was published as a *folletín* in 1896 in the anarchist *Ciencia Social*. It is not known how much Joaquín Dicenta, Spain's first social dramatist, knew about Hauptmann and his work, but it is interesting that both playwrights gave the proletariat such a dominant role on the stage within only two years of each other, Hauptmann with *The Weavers* in 1893, and Dicenta with *Juan José* in 1895.

The nineteenth century witnessed many changes on the Spanish stage, especially as it developed into the modern theater as we know it today. Brockett describes the condition of the Spanish theater as "so chaotic that a state council was created to establish guidelines for its regulation" (532). Some of the changes that came about as a result of this "state council," formed in 1849, include the renaming of the Teatro del Príncipe to the Teatro Español, the complete remodeling of the physical structure, including the addition of gas lighting, and a modernization of the stage machinery. These modifications are important in that they provided the dramatist with the possibility of a more realistic setting, pushing the Spanish stage to join its European neighbors in their move towards realism.

José Echegaray is the one dramatist who dominated the Spanish stage during the final twenty-five years of the nineteenth century. Despite his many critics and the questionable quality of many of his dramas, Echegaray was by far the most popular dramatist before the turn of the century. Besides catering to the public's taste for melodrama, Echegaray owes his popularity, in part, to the fact that there was a considerable lack of worthy rivals when he first appeared on the scene. López de Ayala died in 1879, and Tamayo y Baus produced no dramas after 1870. Other well-liked dramatists also stopped writing for the stage: Núñez de Arce quit after his famous play *El haz de leña* in 1872; Zorrilla finished his dramatic career in 1849, and Hartzenbusch in 1860. Benito Pérez Galdós, like Jacinto Benavente, did not begin his dramatic career until the last decade of the century, and even Joaquín Dicenta's dramatic career was not successful until the 1890's.

Echegaray, who was a famous mathematician, a professor, a physicist, a political economist, a government minister, and an orator before he produced his first play, resuscitated Romantic drama in his plays by initiating a new genre: neo-Romanticism. Even his thesis plays are Romantic in their sensationalism and melodramatic themes. There are several stages to Echegaray's career. His first plays are essentially Romantic, many of them historical dramas, in which the themes of truth, love, and honor are explored, but unlike his Romantic predecessors who populated their dramas with the legendary and the heroic and their great passions, Echegaray explores upper class society and their more common problems such as jealousy. In effect, Echegaray not only revived Romantic drama in all its high-spirited lyricism, he also combined it with the modern theater of ideas and social problems.

Another category of Echegaray's drama is the thesis play, which includes his best work. Echegaray's masterpiece, *El gran galeoto* (1881), contains universal ideas that apply to all mankind and to all of human history. He explores the evils of slander and gossip at such a depth that the audience is left with no other choice but to reject any appearance of calumny. Following the success he enjoyed with *El gran galeoto*, Echegaray soon began to imitate Henrik Ibsen. Some of the plays that fall into this category are *Vida alegre y muerte triste* (1885), *El hijo de don Juan* (1892), and *El loco Dios* (1900). The abrupt change from passionate Romantic themes to the ultra-realistic and symbolic tragedies that mirrored Ibsen's work was a difficult jump for Echegaray, for he was truly a Romantic at heart. His dramatic career ended with the turn of the century, but he was still recognized for his great contribution to the Spanish stage when he was awarded half of the Nobel Prize for Literature (he shared it with Mistral) in 1904. Echegaray's influence on Joaquín Dicenta is undeniable, for Dicenta's first dramas follow Echegaray's lead by examining with a romantic twist those problems suffered by the upper middle classes.

While Echegaray was monopolizing the Spanish stage with his neo-

Romantic melodramas, there were several dramatists who wished Spanish drama to develop into a more realistic approach. These dramatists and their early attempts at realism are precursors to the social drama that came to the forefront in the 1890's, and their plays are excellent examples of how social drama developed in Spain. While some of their plays were imitations of Echegaray, there were several innovative techniques that proved their plays more realistic in dealing with contemporary society. Among these playwrights are Eugenio Sellés (1842-1926), Leopoldo Cano y Masas (1844-1934), and Enrique Gaspar (1842-1902).

Eugenio Sellés in *El nudo gordiano*, his first theatrical success, takes a new approach to Echegaray's style; like his master Echegaray, Sellés portrays contemporary Madrid and places the idea of honor at the forefront of the drama. Unlike Echegaray, however, Sellés moves one step down the social ladder, treating the lower-middle class rather than the upper-middle class. Sellés' most innovative technique is his frank treatment of the necessity of divorce in a marriage turned sour. In this play, however, divorce is not an option because of the fear of social condemnation; the solution is either violence (murder) or escape to another country where divorce is more acceptable. The husband in *El nudo gordiano* murders his unfaithful wife and accepts his punishment with honor. This theme is reminiscent of Calderón's *El médico de su honra*. The play was extremely popular, and according to Gies, "By 1880 the play was in its fifteenth printing, the first fourteen having been sold out in less than two years" (*Theatre* 323). Undoubtedly, Dicenta was familiar with this drama, and in several of his early plays he too attacks the insolubility of marriage in late nineteenth-century Spain. Sellés, however, lacked Dicenta's keen eye for the stage, and the majority of his plays are "seriously handicapped by an apparent lack of understanding of characterization and a commensurate lack of technique" (Klein 53). His contribution to the development of the social drama is undeniable, as he is one of the first Spanish dramatists to explore social issues that would be immediately significant to the theater-going public.

Other precursors to the realistic social theater are Leopoldo Cano y Masas and Enrique Gaspar. Cano, in his well-known *La pasionaria* (1883), mixes the middle class with the lower class and explores the abuse that the later suffers from the former. This new approach indicates Cano's interest in the oppression of the lower classes, a common characteristic among social dramatists. In this play, Cano condemns a society that ostracizes a single mother and her illegitimate child while supporting the seducer who abandoned her. Another innovative technique used by Cano is his inclusion of dialect to reflect the actual speech patterns of the servants. The use of language to represent reality is a definitive move towards realistic drama.

Enrique Gaspar, a far more successful dramatist than both Sellés and Cano, contributed greatly to the development of realism in his ability to create a drama in which the characters, plot, and dialogue all revolve around a central issue. Many of Gaspar's dramas are thesis plays full of social criticism, and in at least three of them, Gaspar studies the problems of marriage. In his final play, *La eterna cuestión* (1895), Gaspar succeeds in creating a domestic problem that is so real, too real, in fact, that the audiences were "terrified" (Peak 101). María, who is married to Carlos, has been having an affair with Enrique for years when she suddenly finds out that her lover is in love with her daughter. She begs Enrique to kill her as she pleads for forgiveness from her daughter. They both refuse, and in doing so provide for her the worst punishment possible. Peak describes the reason why *La eterna cuestión* had such a strong effect on audiences:

> They felt that such a tragedy might enter the lives of their friends, or their own. The actors spoke the language of the contemporary environment, and behaved in general in a manner appropriate to actual human beings. The final horror was the absence of vengeance, which utterly annihilated whatever feelings of complacency still remained to the moral mind of the Spaniard. (101)

Gaspar's drama shows a definitive break from the Echegarayan drama that had entertained audiences since the 1870's. Gaspar abandoned all sense of fantasy or romantic technique and provided realistic characters who represented events that were entirely possible in contemporary Madrilenean society.

Like Gaspar, Benito Pérez Galdós (1843-1920) avoids anything unrealistic in his attempt to stage several of his novels and original plays. He too breaks free from the neo-Romantic mold made popular by Echegaray. Galdós, whose novels gained worldwide attention, decided to move his social criticism from the novel to the stage. Although Galdós was not as successful a dramatist as he was a novelist, he was determined to put his work on stage, and despite his own admission of defeat, his drama, when placed in the context of all of Spanish drama during the last quarter of the nineteenth century and into the first decade of the twentieth century, remains important in the development of realism on the Spanish stage. Before his first play was represented on stage, Galdós expressed his opinion of the decadence of Spanish theater in an article in *Nuestro Teatro* (1885) (Brett 810). He claimed that audiences craved real characters whose actions are logical and not ruled by the extreme passions evident in many of the contemporary neo-Romantic plays. Galdós wrote twenty-one plays, among which *Realidad* (1892), *La loca de casa* (1893), *La de San Quintín* (1894), *Voluntad* (1895), *Doña Perfecta* (1896), *Electra* (1901), and *El abuelo* (1904) are the most well known.

In *La de San Quintín*, Galdós explores the need for a more accepting attitude on the part of the upper classes with regard to the lower classes; for him the ideal society would be one in which there is an amalgamation of the social classes. He, like Gaspar before him, sympathizes with the lower classes and condemns the prejudiced upper classes for their narrow views. In *Electra*, one of Galdós' best-received plays, he attacks the Catholic Church and Spain's refusal to accept progress. The title character, Electra, represents Spain; she suffers from the wrongdoings of her ancestors, and she is undereducated, immature, and haunted by her past. Galdós' greatest desire is to remove Spain from the dark clutches of the past and bring her into the twentieth century where she will embrace progress, truth, personal freedom, and scientific objectivity. If Spain is able and willing to accept the achievements of science, as the other countries of Europe have done, she will progress and be regenerated. *Electra* was extremely popular, and following its premiere on January 30, 1901, riots erupted in the streets of Madrid. It even had commercial value as "there began to appear in Spain Electra chocolates, Electra cigarettes, Electra hats…" (Gies, *Theatre* 345). The review in *El Globo* praises its contemporary appeal to the public:

> *Electra* no es solamente una obra dramática de singularísimo mérito, sino un hermoso, brillante, magnífico manifesto de las aspiraciones de la juventud intelectual española, que al aprestarse en estos días a dar batalla al clericalismo, ha encontrado en Pérez Galdós su indiscutible jefe. (Gies, *Theatre* 345)

Despite Galdós' several theatrical successes, his plays and adaptations were never received with the same praise as his novels. His contribution to the development of realistic theater, however, is great, for he brings his vast knowledge and success as a novelist to the stage by rejecting the popular Echegarayan melodrama and by experimenting with a more realistic approach in his criticism of contemporary society.

The drama in Spain in the last decade of the nineteenth century underwent major changes compared to the plays that dominated the stage prior to the 1890's. The emergence of a new social class, that of the miserably poor, exploited working community, both rural and urban, provided dramatists with new material for the stage. The common man, who before had taken unimportant parts such as the roguish servant, suddenly found himself portrayed with great dignity as he played the new role of hero. As the social drama developed out of realistic drama, the hero was more likely to be found in the humble working class rather than in the middle class. Social drama, by nature, is theater that seeks to explore unjust social structures by focusing attention on class struggle.

These social plays may or may not include proposals for reform. In Spain, social drama generally refers to those plays in which the working class fills the primary roles on stage, a working class that is conscious of social injustice and the need for change. Joaquín Dicenta is generally credited for being the first Spanish dramatist to give the oppressed primary roles on stage; however, he was not alone in his effort to criticize the unjust division between the classes.

Several months after the landmark premiere of Dicenta's *Juan José* in October of 1895, José Feliú y Codina (1847-1897) staged *María del Carmen* (February 4, 1896), a noteworthy rural drama that was characterized by its treatment of the abuse suffered by the *huertanos* of rural Murcia. It was so acclaimed that it received the award for the best drama of the year by the Real Academia, the "Premio Piquer" (Paco de Moya, "María" 67). With the premiere of *María del Carmen*, Feliú y Codina initiates a new sub-category of social drama, the rural drama that became popular in the last few years of the nineteenth century and remained so for the first thirty years of the twentieth. Paco de Moya describes the common characteristics of rural drama:

> Se caracteriza de modo externo por la localización a que su nombre alude y por el empleo de un lenguaje que, con apariencias de dialecta, es simplemente vulgar. Temáticamente suele presentar conflictos que giran en torno a la honra y al amor, reflejando las pasiones humanas en un estado primario y radical, favorecido por el ambiente en que se desarrollan. ("María" 65)

Paco de Moya credits the influence of naturalism in the development of rural drama, as well as the already established trend of *costumbrismo regional*. There is also a connection with the "dramas campesinos" of the Golden Age. The play is set in the *Huerta* of Murcia, and Feliú y Codina exhibits a vast knowledge of the surrounding rural regions, including detailed descriptions of the traditional costumes worn by the *huertanos*, as well as certain customs such as the Thursday "mercao" in the city. Paco de Moya describes the value of Feliú y Codina's contribution to the development of rural drama in Spain:

> Su interés es grande por encontrarse en el origen de este subgénero dramático y por ofrecer un cuadro bien dibujado y muy exacto de costumbres, tipos y situaciones de la huerta murciana a fines del pasado siglo. ("María" 75)

Angel Guimerá (1869-1926) brought fame and recognition to Catalonia, his homeland, through his poetry and drama. He wrote about thirty plays, and even though he wrote them in Catalan, they are important in the study of the development of Spanish realistic theater in that they were translated into Spanish by such playwrights as Enrique Gaspar and José Echegaray and many times were performed in Spanish before being represented in the original Catalan. Gies notes Guimerá's evolution towards the social drama:

> Guimerá became more interested in the sociology of his environment than its costumbrista or Romantic elements. His main characters tended to be the working man and the peasant rather than the *bourgeois gentilhomme* or the noble bandit. (*Theatre* 308)

One of Guimerá's most famous plays is *Terra baixa*, which was first performed in the Teatro Español on November 30, 1896 after having been translated to Spanish by José Echegaray. Coming one year after Joaquín Dicenta's landmark *Juan José*, *Terra baixa* has many similarities, yet instead of placing the protagonists in the city, Guimerá places them in the lowlands (*tierras bajas*), thus establishing a connection with Feliú y Codina's success with rural drama earlier that same year. *Juan José*, *María del Carmen*, and *Terra baixa* all center on the poor working class and their oppression by the ruling class. All three dramas point to social injustice, yet not one of them puts forth any plausible solutions; in fact, both Juan José and Manelich, the poor shepherd of *Terra baixa*, resort to murder when pushed beyond their limit.

The popularity of *Terra baixa* was widespread; it was translated into Portuguese, Italian, French, English, German, Swedish, Russian, Czech, Serbian, Dutch, and Yiddish (Gies, *Theatre* 308). Although *Terra baixa* is more a psychological, symbolic drama than a realistic play, it contains hints of naturalism in the fatalistic view that the oppressed are incapable of escaping violence and murder. Guimerá's treatment of rural semi-feudalism categorizes this play as a social drama, and had he written it in Spanish rather than Catalan, it is possible he would have enjoyed similar fame as Dicenta.

Another of Dicenta's contemporaries, Vicente Medina (1866-1937) also makes a name for himself by giving low-class members of society the primary roles on stage. His first play, *El rento* (1898) is a continuation of the trend set by the initiators of rural social drama, Feliú y Codina and Guimerá. In general, Medina's plays are characterized by their simple structure, respect for the unities, lack of complexity in the plot, the use of prose, and attention to contemporary issues (Paco de Moya, Introducción 35). *El rento* (1898) shares many of the same characteristics of *Juan José* (1895), *Tierra baja* (1896), and *María del Carmen* (1896), as it explores the hardships of two poor families in debt and their exploitation by members of the ruling class.

It is obvious that Joaquín Dicenta was not alone in his desire to give the poor working class a voice on the stage in his attempt to criticize the extreme abuse and exploitation by the ruling class. Before his famous *Juan José*, a realistic tradition had already been established by such dramatists as Eugenio Sellés, Leopoldo Cano y Masas, Enrique Gaspar, and of course, Benito Pérez Galdós, among others. Even José Echegaray contributed somewhat to this new trend in his thesis plays. These playwrights helped open a door for Dicenta, enabling him to develop plays that, although controversial, the Spanish theater-going public was finally ready to embrace with open arms.

2
Life, Works, and Critical Reception of Joaquín Dicenta

LIFE AND WORKS

JOAQUÍN DICENTA BENEDICTO WAS born on February 3, 1863 in Calatayud, "a mitad de camino" between Alicante and Vitoria as his parents, Manuel Dicenta and Tomasa Benedicto, were in the process of relocating the family to Vitoria (Sánchez Portero 139). Manuel Dicenta, a Lieutenant Colonel of Hussars, had been transferred to Vitoria where he was to assume military command. Five years after the birth of Joaquín Dicenta, the elder Dicenta suffered an injury in the Carlist War that left him mentally unbalanced for the seven remaining years of his life. Immediately following this severe head injury, the family moved to Madrid hoping to find a cure for Manuel Dicenta's mental illness, yet they soon realized that he would never be the same again. They moved once again to Alicante where friends and family were able to help Tomasa Benedicto as she dutifully cared for her husband in his last years. Having lost his father at such an early age, Joaquín Dicenta struggled through his life without any solid paternal discipline. Years later, in an interview with José María Carretero (*El Caballero Audaz*), Dicenta discussed those painful moments of his childhood:

> Siete años vivió con su locura. Durante ellos, mi pobre madre sufrió como una mártir, porque se opuso a que fuera recluido. Con él quiso subir el calvario de su demencia. A los siete años de su desvarío, un día le sorprendió la muerte en medio en la calle. Tenía yo entonces doce años, y era la mismísima piel del diablo. (*Galería* 633-34)

As a result of the loss of a father figure at such an early age, Dicenta grew very close to his mother and developed a sensitivity that is evident in his plays. In

Idos y muertos (1911[1]), a short novel written at the request of Eduardo Zamacois, a dramatist who became famous for his contribution to the *género chico*, Dicenta relives part of his youth. Dicenta dedicates the first chapter of *Idos y muertos* to the abbot of the "Colegiata de Alicante," Don Francisco Penalva, because he was able to summarize Dicenta's character in one sentence. Dicenta describes the occasion when he had been in a fight with another student, and full of rage, Dicenta beat him so badly, that had his friends not pulled him away, he would have killed his opponent. The next day, after having been rebuked by the abbot, Dicenta burst into tears, grabbed the hands of the injured boy and cried: "¡Perdóname, Emilio! ¡ Perdóname!" (*Idos* 87). Upon witnessing this, the abbot said to Dicenta: "¡Ay, Joaquinito, Joaquinito!... Extraña criatura eres tú. Hay dentro de ti un ángel y un demonio riñendo formidable pelea. ¿Cuál de ellos triunfará?" (*Idos* 88).

The information that is available concerning Dicenta's early education is both confusing and contradictory. Jaime Mas Ferrer indicates that Dicenta's biographer, Andrés González Blanco, made many errors about specific dates and events in his study, *Los dramaturgos españoles contemporáneos* (1917). In the introduction of the Cátedra edition of Dicenta's most well-known play, *Juan José* and in his study of Dicenta, *Vida, teatro y mito de Joaquín Dicenta* (1978), Mas Ferrer clarifies these dates and points out what he believes to be true about Dicenta's life. Unfortunately, however, neither critic is without errors, and due to the contradictory nature of the information on Dicenta's early life, one must piece together a successive history from other sources as well as the two accounts provided by González Blanco and Mas Ferrer.

Dicenta, as stated earlier, describes his youth, which he spent in Alicante, in his short novel *Idos y muertos*, yet Andrés González Blanco claims that Dicenta first studied in "Jetafe, donde hizo las primeras letras en el Colegio de Escolapios" (*Dramaturgos* 208). Jaime Mas Ferrer, however, claims to quote Angel Salcedo to the fact that Dicenta passed his childhood in Alicante: "Toda la infancia de Joaquín Dicenta transcurrió en Alicante" (*Vida* 15):

Aceptamos la versión de A. Salcedo, máxime cuando a raíz de nuestro viaje a Madrid, tuvimos la suerte de conversar con los nietos de Dicenta, Pedro y Fernando, y nos confirmaron nuestras dudas, afirmando que el libro de González Blanco, *Los dramaturgos españoles contemporáneos*, tiene

---

[1] There is no record of the first publication of *Idos y muertos*, yet after a careful reading, I deduce that it must have been written in 1911 since Dicenta writes that his dear friend, Manuel Paso, had passed away ten years earlier (107). Manuel Paso died in 1901. *Idos y muertos* was published posthumously in 1922 in a collection of short novels entitled *Novelas*.

muchos errores de apreciación. (*Vida* 15)

However the quote which Mas Ferrer attributes to A. Salcedo is in fact from Antonio Sánchez Portero's study, *Noticia y antología de poetas bilbilitanos* (139). Despite this significant error on the part of Mas Ferrer, both he and Sánchez Portero were able to speak with Dicenta's grandchildren to discover the truth about the errors made by González Blanco. Sánchez Portero states:

> En uno de los viajes que hemos hecho a Madrid, conocimos a D. Pedro Dicenta, nieto de D. Joaquín, quien trabaja infatigablemente reuniendo datos, recortes de prensa y publicaciones sobre su abuelo. Es justo que le manifestemos nuestro agradecimiento por los datos que nos ha facilitado.... (*Noticia* 145)

Mas Ferrer contends that there are other errors in González Blanco's biography concerning Dicenta's early education, giving as example González Blanco's statement that Dicenta attended the Instituto de Alicante. However, Vicente Ramos, in his study of Carlos Arniches, offers a detailed account of Arniches' childhood, including his fellow classmates at the Colegio San José (Alicante), Rafael Altamira and Joaquín Dicenta. In one specific passage Ramos describes an early act of rebellion led by the young Dicenta and his friends Altamira and Arniches, "entonces chiquillos traviesos" (17). We thus have an eyewitness account of Dicenta's early life, which should be accepted as accurate, especially because of the testimony of Dicenta's early tendency towards rebellion that characterized his entire life and is evident in his plays.

After receiving his "título de Bachiller," Dicenta and his mother moved to Madrid, where Dicenta began to develop his talent. In his detailed study of the Spanish stage of the nineteenth century, *El arte escénico en España*, José Yxart discusses the tendency of many families who have migrated to the city (Madrid) to push their young sons into the three traditional fields that would reflect their social status: law, medicine and engineering. Instead, Yxart describes, these young men soon abandon these careers in favor of journalism and playwriting (84). Dicenta easily falls into this category as he attempted to please his mother by following her advice as he planned his future. Upon arrival in Madrid, Dicenta immediately enrolled in the Academia de Artillería de Segovia. Dicenta was soon expelled due to his inability to conform to the strict discipline required of him. In his interview with José María Carretero, Dicenta describes his failure: "Mi carácter rebelde está poco de acuerdo con la disciplina, por cuya razón al año de estar allí, me tuvieron que expulsar" (*Galería* 634). Mas Ferrer blames Dicenta's poetic tendency as one of the reasons he was expelled. One day a superior caught Dicenta composing poetry when he should have been following orders. Once confronted, he rebelled against his authorities and was forced to leave the institution. According to Mas Ferrer, Dicenta spent two years at the Academia between 1877 and 1878 (*Vida* 17); Dicenta's testimony, however, quoted above, suggests he spent only one year in the Academia. After failing to initiate a military career in the Academia, Dicenta immediately enrolled in Law School in Madrid in 1879. In this, too, he was unsuccessful because he was unable to devote the time necessary to his studies. He abandoned this career only after the first few months of classes because, according to Mas Ferrer, "la vida bohemia empieza a atraerle" (Introducción 13). Again, with the encouragement of his mother, he enrolled in Medical School in 1880, but his bohemian lifestyle was unsuited to such a profession. He remained there for two years (1880-1881), after which he dropped out of classes and sold his books for money "para convidar a una chalequera" (*Idos* 91). Dicenta explains: "dejé las aulas para novillear con ella por los boscajes del Retiro" (91). Dicenta claims that he wrote his first verses for a woman, stating:

> A una mujer debo la orientación que me llevó por los caminos literarios…. Ella literateaba unas miajas, y yo quise imitarla. Repito que eran malos mis versos; tan malos como fueron para mi espíritu, lleno de románticas candideces, mis amores con la poetisa. (*Idos* 99)

After abandoning Medical School, Dicenta decided that he could no longer live off his mother's small widow's pension, and he determined to become independent: "Me parecía indigno de un hombre, apto para el trabajo, vivir á expensas de una mujer que apenas si para ella tenía suficiente con su mezquina viudedad" (*Idos* 101). By then Dicenta was only seventeen years old. In his interview with Carretero he explains,

> A partir de aquel día, que contaba yo diecisiete años, empezó para mí la bohemia del artista joven y sin recursos que ansia compartir la gloria, y, obre todo, ¡que quiere vivir y comer alguna vez que otra! (*Galería* 634)

Dicenta never forgot his mother and her love for him, and his devotion and respect for her is obvious in his plays as many of the mothers he creates possess great dignity and honor. (One obvious example is Andrés' mother in *Juan José*.) Without the help of his mother's widow's pension, Dicenta soon learned to survive by taking all types of odd jobs. One of the many was his contribution to several unimportant periodicals, which fed the literary interests that were to define his life. One particular journal entitled *El Edén*, published by a perfume house, provided Dicenta the opportunity to publish his first poetry, which was later republished in his book of poems *Del tiempo mozo* in 1912. González

Blanco points out that *El Edén*'s contributors were not paid money but rather articles of perfume that they probably gave to their female companions who helped support their bohemian lifestyle (*Dramaturgos* 210).

In his youth, Dicenta contributed to several different periodicals, among them *La Piqueta, El Motín, La Avispa, La Opinión, La Lucha, El Radical, El Mundo, La Regencia, El Universal,* and *La Gaceta.* These newspapers had in common their short existence and their antigovernmental hatred. The majority of Dicenta's articles focused on the poor working class, those suffering great injustices and severe oppression. In *Idos y muertos,* Dicenta describes how he became so interested in the plight of the lower classes: "Inclinaciones invencibles llevaban mi trato más hacia la gente del pueblo, que hacia los burgueses y aristócratas" (123). By "inclinaciones invencibles" Dicenta means his weakness for women. He continues:

> Hez del pueblo, criaturas empujadas por la miseria á los bajos fondos sociales, me enseñaron á estimar en el historial de sus vidas á la clase trabajadora.... A conocerlas á ellas, quise conocer el vivir de su clase, darme cuenta precisa de los desamparos y abandonos que tales espumas arrojaban á mí. Estudiando la vida horrible de la mujer y hombres del pueblo en el taller, en la obra, en la fábrica y en el terruño, aprendí á admirarlas en sus honradeces, á compadecerles en sus culpas, á sentir ansias de reclamar para ellos la justicia que no se les hace y el pan que se las regatea. (*Idos* 123-24)

In an effort to explain the reason he was drawn towards the dregs of society, Dicenta describes his heritage:

> Sobre uno de mis escudos triunfaba la corona ducal; cruzada era por raya de bastardo. Cierto señor duque tuvo la deferencia de hacer madre á una villana de su feudo. De aquel obsequio vengo por una de mis líneas.... La villana, gozada por el feudal señor, tuvo más influencia sobre mí, á través de los siglos, que todos los nobles duques y duquesas á las villanas subsiguientes. (*Idos* 89, 125)

In April of 1895, just months before the premiere of *Juan José*, together with his cousin Ricardo Yesares, Dicenta founded the newspaper *Democracia Social*. Dicenta and several of his friends, Ricardo Fuente, Antonio Palomero, Luis París, Manuel Paso, Montalvo, Carlitos Soler, Rafael Delorme, Eduardo Zamacois, and Ernesto Bark, worked together to write articles. Rafael Pérez de la Dehesa describes the social criticism that was central to *Democracia Social*: "En las páginas de esta revista… predominan artículos, cuentos o poemas de un fuerte sentimentalismo que pintan vívidamente la situación de miseria y desesperación de las clases trabajadoras" (39). Dicenta was the director of this short-lived publication; it only survived a month. He, together with his cousin and friends, used the newspaper to fight against misery and hunger for a better world for all people and for a better future for themselves. He describes the failure of *Democracia Social*: "Pobres Quijotes de una caballería nueva, caímos nosotros y cayó la *Democracia Social*, que de Rocinante nos servía, despalillados, rotos al embate de las aspas contra las cuales embestimos" (*Idos* 137). The following year, 1896, Dicenta and his friends, not discouraged by the failure of *Democracia Social*, embarked upon a new project, another periodical that they eventually named *Germinal*, after Zola's famous novel published in 1885. Dicenta, again the director, solicited contributions not only from his fellow authors from *Democracia Social* but also from Nicolás Salmerón y García, Valle-Inclán, Urbano González Serrano, Alfredo Calderón, Benavente, Felipe Trigo, González Anaya, Rusiñol, Blasco Ibáñez, and Verdes Montenegro, among others (Pérez de la Dehesa 50).

Dicenta spent the entire decade of the 1880s and the first half of the 1890s in extreme poverty and misery. He began to lead the bohemian lifestyle that was popular among certain young Spanish intellectuals at the time; he and his contemporaries formed a group called "Gente nueva." This pre-generation of 1898 group of young writers who frequented the intellectual circles in Madrid consisted of the following: Joaquín Dicenta, Manuel Paso, Alejandro Sawa, Luis Bonafoux, Pedro Barrantes, Marco Zapata, Reparaz, Luís Paris, Torromé, Ruiz Guerrero, Maifrén, Muñiz de Quevedo, Manolo Cid, Mariano del Cavia, and Pedro Luis de Gálvez, among others (*Vida* 19 and *Idos* 103). They had in common their rebellious and nonconformist natures and their constant desire to fight against social injustices through their poetry, novels, plays, and articles. Dicenta describes his view of the artistic Bohemia in *Tinta negra*, a series of chronicles and stories concerning social problems published in 1891:

> La bohemia del arte es muy distinta. Soportar la miseria, pero soportarla, no como a un compañero, como a un enemigo a quien es necesario vencer a todo trance en lid honrosa y noble; protestar por medio del trabajo..., dirigir los ojos a la cumbre, contemplarla con la alegría de la esperanza e ir a su encuentro paso paso, sin humillaciones, sí, pero también sin orgullos necios y sin retraimientos estériles... (*Tinta* 39)

For Mas Ferrer, Dicenta's rebellious nature stemmed from his choice to lead a bohemian lifestyle: "Dicenta fue un bohemio y, como tal, un ser rebelde; ambos vocablos—bohemia y rebeldía—a finales de siglo eran sinónimos" (Introducción 19). (We noted above, however, that according to Vicente Ramos Dicenta was already a rebel in secondary school.) For Manuel Machado, Dicenta was a courageous rebel from his early youth: "siguió mostrando el alma valiente y rebelde de su primera juventud" (58). Also, for Machado, Dicenta learned the essential truth of Juan José during his bohemian days: "Dicenta encontró a Juan José en la taberna, y Juan José era verdad. Dicenta, en cambio, era mentira" (*Año* 151).

Dicenta's youth was very turbulent. González Blanco compares him to the Romantics de Musset and Byron because, like them, he led life at the extremes. One of his early poems, entitled "¿Para qué?," first published in 1884 in *El Edén* describes his disillusionment with a life of wine, women and gambling:

> Mujeres, vino, juego; tres placeres
> a los que mi existencia consagré
> despreciando consejos y deberes.
> De jugar y beber me retiré.
> De lo otro, no. De lo otro, ¿para qué?
> Ya me irán retirando las mujeres. (*Del tiempo mozo* 45)

Dicenta rebelled violently against social injustices and prejudice, emphasizing the importance of individuality and personal freedom. H.B. Hall explains Dicenta's rebellious nature in his essay, "Joaquín Dicenta and the Drama of Social Criticism":

> The consequent lack of paternal discipline, his mother's indulgent sacrifices, the family atmosphere of impoverished gentility, and the repressive character of his early schooling, all undoubtedly contributed to the aggressiveness, the conscious plebeianism of this young rebel with literary leanings who after attempting a succession of different careers in Madrid, not unnaturally turned to journalism and strove to keep himself by writing for the radical press. (44-45)

Dicenta's interest in literature began at a young age: "Desde niño fuí aficionado á las bellas artes y muy dado á lecturas de versos, novelas, dramas y libros históricos y filosóficos" (*Idos* 97). Dicenta describes his love for theater and especially that of José Echegaray: "[yo] hacía los imposibles para buscarme la peseta, y comprar una entrada, y plantarme en el paraíso y presenciar los estrenos del maestro" (*Idos* 97). It was not until 1887, when Dicenta published a book of short stories, that he took his first steps away from journalism and began his literary career. In 1887 he published S*poliarium*, a book of short stories, which contains the story "Juan José," the first mention of the famous title character of what would be his 1895 success. This group of short stories contains early evidence of Dicenta's treatment of social issues. Also during 1887, Dicenta finished his first play, *El suicidio de Werther*. In *Idos y muertos*, Dicenta describes in detail the circumstances that preceded the premiere of his first drama. On four different occasions, Dicenta, with drama in hand, went to the Teatro Español to ask both playwrights and the managers of the acting companies to review his work. Each time, Dicenta was rudely refused and humiliated:

> Echegaray, hundido en su butaca, me miraba por encima de las gafas, como diciendo: ¿Qué traerá este mocito? Calvo, me dejaba con la palabra en la boca, y con el manuscrito en la diestra, para atender á sus aduladores; Vico me daba palmaditas guasonas. Cano no me prestaba atención alguna; tenía el hombre entonces un empacho de Pasionaria y se creía un Dios; Sellés me alargaba la mano y seguía adelante... Todos, cual más cual menos, me querían dar á entender que yo era en el saloncillo un estorbo. Hasta el portero refunfuñaba al abrirme la puerta. (*Idos* 146)

Dicenta decided that he had had enough and that he would never again return to suffer the same humiliation. His mother took it upon herself to find someone who would give Dicenta's first play a reading, so she went to the celebrated dramatist Manuel Tamayo y Baus and introduced herself, saying:

> A usted acudo para pedirle consejo primero y protección después, si la persona la merece. Se trata de mi hijo, señor. Ha escrito un drama; él cree, y yo también—al cabo soy su madre—que el drama tiene condiciones. Los actores se niegan á escucharlo. Mi hijo, cansado de inútiles esperas, ha resuelto no volver en solicitud. Está desesperado. Cifraba en el drama todo su porvenir. ¿Quiere usted leerlo y decirme su leal opinión? Doy este paso á espaldas de mi hijo. (*Idos* 147-48)

After several weeks, one morning Dicenta was hurredly awakened by his mother who told him that Tamayo had climbed the one hundred and six steps to their tiny apartment in order to see the young dramatist and was waiting in the living room. Upon seeing Dicenta, Tamayo exclaimed "¡Venga usted joven, venga usted acá y venga un abrazo! Lo merece quien ha escrito ese Suicidio. Está muy bien.... Es usted un poeta y un autor dramático" (*Idos* 149). On February 23, 1888 *El suicidio de Werther* was performed by the Calvo-Vico company in the Teatro de la Princesa. Dicenta's first play marks a continuation of the neo-Romantic style that had dominated the stage since Echegaray. Although Romantic in nature, Dicenta's first drama draws attention to the suffering of those who are judged by society because of the lack of a legitimate family name.

Dicenta emphasizes that a person's worth is to be based on his works and not on his ancestry or lack thereof.

Many of Dicenta's plays directly reflect his own early struggles, his experience of poverty and misery among the lowest of the social classes and of the suffering of those who were the victims of discrimination. Yet, as he slowly began to achieve some success in his productions, Dicenta found himself among those who were of a higher social class, including his aristocratic bride, Purificación de Orduña y Zarauz, whom he married on June 25, 1888. This marriage, however, did not provide the young dreamer with the support and inspiration he required to be a successful dramatist. Dicenta had married a woman who was incapable of understanding him as an artist. His unhappy marriage provided much material for his creation in several plays of the role of the misunderstood artist. The marriage failed due to their incompatibility: "D. Joaquín era un soñador y un romántico, su esposa era práctica y realista" (Sánchez Portero 140). Dicenta continued to live in an artistic youthful world, while Doña Purificación, who was older than he, was very much a part of her materialistic surroundings. She showed no respect for his talent as a dramatist, nor did she understand his bohemian way of life. Sánchez Portero's study *Noticia y antología de poetas bilbilintinos* includes a reference to a determining event in the failure of Dicenta's marriage. After finishing a particular short story in the middle of the night, the triumphant Dicenta awoke his wife to read it to her. Not understanding how important this accomplishment was to her husband, Doña Purificación ignorantly asked him: "¿Y cuánto es lo que te van a dar por eso?" (*Noticia* 140). Sánchez Portero describes Dicenta's anger and oversensitive reaction to his wife's indifference to his artistic achievment: "Enfadado don Joaquín, herido en lo más profundo de su sensibilidad, se marchó de casa y desde entonces no quiso saber nada de su esposa" (*Noticia* 140). In his heartbroken disillusionment, poor Dicenta determined that he would never see her again. The heartbreak of the artist is covered in the drama, *Luciano* (1894), and the novel, *Mi Venus* (1915). Furthermore, Dicenta, like Galdós, demanded the acceptance of divorce in several of his works: *La mejor ley* (1889), *Los irresponsables* (1892), and the previously mentioned *Luciano*. His marriage to Doña Purificación lasted only six months, and not long after their separation, Dicenta fell in love with Amparito Triana, a gypsy whom he had encountered in a run-down bar in Madrid and who understood and supported his ideals as an artist. Amparito provided Dicenta with the inspiration and moral support that he so needed. Dicenta's relationship with Amparito is further explored in *Amparo*, a play written by Dicenta's son, also named Joaquín Dicenta. The elder Dicenta and his lover lived together without the possibility of marriage in a nation where divorce was neither legally possible nor socially accepted. We recall, of course, the relationship, without the benefit of clergy, between Juan José and Rosa in

Juan José, and the decision of the two main characters of *Los irresponsables* to live the rest of their lives together without marrying. Amparito and Dicenta too decided to practice free love. Mas Ferrer notes Amparito's devotion to Dicenta in his years of penury:

> Con respecto a Amparito, se ha dicho que *Juan José* no hubiera visto la luz de los proscenios, si ella, en los momentos de más penuria y estrechez, no hubiera velado para que al dramaturgo no le faltara lo imprescindible para escribir. (*Vida* 27)

Mas Ferrer also relates a story told to him by Pedro Dicenta, Joaquín Dicenta's grandson: "...el *Juan José* se terminó de escribir a la luz de las cerillas que ella [Amparito] mantenía con sus dedos, mientras Dicenta trabajaba" (*Vida* 27-28). Sánchez Portero also refers to this event:

> Cuando le faltaba poco para terminar *Juan José*, interrumpió su labor abrumado por la falta de tabaco, de café, de luz... Amparito se lanzó a la calle y al poco rato volvía con todo lo que necesitaba el escritor... (*Noticia* 141)

Dicenta acknowledges Amparito's positive influence on his life. In Dicenta's poetry, dramas, and novels, there are many women who provide an inspiration and love that is a reflection of Amparito's love for Dicenta. Little is known about the family life of Dicenta except for a brief reference in his interview with José María Carretero (*El Caballero Audaz*) in which he claims he has five children, yet there is no evidence to suggest that he had these children with Amparito (*Galería* 635). On the other hand, Antonio Sánchez Portero writes that Dicenta had six children (*Noticia* 142). As mentioned previously, Dicenta did have a son who carried his name, Joaquín Dicenta, who was known for his poetry and also for his dramas, which met with less success than did those of his father. Another son, Manuel Dicenta, was "uno de los más eminentes actores de la actualidad," according to Sánchez Portero in 1969, two years after the death of Joaquín Dicenta, the son (*Noticia* 143).

Following the break-up of Dicenta's marriage to Purificación and Dicenta's decision to live outside of marriage and against the contemporary moral code with Amparito, Madrid closed its doors to the talented young artist. It is not surprising that his next several plays, including *La mejor ley* (1889), *Los irresponsables* (1890), and *Luciano* (1894), treat the theme of failed marriages and the pursuit of free love. Although *La mejor ley* was poorly acclaimed, the approach in *Los irresponsables* to the evils of marriage created quite a stir among both audiences and critics and gave Dicenta the reputation of a coming dramatist. González Blanco notes the success of the drama:

> ...este drama fue muy bien acogido por la crítica... Fue sin duda el primer drama que contribuyó a afianzar y robustecer su personalidad literaria, pues dio lugar a apasionadas polémicas entre periodistas" (*Dramaturgos* 215).

Unfortunately, however, this success did not provide him with the financial security he so desperately needed. He and Amparito continued to live in poverty.

For financial reasons, Dicenta was forced to take a salaried position in San Sebastián as the director of a newspaper, *La Unión Liberal*, which was primarily supported by the upper class. The local oligarchy used this newspaper to support their conservative ideals. It must have been difficult for Dicenta to work for this newspaper, knowing that he was only furthering the oppression of the poor working-class communities. While he was in San Sebastián, Dicenta wrote a series of chronicles and stories that treat social issues, *Tinta Negra*, in 1891, which unfortunately was not widely known. Also in 1891, Dicenta changed his approach to drama by writing a one-act historical drama, *Honra y vida*. This short play treats the ancient legend of King Pedro the Cruel and focuses mainly on the theme of honor. Dicenta, feeling homesick for his contemporaries in Madrid and craving a return to the stage, finally left his position as director of *La Unión Liberal* in 1892 and returned to Madrid where he started writing for *El Resumen*.

Several years passed before the premiere of Dicenta's next play, and the change in his technique and outlook is immediately evident. On February 25, 1894 *Luciano*, Dicenta's first prose drama, appeared. *Luciano* is a thesis play that gives the title role to an artist who experiences the same problems in his marriage as Dicenta. The characters in the autobiographical *Luciano* are victims of an uncaring society that judges people for their family position rather than their own personal worth. Having abandoned the use of verse in this drama, Dicenta takes a step towards a more realistic approach to writing plays. Only two weeks later, Dicenta staged his first *zarzuela*, *El duque de Gandía*, a Spanish opera that was well received by the public after it was performed in the Teatro de la Zarzuela. It was written in the popular mode of the time and is characterized by its neo-Romantic tendencies. For Dicenta, it represented a new phase of his art as he incorporated music into his plays. Together with *Luciano*, *El duque de Gandía* helped make Dicenta better known among the public and critics alike. Both plays, although completely different, were successful, and although they did not provide Dicenta with the financial security he longed for, they did allow him to enjoy his new status as a dramatist with much to offer. Having finally gained the attention of the public, Dicenta continued to dedicate more of his time to writing plays.

Dicenta's next play marks a definite break with the neo-Romantic dramas of the 1890's, as he abandons the imitation of other successful dramatists. In 1895 Dicenta received the acclaim that he had longed for with the production of *Juan José* on October 25 in the Teatro de la Comedia in Madrid. Dicenta was so praised for this new drama that a banquet was given in his honor:

> Y pocos días después del apoteósico estreno, el 11 de noviembre de 1895, organizaron en su honor el banquete más famoso que se había celebrado en Madrid en muchos años, al que asistieron las personas más significativas de la capital. (Sánchez Portero 141)

Dicenta, true to his character, was accompanied by his gypsy lover, Amparito, and having not yet financially benefited from the success of *Juan José*, the couple arrived poorly dressed. His friends and family chastized him for his attire but most of all for having brought Amparito to such a prestigious event. Dicenta was outraged by their behavior towards Amparito, and turning his plate upside down, he wrote upon it the following sonnet:

> Cuánto sufrí, y ¡qué solo!… Ni un amigo;
> ni una mano leal que se tendiera
> en busca de la mía; ni siquiera
> el placer de creame un enemigo.
> De mi angustia y dolor solo testigo,
> de mi penosa vida compañera
> fué una pobre mujer, una ¡cualquiera!
> que hambre, pena y amor partió conmigo.
> Y hoy que mi triunfo asegurado se halla,
> tú, amigo por el éxito ganado,
> me dices que la arroje de mi lado,
> que una mujer así deshonra. ¡Calla!
> Con ella he padecido y he triunfado.
> El triunfo no autoriza a ser canalla. (*Mozo* 153-154)

Prior to *Juan José*, the tendency on the Spanish stage was either Romantic or realistic. The two best examples are José Echegaray and Benito Pérez Galdós. Their plays portrayed the upper class and its problems. Dicenta is the first Spaniard to take the principal roles away from the traditional Romantic hero and the upper class and give these roles to artists and humble working-class individuals. The critics did not ignore the value of this new type of drama. Newspapers of diverse political tendencies remarked on the revolutionary, contemporary nature of *Juan José*. Fernández Shaw wrote in *La Época*:

> El señor Dicenta es, sin duda alguna, entre los autores de la nueva generación, el más inspirado, el más genial, el que con más iniciativa y con arte más extraordinario, sabe llevar a la escena las grandes luchas de la vida contemporánea, "pensando alto, sintiendo hondo y hablando claro"... (qtd. in Mas Ferrer, Introducción 57)

El Resumen also praised Dicenta's talent:

> El autor de *Juan José*, por voto unánime de la opinión docta, se encuentra desde anoche en lugar preferentísimo entre los primeros cultivadores del teatro genuinamente español, del teatro nacional moderno: revolucionario, atrevido, regnerador. (qtd. in Mas Ferrer, Introducción 57)

The opening night of *Juan José* represents the beginning of Social Theater in Spain. Although it is possible that there were other social dramas prior to October 25, 1895, Dicenta's masterpiece represents a new beginning for Spanish theater. Its first appearance on stage has an interesting history. Emilio Thuillier, the actor who was to play the unforgettable protagonist, was immediately impressed by *Juan José* upon his first reading of the play; however, he discouraged Dicenta from showing it to the director of the Teatro de la Comedia, Emilio Mario. Thuillier felt certain that Mario would not accept a "drama de alpargata" (García Pavón 37). By chance, Emilio Mario was left with a two-week space for which he had nothing programmed, and after Thuillier approached him with Dicenta's latest drama, he decided to ask Dicenta to fill the hole. Mario refused to participate in the performance, and so did María Tubau, the leading actress of the Teatro de la Comedia. García Pavón summarizes their harsh reaction: "¡Un drama de gentuza y oliendo a vino!" (37). Although the actors appreciated the value of the new play, they were uncomfortable with the novelty of the theme and feared scandal. Pavón cites three reasons for the success of *Juan José*, despite the concerns of the theater directors and actors: 1) The value of the work, 2) the innovative manner in which Dicenta explores the age-old theme of honor while portraying common working-class individuals, and 3) the fact that the "cuestión social" forms the dramatic climax of the play (38).

Following the great success of *Juan José*, Dicenta was able to fulfill immediately his desire to transform the Spanish stage. Heralded by his contemporaries as the initiator of Social Drama in Spain, Dicenta chose to treat the social question in his next play, *El señor feudal*, which premiered in 1896. For H.B. Hall, however, the very fact that Dicenta was conscious of his role as Spain's first social dramatist caused *El señor feudal* to be a failure. Dicenta turned quickly away from social drama, and in 1898 he saw the premiere of his next play, *Curro Vargas*, a lyrical drama that bears a striking resemblance to Pedro de Alarcón's *El niño de la bola*. After the debut of *Curro Vargas* in the Teatro de Parish, Dicenta was accused of plagiarism, and controversy ensued (Mas Ferrer, *Vida* 101). Written in collaboration with Manuel Paso, who was one of the members of "gente nueva," and with the music of Ruperto Chapí, *Curro Vargas* proved to be a positive step in Dicenta's career as a dramatist despite the harsh accusations of plagiarism. Mas Ferrer summarizes the impact of *Curro Vargas* on Dicenta: "Esta obra, junto con el *Juan José*, fue la que más beneficios económicos dio a nuestro autor" (*Vida* 101). Also in 1898, Dicenta published a series of *Crónicas* (a collection of articles from his column in the republican newspaper *El Liberal* in 1897).

In March of 1900, Dicenta's next play, *La cortijera* first appeared. It is a lyrical drama written in colaboration with Paso and the music of Chapí. Unfortunately, *La cortijera* enjoyed much less public approval than *Curro Vargas*. *El tío Gervasio* and *El león de bronce*, both one-act monologues, were performed shortly after *La cortijera*, yet they too were soon forgotten. In 1902 *Raimundo Lulio* made its debut in the Teatro Lírico. Reviving the medieval legend of Ramón Lull, *Raimundo Lulio*, an opera of three acts with music by Ricardo Villa, indicates Dicenta's continued success in the art of lyrical dramas.

In 1902, following the six-year absence of social dramas after the failure of *El señor feudal*, Dicenta finally returned to society's mistreatment of the poor working class in *Aurora*, a social drama in which the title character is a poor seamstress who manifests more positive characteristics than the people of higher social classes. Unfortunately for Dicenta, however, he never equaled the success he achieved with *Juan José* even though he continued writing dramas until his death. He dedicated the next few years to writing *comedias*, travel diaries, social chronicles, monologues, and *zarzuelas*: *De tren a tren* (*comedia*, 1902), *Espumas y plomo* (impressions of his trip to the Canary Islands and the mines of Linares, 1903), *De la batalla* (a volume of short stories similar to the previous *Tinta negra*, 1903), *Pa mí que nieva* (*modismo*, 1904), *Juan Francisco* (lyrical drama, 1904), *La conversión de Mañara* (*comedia*, 1905), *De piedra a piedra* (impressions of his trip from the Monasterio de Piedra to Monserrat, 1905), *Amor de artistas* (*comedia*, 1906), *Traperías* (chronicles with a social theme, 1905), *Desde los rosales* (impressions of his trip to San Vicente de la Barquera and the mountains, 1906), *El vals de las sombras* (lyrical remake of *De tren a tren*, 1906), and *Marinera* (monologue, 1907).

Dicenta's next significant play, *Daniel* (1907), is the drama that represents Dicenta's best treatment of the social question,. This is the story of an old miner who takes vengeance on his oppressors by killing an entire group of wealthy individuals who have just finished an elaborate banquet in the very mine that caused him to lose two sons, his wife, and his health. Performed in the Teatro Español by the famous Guerrero-Mendoza acting team, *Daniel* stands out from Dicenta's previous social dramas because the social criticism itself is the actual source of all the dramatic action; it is not on another level behind other themes such as love and honor. The primary theme in *Daniel* is the plight of the miners who suffer greatly because of the conditions in which they work and the poverty caused by those who exploit them. *Daniel*, as Dicenta's final social drama, marks the end of Dicenta's attempt to revive the success he had achieved with *Juan José*.

Despite the fact that Dicenta seemed to have abandoned the social drama that made him famous, he continued to publish plays until his death, although never with the productivity he experienced in the past. In 1907, following the performance of *Daniel*, Dicenta published *Lorenza*, a drama of three acts written in prose. Four dramas were performed in 1908: *El crimen de ayer*, *Los majos de planta*, *Confesión*, and *Entre rocas*. In *El crimen de ayer*, Dicenta examines the traditional view of the family. The female protagonist of *El crimen de ayer*, suffers a great humiliation: not only has she been abandoned by her lover (like Juan José), but also she is faced with a more serious situation; her lover leaves her alone to raise their child (Fernando's mother in *Suicidio de Werther*). She, like Juan José, decides to punish the cause of her pain; she murders her baby's father, Julián. *Los majos de plante* is a *sainete* written in collaboration with Pedro de Repide, one of Dicenta's friends who never achieved the fame as did Dicenta. *Confesión* is a one-act comedia written in prose, and *Entre rocas* is another of Dicenta's lyrical dramas that depends on the musical talents of Ruperto Chapí. Dicenta continues to write short lyrical dramas, and in 1909 *Los tres maridos burlados*, a *zarzuela* also written in collaboration with Pedro de Repide, was first performed. It contains the music of Vicente Lleó.

Over the next few years Dicenta completely abandoned dramas as he dedicated his time to writing travel diaries, novels, and poetry. In 1910, Dicenta published *Por Bretaña*, a description of his journey to the Brittany Coast. Also in 1910, Dicenta published *Rebeldía*, a novel that explores the theme of true love. In 1912, Dicenta published yet another novel, *Los bárbaros*, and in that same year he put together a collection of his poetry, *Del tiempo mozo*. In 1913, Dicenta published his final dramas, *Sobrevivirse* and *El lobo*, both dramas dealing with men who are facing the end of their lives. *Sobrevivirse* requires a close examination in that the protagonist is a dramatist who suffers a stroke, and as a result of his paralysis, loses all that he had once enjoyed. In the final scene the dramatist swallows poison, sacrificing his own life for the happiness of his loved ones. It is a complicated play full of tragic overtones. *El lobo*, on the other hand, is an inspirational drama, unlike any other written by Dicenta. El Lobo is an old man, having served most of his life in prison for his crimes. Through el

Lobo, Dicenta shows that even the most hardened of criminals is able to recognize his tender side when confronted with humanity and sympathy, in this case in the form of a little girl. Both of these late dramas treat some aspect of the social question (albeit in a minor way), and the final one, *El lobo*, returns to the orphaned and imprisoned protagonist reminiscent of the title character of *Juan José*.

In the years remaining until Dicenta's death on February 21, 1917, Dicenta published two more novels, *Encarnación* (1913) and *Mi Venus* (1915), and two more travel diaries, *Mares de España* (impressions on board "Felisa" as he traveled around Spain by boat 1913) and *Bajo los Mirtos* (a description of his trip to the island of San Simón in Galicia 1916).

With his bohemian lifestyle, Dicenta found himself physically exhausted by the time he reached his fifties. By 1916 Dicenta was already suffering from an illness that would eventually cause his death. He chose to seek better health on the southern coast of Spain just as his father had many years before. Several days before he died he said to his doctor: "Cónstele a usted que ha llegado el fin de mi vida y que muero fuera de toda confesión religiosa, manteniendo mis ideales y mirando cara a cara a la muerte" (González Blanco 278).

CRITICAL RECEPTION

Dicenta's work continues to be important in the study of the development of the Spanish stage at the end of the nineteenth century, and it remains a part of the core curriculum of Spanish university courses today.[2] However, most of the criticism that is written about Joaquín Dicenta's works centers on the landmark production of *Juan José* in 1895, and up until the publication in 1978 of Jaime Mas Ferrer's study *Vida, teatro y mito de Joaquín Dicenta*, no comprehensive study was ever attempted. Even Mas Ferrer's study is incomplete, as he only covers selected dramas and simply lists other works written by Dicenta. The detailed critiques of *Juan José* will be saved for Chapter Four where I examine Dicenta's masterpiece in more detail. What follows here is a chronological summary of the criticism to date of Joaquín Dicenta's works.

José Yxart provides an insightful study of the history of the Spanish stage in the nineteenth century in the the two volume set *El arte escénico en España* published in 1894, one year prior to Joaquín Dicenta's *Juan José*. The second volume, published in 1896, explores the development of the *género chico* as well as other end-of-the-century dramatists such as Feliú y Codina and Ricardo de la Vega. His exploration of the history of the Spanish stage in the nineteenth

---

[2] See <http://orion.ulpgc.es/filologia/VSSWeb5c2LITESP3.htm> for the requirements to obtain a degree in the study of Spanish literature at the Universidad de Las Palmas de Gran Canaria.

century is indispensable; unfortunately, however, due to his untimely death in 1895, Yxart did not have the opportunity to witness Dicenta's masterpiece and therefore only barely mentions the budding dramatist, discussing briefly *Luciano*.

In an article in *La España Moderna* in 1908 Gómez de Baquero treats Dicenta's newest drama, *El crimen de ayer*, which premiered that same year. As an introduction, Gómez de Baquero also discusses the nature of Dicenta's drama. In describing Dicenta as "un romántico," Gómez de Baquero compares Dicenta to Zola, stating that Zola too was "un gran romántico" (155). He claims that those who think that Dicenta should provide a more realistic approach in his dramas forget that "esto es lo último que puede pedirse á un romántico" (156).

Manuel Bueno, in his study *Teatro español contemporáneo* (1909), which includes separate chapters dedicated to the dramatists José Echegaray, Angel Guimerá, Benito Pérez Galdós, Joaquín Dicenta, Jacinto Benavente, Linares Rivas, the Quintero brothers, and Santiago Rusiñol, compares Joaquín Dicenta to Victor Hugo: "Los caracteres, las almas, son tan arcaicos y legendarios como los personajes del teatro de Víctor Hugo" (113). Bueno, to my mind erroneously, declares the entirety of Dicenta's dramas to be Romantic and continues to compare him to Calderón de la Barca and Echegaray, indicating the important role that "honor" plays in *Juan José* and other dramas. Bueno claims that "el culto de la mujer y la admiración del valor personal" provide the nucleus of Spanish Romanticism, of which Dicenta plays a part with his neo-Romantic tendencies (114). Bueno questions the social impact of *Juan José*, *El señor feudal*, and other dramas, denying the depth of Dicenta's argument:

> Nuestra avidez sociológica no llega á advertir en el teatro de Dicenta más que esta sencilla verdad: que hay mucho dinero en pocos bolsillos y muchos bolsillos con poco ó ningún dinero. Nada más. (115)

One of Dicenta's contemporaries, José María Carretero (*El Caballero Audaz*), describes his interview with Dicenta in an article he published in *La Esfera*. His illuminating account is reproduced in his collection of interviews from *La Esfera* entitled *Lo que sé por mí: confesiones del siglo* (1915), later republished in *Galería: más de cien vidas extraordinarias contadas por sus protagonistas y comentadas* (1948). Carretero presents a fascinating glimpse of Dicenta as he openly discusses his past, his success, and his interests. Carretero describes Dicenta's personality:

> Dicenta es un hombre de trato encantador; tiene lo que se llama "don de gentes." Su charla es sincera, fraternal, llena de ingeniosidades; tan pronto grita y se impone, varonil, como tiene ingenuidades de chiquillo. El asegura

que dentro de su corazón un ángel y un demonio riñendo formidable gresca. Yo lo creo. (134)

He continutes with Dicenta's physical description:

> Más bien bajo que alto, enjuto de carnes y de movimientos nerviosos y gallardos. Su rostro, pulcramente afeitado y rugoso, es altanero; sus ojos, azules, son pequeños y redondos; su nariz, larga y encorvada como el pico de un ave de rapiña; su boca, carnal, delatora de una sensualidad inaudita, y sus orejas son largas y puntiagudas como las de un fauno... No es viejo; pero ya las canas van invadiendo su cabeza redonda y llena de manchas plateadas. (134-135)

As the interview begins, Carretero questions Dicenta about his work habits. Dicenta explains that he writes with ease "una crónica la hago en una hora, generalmente" (136). Dicenta continues to describe his youth and the poverty in which he lived before the success of *Juan José* in 1895. Carretero interrupts Dicenta to ask him "¿Cuál es el vicio que más le domina?" (139). Dicenta replies:

> El vicio mayor mío ha sido el alcohol, con el cual he luchado por quitármelo, y no lo he conseguido... Las mujeres también me tiran bastante; pero esto no lo considero vicio. (139)

Dicenta continues to describe his favorite autores: "En el libro, Galdós; y en Francia, Víctor Hugo. En el teatro español, Echegaray y Benavente. A Echegaray el teatro le debe mucho" (139).

Andrés González-Blanco, Dicenta's only biographer, offers a detailed study of Dicenta's personality, tracing his development from childhood to death in his study, *Los dramaturgos españoles contemporáneos* (1917). Unfortunately, many of the dates and events he describes are erroneous, forcing the reader to verify the dates of the premieres of Dicenta's plays in other sources. González-Blanco's study, however, proves beneficial in his detailed descriptions of Dicenta's life and works. He describes Dicenta's youth as "borrascosa," and compares him to the Romantics de Musset and Byron. González-Blanco believes that Dicenta was fortunate that his first drama was not *Juan José*, *Aurora*, or *Daniel*, "porque entonces, al presentárselo a D. Manuel Tamayo, éste lo hubiera repelido con indignación o al menos con excusas" (213). González-Blanco praises Dicenta's talent, claiming that his choice to explore the suffering of society's victims in no way lessons his art:

> En vano se nos quiere representar al autor de *Luciano* como un adulador de los bajos instintos de la plebe, incapaz de sentir el arte superior y exquisito; hay arte y mucho arte en Dicenta y hay, sobre todo, un deseo de infundir en el pueblo ese aliento divino del arte. (229)

González-Blanco explains that although he credits the newspapers for much of the information he presents concerning Dicenta's plays and their premieres, he also relies heavily on his own memory as he has been fortunate enough to attend all of the first performances of Dicenta's works and witness the reactions of the public. Despite the many errors, González-Blanco's firsthand experience is invaluable in the study of Joaquín Dicenta and his works.

Enrique Díez-Canedo relates Dicenta's success in his study *Conversaciones literarias: primera serie 1915-1920* (1921), a compilation of articles he had previously published in *España* and *El Sol*. Díez-Canedo states that Dicenta's literary contributions all reflect his "espíritu batallador, su afán de reivindicaciones sociales, su amor a los caídos y a los humildes" (47). According to Díez-Canedo, despite the social nature of many of Dicenta's plays, he was above all a Romantic: "No un romántico de cota de mallas o de laúd a la espalda: Joaquín Dicenta era un romántico de blusas" (49).

José Francos Rodríguez, one of Dicenta's friends since childhood who shared with Dicenta his hatred of "convencionalismos y tapujos," discusses the circumstances surrounding the premiere of *Juan José* in his 1927 *Contar vejeces, de las memorias de un gacetillero* (172). He describes Dicenta's dissatisfaction with minimal fame and his desire to be very famous:

> A Dicenta, que tuvo un feliz principio de carrera con el estreno de *El suicidio de Werther*, no le bastaba con vivir a la sombra de la fama corriente; apetecía la cúspide; no acomodarse en las laderas donde sopla el viento apacible del bienestar común, sino arriba, en lo más alto, donde rugen los huracanes y se triunfa definitivamente se sucumbe. (170-171)

In 1929 Fernando Castán Palomar published an anthology of poetry, including several poems by Joaquín Dicenta. In the prologue to these poems Palomar briefly summarizes Dicenta's life, describing the great success of *Juan José*. In comparing Dicenta with Echegaray, Palomar praises Dicenta's drama, emphasizing its Romantic characteristics:

> En la forma, Dicenta es más vigoroso, más realista, más sincero. Un espíritu de combate, un afán apostólico de deshacer rutinas, y sobre todo, un anhelo valiente de justicia, laten definitivos en las obras de Dicenta; romanticismo, bello y admirable romanticismo, que tiene un fervoroso abolengo español;

el amor y el honor emparejan en él con sinceridad, con calor, con realidad de idea firme e inquebrantable. (8)

Just as Carretero describes his personal experiences with Joaquín Dicenta, Luis Ruiz Contreras also relates an enlightening account of several meetings he had with the famous dramatist in his revealing study *Medio siglo de teatro infructuoso* (1930). Ruiz Contreras was a renowned critic who had translated a number of European dramas into Spanish including Émile Zola's *Thérèse Raquin* and Henrik Ibsen's *Jean-Gabriel Borkman*. Upon his first meeting with Dicenta, Ruiz Contreras did not know the dramatist or his work, and in fact, Dicenta was relatively unknown to most critics. Ruiz Contreras indicates that at that time Dicenta had only written *El suicidio de Werther* and *La mejor ley*, placing their meeting sometime between 1889 and 1890. Ruiz Contreras reveals an illuminating perspective of Dicenta as a young artist struggling to become a famous dramatist. Ruiz Contreras describes Dicenta's physical appearance:

Y me tendió la mano un joven de mediana estatura, buen talle, perfil correcto, bigote cuidado; en la boca una leve mueca triste, aspirante a sonrisa irónica; ojos felinos que, seguros de impresionar favorablemente, doraban el verde claro de sus pupilas; un poco de socarronería; mezcla de gracia elegante y desenfado vulgar. (121)

Two years later they meet again, and this time they discuss a particular drama that Dicenta had begun several months earlier but which had been interrupted by "las angustias del vivir" (181). Dicenta explains that he had only written one act, and after Ruiz Contreras shows interest in the dramatist's work, Dicenta reads aloud the first act of *Juan José* to him. Anxious to know Ruiz Contreras' opinion, Dicenta questions him. Ruiz Contreras responds prophetically: "Otros dos actos como ese, y habrá escrito usted uno de los más hermosos dramas castellanos" (181). To Dicenta's excited exclamation "¿No me engañas?", Ruiz Contreras replies: "Ni sabría engañarte ni me puedo equivocar. El público sentirá lo que yo he sentido. Lo que penetra en la entraña lo comprende todo el mundo. ¡Al trabajo!" (181). Dicenta, after his success with *Juan José*, gave the original manuscript to Ruiz Contreras as a token of appreciation. Ruiz Contreras was touched by Dicenta's gratitude, given Dicenta's rebellious nature: "Joaquín Dicenta, el arisco, el burlador, el indomable, sentía esa dignidad que tiene por nombre 'agradecimiento'" (182). Ruiz Contreras fondly believed that his "entusiasmo fué la llama que reanimó su adormecido pensamiento" (182).

Edwin S. Morby describes Joaquín Dicenta as "probably the most confirmed self-plagiarist in Spanish letters" in his 1941 study "Notes on Dicenta's Material and Method" (383). For Morby, many of the plots of Dicenta's plays can be found in earlier plays, articles, or short stories. Morby believes that the reason that Dicenta borrowed so much from himself in writing and rewriting his dramas stems from Dicenta's inability to escape his journalistic past. Morby writes: "Dicenta merely seems to have found creation difficult without a sketch to work from"; Dicenta's sketches are "usually journalistic, and probably always written for publication in a newspaper" (392). Although Morby has illuminated a truth about Dicenta's tendency to create dramas from earlier prose, he completely ignores Dicenta's talent not only in the creation of fiction but also in his versatility, in exploring the same theme in several genres.

In 1946 José Deleito y Piñuela published *Estampas del Madrid teatral fin de siglo*. Not only is this study valuable for the detailed information he discloses about the actors, theaters, and dramatists that were at their height at the end of the nineteenth century, but also it contains nearly one hundred photographs of these dramatists and actors. Deleito y Piñuela's discussion of Dicenta includes an analysis of Dicenta's first drama, *El suicidio de Werther*, in which he describes how it arrived on the stage, who played the major roles (Rafael Calvo as Fernando), and the success it achieved. Like Manuel Bueno, Deleito y Piñuela compares Dicenta to Pedro Calderón de la Barca and José Echegaray, especially in this first drama, which is fully cloaked in neo-Romantic characteristics. Deleito y Piñuela describes Dicenta's evolution from his first play through *Los irresponsables*, *El duque de Gandía*, and *Luciano* to his biggest success, *Juan José*. Deleito praises Dicenta's talent, lamenting his decision to abandon verse for prose: "sacrificio doloroso para tan gran dominador de la rima" (199).

In 1952, the British critic H.B. Hall published the article, "Dicenta and the Drama of Social Criticism," in *Hispanic Review*. Hall briefly discusses Dicenta's background, including his childhood and the years before he began writing dramas, and he also describes Dicenta's rejection of Christianity, emphasizing Dicenta's belief that man is capable of improving his society without the aid of any supernatural being. Of interest is Hall's definition of successful social criticism on the stage: first, there must be a "certain harmony of outlook between dramatist and audience," and second, "there must also be a sufficient degree of realism in the presentation of the theme for the public to recognize themselves and the contemporary situation on stage" (47). Hall claims that in the mid 80's, just as Dicenta started his career as a dramatist, this harmony had not yet occurred on stage, for Echegaray, with his not so realistic dramas, was in full control. Hall provides insightful yet brief critiques of many of Dicenta's dramas, including *El suicidio de Werther*, *La mejor ley*, *Los irresponsables*, *Luciano*, *El señor feudal*, *Aurora*, *Amor de artistas*, *Daniel*, and *El lobo*, but his best critique is of *Juan José*. (See my study of *Juan José* in Chapter Four.) Hall concludes that Dicenta made an important contribution to the Spanish stage:

[Dicenta] brought to the theatre an awareness of the conflicts taking place in society, as distinct from 'society.' He furthered the development of a natural prose dialogue, and extended the range of stage *costumbrismo* by the introduction of realistic scenes from the lives of the proletariat. (66)

Hall's final sentence concedes, however, that Dicenta was "too old-fashioned and too radical" for the Madrid audiences of the late nineteenth century (66).

Gonzalo Torrente Ballester, in his study *Teatro español contemporáneo* (1957), defines Dicenta's contribution to social theater in Spain: "La novedad del teatro social de Dicenta no consiste en sacar a escena al pueblo, sino en sacarlo investido de derechos que suponen el movimiento proletario del siglo" (60-61). Social theater "se dramatiza la lucha de clases de forma más o menos enmascarada" (60). Rather than explore Dicenta's most famous social drama, *Juan José*, Torrente Ballester discusses *El señor feudal* which "me parece mucho más significativo que *Juan José*" (61). Torrente Ballester recalls a conversation he once had with Manuel Dicenta, Joaquín Dicenta's son who became a famous actor. Manuel Dicenta explained that although his father was not a believer, he did respect religion and in general the highest traditional values. With this as his argument, Torrente Ballester denies that Joaquín Dicenta was a socialist, but rather "un tipo, muy español y muy ibérico, de liberal socializante" (63). Torrente Ballester also denies the evidence of class struggle in Dicenta's plays, especially in *El señor feudal*: "No es la conciencia de clase... sino la conciencia moral" (64).

Francisco García Pavón's *El teatro social en España: 1895-1962* (1962) is a valuable source of information concerning Spain's early social theater. García Pavón defines social theater and carefully explores its development from the pre-Dicenta Galdosian dramas to Lauro Olmo's *La camisa* (1961). He limits social theater to those dramas that are dominated by "la cuestión social" (18). That is,

> aquellas obras y autores que centran su atención en la lucha de clases; en el drama humano surgido de unas estructuras sociales injustas; en el teatro, en suma, que se limita a exponer estas injusticias de manera tácita o expresa y propugna unas fórmulas revolucionarias o evolucionistas para su corrección. (18)

García Pavón offers a detailed critique of *Juan José*, *El señor feudal*, and *Daniel*, and even includes a photograph of a tavern scene from *Juan José*. In his discussion of *El señor feudal*, García Pavón defines four common characters that are present in a social drama: first, the "burgués explotador" who is egotistical, cruel and without virtue; second, the "obrero masa," who is undecided and incapable of rebellion without a ringleader pushing him/her; third, the "proletario consciente," he or she who is the director and coordinator of strikes and riots, who would die for the sake of justice, and/or who is imprisoned and abandoned by his/her companions, the "obreros masa"; and finally, the "viejo obrero honrado:" a conformist who loves order and his work, rejects new revolutionary ideas and violence, but ends up taking vengeance for his son or daughter (57). García Pavón claims that *Juan José*, which lacks these fundamental characters, was not a social drama even though it "resultó el más bello drama social de nuestra historia literaria" (58).

Two years after García Pavón's illuminating study of Spanish social theater, J. Hunter Peak published *Social Drama in Nineteenth-Century Spain* (1964). As the title suggests, Peak limits his study to the nineteenth century. Even though Peak does not define social drama in his study, it is easy to deduce that he is not in agreement with García Pavón's definition. For García Pavón, social drama is limited to those plays that focus on class struggle and the suffering caused by unjust social structures with the primary emphasis on the working classes. Dramas that fit that definition begin with Joaquín Dicenta's *Juan José* in 1895 (as García Pavón's title indicates: *El teatro social en España: 1895-1962*). Peak, however, uses a much broader definition of social theater; for him, social drama defines any play that offers a moral that suggests change in contemporary society. Peak begins his examination of social drama with Leandro Fernández Moratín, giving him full credit for "initiating this form of drama on the modern Spanish stage" (29). His study includes detailed plot summaries and analyses of the drama of the following playwrights: Leandro Fernández Moratín, Martínez de la Rosa, Manuel Gorostiza, Bretón de los Herreros, Ventura de la Vega, Manuel Tamayo y Baus, Adelardo López de Ayala, Luis de Eguílaz, José Echegaray, Rodríguez Rubí, José Marco y Sanchís, Eugenio Sellés, Leopoldo Cano y Masas, Enrique Gaspar, Gaspar Núñez de Arce, Joaquín Dicenta, and Benito Pérez Galdós. Peak claims that these dramatists portrayed social issues on the stage, a tradition that peaked with Joaquín Dicenta's *Juan José*.

In his analysis of Dicenta, Peak states that "Dicenta's chief claim to fame is his interest in the lowest economic groups" (106). Peak analyzes in detail *Los irresponsables*, *Juan José*, *El señor feudal*, and *Daniel*, praising Dicenta's technique and giving Dicenta credit for enlarging considerably "the scope of Spanish drama" (161). His analysis, however, is at times seriously flawed. Peak describes *Los irresponsables* as Dicenta's first play when in truth Dicenta had already published and produced *El suicidio de Werther* and *La mejor ley*. Peak also erroneously claims that "all of Dicenta's dramas deal with the proletariat" (161). A study of the entirety of Dicenta's work reveals that this is not the case. Peak continues to argue that "all of Dicenta's plays end violently and pessimistically. Not a note of optimism is to be discerned in any of Dicenta's works" (162). Although Peak provides a valuable history to the drama that leads up to the landmark production of *Juan José*, his analysis of Dicenta indicates that he had only read the four plays he discussed, and his uninformed opinions are based upon an incomplete picture of what constitutes the theater of Joaquín Dicenta. Francisco Ruíz Ramón describes Dicenta in his *Historia del teatro español* (1967) as a true dramatist, not a journalist who turned to playwriting in order to use the stage as an instrument to effect change in society. Ruíz Ramón diminishes Dicenta's role as a social dramatist, however, by claiming that Dicenta treated the "choque de personas morales" more than the "choque de clases" (427). He continues: "Los representantes de las clases sociales, conflictivamente enfrentados, representan mucho menos una clase social que un individuo moral" (427). Ruíz Ramón quotes Torrente Ballester several times as he attempts to disprove the social nature of Dicenta's works and to overemphasize Dicenta's concern with moral issues instead of social issues. Finally, Ruíz Ramón compares Dicenta to Gerhart Hauptmann:

> El dramaturgo no consigue convertir la nueva mentalidad, patente en la palabra del personaje, en fuente directa y determinante de la acción, como ocurre, por ejemplo, en *Los tejedores* (1892) de Hauptmann. El drama social se queda a mitad de camino entre la nueva mentalidad de carácter moral e individual. (430)

Rafael Pérez de la Dehesa, in his study *El grupo Germinal: una clave del '98* (1970), begins his discussion of Joaquín Dicenta by quoting José María Salaverría who described the importance of *Juan José* to the Generation of '98: "tuvo la significación del *Hernani* victorhuguesco" (17). Pérez de la Dehesa limits his study to *Juan José* and *El señor feudal*, with more emphasis placed on the former. He reproduces detailed reviews of the great success achieved by *Juan José*, quoting from the *Revista Contemporánea, El País* and other journals. Pérez de la Dehesa also gives a useful summary of the criticism that exists to date (1970) of Dicenta's masterpiece, which I will discuss in more detail in Chapter Four.

Jesús Rubio Jiménez presents a valuable study in his 1982 *Ideología y teatro en España (1890-1900)*. He traces the development of social theater in Spain to foreign influences, especially Émile Zola and Henrik Ibsen. Rubio Jiménez discusses in detail the influx of realistic European drama and its influence on the dramatists of the last decade of the nineteenth century. He dedicates nearly a dozen pages to *Juan José* and its importance in the development of social theater in Spain, providing, as had Pérez de la Dehesa, summaries of reviews and critiques of the premiere of *Juan José* in 1895. He offers a detailed analysis (to be discussed later) of *Juan José*, maintaining that it is not a social drama but rather a melodrama with a thesis.

The first publication dedicated entirely to Joaquín Dicenta and his drama is Jaime Mas Ferrer's *Vida, teatro y mito de Joaquín Dicenta* (1978). In his introduction Mas Ferrer explains his goal: "no pretendíamos estudiar la obra en general del bilbilintano, sino limitarnos al estudio de una parcela: la producción dramática" (9). Mas Ferrer begins his study with a narration of Dicenta's life; however, the account is full of errors and inconsistencies. In Chapter Two, Mas Ferrer lists Dicenta's non-dramatic work, "crónicas de viaje," "artículos y cuentos," "novelas largas y cortas," "poesías," and "traducciones" (43-45). In Chapter Three, Mas Ferrer describes the state of the theater upon Dicenta's arrival on the theatrical scene. Mas Ferrer's discussion of Dicenta's drama is divided into three sections: miscellaneous drama, musical pieces, and finally, social drama. Mas Ferrer analyzes in detail the following plays: *El suicidio de Werther, Honra y vida, La mejor ley, Los irresponsables, Luciano, Amor de artistas, Lorenza, El crimen de ayer, Sobrevivirse, El lobo, Juan José, El señor feudal, Aurora,* and *Daniel*. Rather than analyze Dicenta's musical theater, Mas Ferrer simply lists their premiere dates. His final chapters treat Dicenta's journalistic career and his death. In his definition of social theater, Mas Ferrer quotes Alfonso Sastre who claims in *Drama y sociedad* that those dramas that pertain to the category of social theater should be characterized by "la índole de los materiales dramáticos recogidos, y la intención del dramaturgo" (107). Mas Ferrer elaborates:

> El primero se basaría en la extracción de la temática dramática de la realidad utilizando para ello una visión 'objectiva' y la segunda perseguía una intención con la finalidad de conseguir algo, enfoque 'subjetivo'... el fin que persigue el autor al exponer ante el espectador una realidad con el objeto de conseguir por medio de una toma de conciencia con el auditoria una reforma o purificación de esa realidad representada. (*Vida* 107)

More recently, Mas Ferrer has written the introduction to the "Catedra" edition of *Juan José* (1992), repeating information from the 1978 publication.

Antonio Castellón's 1994 study, *El teatro como instrumento político en España (1895-1914)*, offers a detailed examination of the five different tendencies on the Spanish stage between the premiere of Spain's first social drama *Juan José* in 1895 and the beginning of the first World War in 1914: "tendencia inmovilista," "tendencia capitalista," "tendencia radical," "tendencia revolucionaria," and "tendencia nacionalista" (19-23). Castellón places Joaquín Dicenta in the category of "tendencia radical," together with Enrique Gaspar, Leopoldo Alas, and Benito Pérez Galdós (21). The theater in this category

> Se trata de un intento, llevado a cabo por la pequeña burguesía radical, para vincular una ideología que marque la diferencia existente entre sus intereses y los de las clases que integran la oligarquía en el poder. (21)

In his definition of social theater, Castellón rejects García Pavón's contention that those dramas that focus their attention on class struggle form social theater, but rather, Castellón claims, such plays are "Teatro Político," as Alfonso Sastre had defined earlier in his study *Drama y sociedad* (25). In his argument, Castellón quotes Alfonso Sastre's definition of both "Teatro Social" and "Teatro Político." First, about social theater Sastre states: " Temas rigurosamente sociales son aquellos que tratan realidades dramáticas en que están interesados grandes grupos humanos" (25). Second, about political theater, Sastre explains: "Estas son las dos caras del teatro político: Denuncia de horror y de miseria, por un lado; esperanza en nuevas estructuras sociales por otro" (25). In the thirty-six pages that Castellón dedicates to Dicenta, he offers nothing new, freely borrowing from previous critics such as García Pavón, Pérez de la Dehesa, and Mas Ferrer without giving them credit. Castellón traces Dicenta's career in journalism, the importance that honor has in his dramas, and his struggle with "las dos Españas": "La España fanática, tradicional, rutinaria e intolerante por un lado, y la España liberal, progresista y científica por otro" (99).

One of the most recent studies of Dicenta is found in David Thatcher Gies' *The Theatre in Nineteenth-Century Spain* (1994). Gies offers a history of the Spanish stage, studying in detail not only the dramatists and their plays, but also paying careful attention to the socio-economic evolution of the theatrical business, including information about the physical structures of Madrid's most well known theaters. His presentation of Dicenta is flattering:

> It was Dicenta, a powerful dramatist as well as a committed champion of the downtrodden, who succeeded best in fusing theatre with social concerns; that is, Dicenta was first and foremost a man of letters who wove into his writing a well-defined social posture rather than a pamphleteer with aspirations to the stage. (325)

Gies credits dramatists such as Félix Mejía (*La Suiza libre*, 1846) and Sixto Sáenz de la Cámara (*Jaime el Barbudo*, 1853) for first bringing the problems of the "underdogs" to the Spanish stage under the mask of historical drama. Others who followed Cámara's lead were Fernando Garrido (*Un día de revolución*, 1855), Francisco Botella y Andrés (*El rico y el pobre*, 1855), and Manuel Ortiz de Pinedo (*Los pobres de Madrid* 1872). In explaining these dramatists and their place in the evolution of social theater on the Spanish stage, Gies emphasizes Dicenta's role in transforming and adapting their ideas to new circumstances with far more success.

3
The Early Plays: 1888-1894

IN THE YEARS BEFORE Joaquín Dicenta's first plays were performed, Dicenta struggled to survive by taking various positions as he pursued a literary career alongside his contemporaries, who called themselves the "gente nueva." While he wrote for several journals, he lived a bohemian lifestyle, and above all he considered himself a misunderstood artist. Dicenta's first dramas adhere to the popular Echegarayan neo-Romantic tradition as well as to the relatively new realistic approach, while establishing Dicenta's tendency to depict social problems, as he protests on behalf of the individual against society.

EL SUICIDIO DE WERTHER (1888)

In 1888, Dicenta began his career as a dramatist with the publication of *El suicidio de Werther*, a four-act play written entirely in verse. Having no prior experience as a dramatist, Dicenta found it difficult to find a producer for his first play. He owed its first performance to his determined mother, who hand-delivered the play to the distinguished playwright Manuel Tamayo y Baus. It was first performed by the Calvo-Vico company on February 23, 1888 in the Teatro de la Princesa in Madrid. As the title suggests, the play is directly related to Johann Wolfgang von Goethe's *Die Leiden des Jungen Werthers* (1774), in which the protagonist, suffering from unrequited love, commits suicide. This tragic story is repeated in Dicenta's play as Fernando, the protagonist, commits suicide while a painting of Werther's suicide hangs gloomily in the background throughout the drama. *El suicidio de Werther* is mostly Romantic in theme as it treats a young artist who, because he is of unknown birth, is mistreated by society and discouraged from initiating a relationship with the only woman he has ever loved. There are indications that hint at Dicenta's future social dramas as the protagonist screams out against a society that allows such misguided prejudice.

PLOT

Fernando, an aspiring young artist orphaned at an early age and condemned by society because he is illegitimate, is in love with María. His goal is to gain her father's acceptance as well as society's approval through his talent at his first art exhibition, where he displays his masterpiece, a painting of the tragic ending to Werther's story. Fernando chose this final tragic moment to depict in his painting in order to emphasize the suffering caused by the unjust social code of the day. After enjoying great success at his art exhibition, Fernando agrees to paint the portrait of a mysterious stranger, Carlota, who he learns later to be his birth mother who had abandoned him as an infant. Don Julián, María's father, recognizes Carlota as a prostitute he once knew, and he chastises Fernando for allowing a woman of such low standards into his studio, especially as he is becoming more recognized and accepted for his talent. Once Fernando realizes that Carlota is his birth mother, he defends Carlota and opposes Don Julián because he feels it is his duty as her son to protect her from Don Julián's insults, even if it means risking his future success and the possibility of a relationship with Don Julián's daughter, María. Because Fernando adheres strongly to the code of honor, he moves into a home he plans to share with his mother, whom he will try to support with the income from his art.

Now that everyone knows that he is the son of a prostitute, Fernando loses the respect he had spent years earning, and he suffers from the new social status that has been put upon him. The situation worsens when Fernando discovers the secret affair between his good friend, Adolfo, and his mother. He considers their relationship an offense to his honor and is so overcome with anger that he challenges Adolfo to a duel. Returning from the duel unharmed, Fernando claims he has killed Adolfo. This new scandal renews public criticism of Fernando, who has lost all hope of gaining the approval of María's father, Don Julián, as well as acceptance from the rest of society. Fernando gives a moving speech in which he expresses his anguish at having killed his friend and at the tragic situation that has been forced upon him by society. He reads aloud a letter that was sent to him by María in which she admits she loves him deeply but refuses to go against her father's wishes. This letter is a copy of the letter sent to Werther by Carlota, Werther's beloved, in Goethe's novel. Fernando suddenly is conscious of the presence of the painting and of the mirror image it creates of his own life; he recognizes himself in the tragic figure of Werther on canvas. Fernando decides that he, like Werther, must take his own life to satisfy the hungry world's desire to ruin him. In this state of total despair, Fernando stabs himself and falls dying beneath the symbolic painting.

TECHNIQUE

El suicidio de Werther follows closely the neo-Romantic tradition of Echegaray. Echegaray, according to José Deleito y Piñuela, heaped great praise on the upcoming dramatist (*Estampas* 60). José-Carlos Mainer, however, diminishes the value of the play:

No tiene otro mérito sino el de anticipar un tema predilecto de Dicenta: el trágico destino que ensombrece, como oscura venganza de sus privilegios espirituales, la vida del artista en el mundo moderno. (*Literatura* 37-38)

Jesus Rubio Jiménez draws a correlation between Dicenta's portrayal of the artist and the literary group to which Dicenta belonged, the "gente nueva": "[Dicenta] introduce personajes artistas con dificultades para adaptarse a la sociedad: Fernando, Felipe o Luciano de alguna manera encarnan los ideales de los escritores de la 'gente nueva'" (*Ideología* 141). The misunderstood artist is a common Romantic theme; Dicenta, however, chooses to explore the tragedy of an artist who is not only misunderstood but also completely alienated by society due to circumstances beyond his control.

In his first play, Dicenta adheres to the popular neo-Romantic technique of the time, using four acts, a minimum number of characters, and verse to express his condemnation of society. The format of the play directly reflects Fernando's decline as Dicenta carefully structures the action, the language, and the setting to fit the theme. Both the action and the language of the play shift from gentle passiveness to violent action, as Fernando realizes that he will never be accepted by society. The setting of the play follows the same format and is divided into two equal halves: Acts I and II take place in Fernando's art studio, which symbolizes hope for the future, and Acts III and IV in the humble home he shares with his mother, Carlota, which symbolizes his stagnant present. This physical transition from wealth, success, and acceptance to poverty, despair, and alienation is immediately evident as a reflection of Fernando's inability to escape the fate that always haunts the Romantic hero. It is as if he were trapped in a downward spiral, culminating with his tragic suicide.

Fernando is unquestionably a Romantic hero: he suffers from unrequited love; he is of unknown origin; he claims to be a misunderstood artist; he is dominated by his passion; he adheres strongly to the honor code; and he commits suicide when he can no longer handle what fate has bestowed upon him. Even Dicenta's dramatic technique is Romantic: most of the play takes place in a gloomy atmosphere, many times with just barely enough light to focus on the main characters; it is written entirely in verse; blood is spilled on stage; and the play contains many of the Romantic expressions and excessive exclamation marks reminiscent of the Duque de Rivas and other Romantic dramatists. Both the emphasis on feeling and the complete disillusionment experienced by Fernando reflect the Romantic nature of the play. Perhaps the most obvious of the Romantic traits of this drama is the unfolding of the plot around the inexorable fate that is common in Romantic dramas, using the symbolic painting of Werther's suicide to foreshadow the inevitable and melodramatic death in the final scene.

IDEOLOGY

Although it may seem to be a simple imitation of Echegaray's neo-Romantic style, *El suicidio de Werther* provides the audience with a taste of the social drama that is to come as Dicenta chastises a society whose narrow-mindedness and condemnation of the innocent drive a social outcast to commit suicide. Fernando, however, is not the only social outcast in this play, for his mother, Carlota, too has suffered from an unforgiving society. Dicenta fills his first neo-Romantic play with many social commentaries, on the lips of an artist who deserves far more respect than he receives and in the lament of a prostitute who is unable to find love even in her own son. Through the characters of Fernando and Carlota, Dicenta expresses his condemnation of society's unjust treatment of the social outcast.

Fernando, the eternal pessimist, continuously laments his tragic situation, stating, "¡vano es mi afán e inútil todo lo que hice para lograrlo!" (17). Dicenta uses Fernando to take advantage of the tragic story of Carlota and Werther by expressing his views on the cruelty of social conventions that discourage two people who truly love each other from being together:

> ¡Revisten tal crueldad,
> tal furia, tal impiedad
> nuestras costumbres sociales,
> que mil hombres, su infinito
> amor, aunque sea honrado,
> lo sufren como un pecado,
> lo guardan como un delito! (23-24)

Fernando argues that as a social outcast he has no hope of acceptance by María's father, no matter how hard he tries or how successful he becomes in his art:

> ¿Qué represento? ¿Qué valgo?
> En sus preocupaciones
> la sociedad me condena
> a sufrir una cadena
> de férreos eslabones... (28)

From the beginning of the play, Dicenta has carefully detailed Fernando's positive qualities, which only make society's rejection of him that much more ridiculous. Fernando, besides being talented, is a hard worker who is completely devoted to his art. He shows great respect for his adoptive father, Don Pedro, whom he truly loves, and expresses his gratitude to him constantly. Above all, however, his devotion to an undeserving woman who had abandoned him at birth truly indicates Fernando's worthiness. He has proven his worth in every possible aspect of his life over which he has had control; unfortunately, however, Fernando's lack of control over his own social acceptance proves he is worthless in the eyes of an unforgiving society.

Years before, Carlota also suffered from society's condemnation, having given birth to a son out of wedlock, and, after being abandoned by the child's father, deserting the infant:

> Muertos mis padres; burlada
> mi fe; cruel mi destino;
> la miseria en mi camino,
> y yo sola, abandonada...
> ¡tuve miedo!... ¡fui cobarde!...
> ¡sentí vergüenza!... ¡y de él me aparté! (52)

After abandoning her son, Carlota was consumed by guilt, and the alienation from all who once loved her nearly drove her insane. She soon turned to prostitution, for which she continues to condemn herself, even though her friend tries to convince her that she was forced into prostitution in order to survive, negating any criminal intent.

Through Carlota, Dicenta gives a voice to the innocent victims of society who have no control over their fate. Not only did she become completely disillusioned at the loss of her lover, but also she was forced to live her life in shame, knowing that she had abandoned her only child. As a prostitute, she has no hope of redeeming herself or of obtaining a respectable place in society. Don Julián represents the general consensus of society as he insults and condemns her. Carlota's reaction to him is like that of a caged animal, victimized and scared. She retreats to the back of the room and tries to hide her face from her oppressor in humiliation, and at times, she lashes out violently in a vain attempt at self-defense. Remembering her friend's encouraging words, Carlota asserts that she is not to blame for all that has happened to her. She claims that even though it is society who has forced her into prostitution, no attempts are made to rehabilitate the social outcast:

> ¡Caemos!... ¿Quién nos escuda?
> ¿Quién a recogernos baja
> del fango? Se nos ultraja,
> pero no se nos ayuda.
> se desprecia nuestro lloro.
> Pedimos gracia, y desdén
> nos brindan; amor también

pedimos y nos dan oro... (57)

Throughout his work and his life, Dicenta demonstrates great pity for women like Carlota who are forced into prostitution, and in *Spoliarium* (1888), a book of short social sketches published the same year as *El suicidio de Werther*'s first performance, Dicenta vows to advise a prostitute whom he once knew to hold her head high against the society that victimized her:

> No bajes la frente; no implores gracia cuando los hombres te insulten; no supliques á las amenazas de la justicia; no temas el desprecio de las gentes ni las execraciones del mundo; míralos cara á cara y diles: "Yo no tengo la culpa. Vosotros me hicisteis caer.... Hoy vendo mi cuerpo al primero que lo compra.... Todo lo bueno que en mí existía he llegado á perderlo por vosotros." (*Spoliarium* 112)

CONCLUSIONS

With a minimum number of characters and in a truly neo-Romantic setting, Dicenta argues two issues in *El suicidio de Werther*. First, he condemns a society that refuses to provide help or support for those who are victimized, those who are of lowly birth, and those like Carlota who have been forced into a degrading position by society, and second, Dicenta denounces the community's inability to accept an honorable man like Fernando, who through no fault of his own is condemned for the actions of his mother. Carlota blames society for having forced her into prostitution, for not helping her regain respect, and finally for condemning her for the very act that was forced upon her. Fernando blames society for remaining completely blind to all of his positive characteristics and condemning him for his mother's actions. Fernando is talented, intelligent, sensitive to others, loyal, respectful, grateful and hard working, yet society continues to condemn him. Because he is unacceptable in the eyes of society, his worth as a person and as an artist is completely disregarded. Throughout the play Dicenta emphasizes that a person's worth is based on his/her works and not on his/her heritage. There is no justice in judging someone's worth based upon the actions of another. Dicenta draws attention to the suffering of those who are judged by society for reasons over which they have no control. Both Carlota and Fernando are condemned to remain in their tragic situation without any hope of returning to the mainstream of society.

LA MEJOR LEY (1889)

Less than a year after *El suicidio de Werther*, Dicenta's next play, *La mejor ley*, was first performed by the Antonio Vico company in the Teatro Español on January 2, 1889. Although it was only politely received by the viewing public, it certainly stimulated discussion as Dicenta explores the problems that exist in a loveless marriage. Unlike *El suicidio de Werther* (1887), *La mejor ley* is set entirely in the realm of the upper class. Continuing in the tradition of Echegaray, Dicenta examines the domestic tragedy of a wealthy couple.

PLOT

The marriage between Gonzalo and Dolores is loveless, which is no surprise since their union was the result of a *mandato paternal*. Dolores, as virtuous as she is beautiful, has no idea that Gonzalo has taken her best friend Mercedes for his lover nor that he is spending all of their wealth on jewels and other luxuries for his insatiable mistress. Pablo, an old friend of Gonzalo, soon arrives to visit after having been away for years. Gonzalo tells Pablo of his predicament, and Pablo is shocked to discover that the poor deceived wife is the young girl whom he once loved years ago and had to give up because her parents had promised her to another man. When Dolores discovers Pablo's presence, the two of them struggle to suppress their old feelings. Dolores knows that she is incapable of neglecting her duty as an honorable wife, even if she is involved in a loveless marriage. Pablo too has enough respect for the institution of marriage that he denies his feelings for Dolores.

Once Dolores learns of her husband's affair, she confronts Gonzalo, threatening to leave him and tell everyone of his dishonor. Although Gonzalo never cared about his wife's feelings as he maintained an extramarital relationship, he is frightened by the thought of public scandal and does not want to separate from his wife. Gonzalo is miserable as his friends and neighbors discover his dishonor, with the result that he quickly arranges to meet with Dolores to discuss reconciliation. While Dolores is waiting for her husband, she and Pablo have an intimate discussion about their love for each other. She tells him that although she loves him, she adheres firmly to the Church's attitude toward matrimony and therefore is unable to imagine dissolving her marriage to Gonzalo. As Pablo prepares to leave, Gonzalo rushes in thinking that Dolores is having an affair with Pablo. Without seeking to verify the truth, he challenges his friend Pablo to a duel. Dolores faints at her husband's hypocrisy and unjust accusation, and as she awakes, she learns that Pablo has been mortally wounded in the duel. Pablo's last breath informs Gonzalo of the truth, and Gonzalo begs his wife to forgive him.

TECHNIQUE

In *La mejor ley*, Dicenta remains true to the neo-Romantic tradition that shaped his first play, yet unlike *El suicidio de Werther*, *La mejor ley* lacks action and suffers from an overabundance of rhetoric. The characters are in a sterile environment where action would seem out of place. It is not until the final tragic murder that the momentum of the play gains speed, only to come to a complete halt. Although the play is weak, it successfully adheres to the neo-Romantic tradition of the time. The importance of honor, the suffering caused by unrequited love, and the preocupation with vengeance shape this play into a typical bourgeois neo-Romantic drama.

Honor is a predominating theme throughout the drama, as Dolores remains the exemplary wife despite temptation. Examples of her profession of honor and deep concern about her reputation are found throughout her dialogue with those around her: "yo, mi honra he de ponerla aun más alta que mi vida" (87). Dolores, ignorant of her husband's affair, remains completely faithful to him, avoiding any possibility that she "pudiera ser mal juzgada" (28). Gonzalo, on the other hand, only finds himself concerned about his honor after the affair is no longer a secret and his wife has left him.

Another Romantic characteristic is the presence of unrequited love and the suffering it causes. Dolores, whose name is symbolic of suffering, complains that she suffers constantly: "lucho con infinitos dolores" (24). The remaining main characters, Pablo, Gonzalo, and Mercedes, are also victims of unrequited love. Throughout the play they each lament their misfortune. Truly, the only one who seems justified in her pain is Dolores, who, because of her commitment to her husband and her honor, accepts her situation and proclaims that she will make the best of it: "a pesar de todo necesito amarle, y trato de triunfar de su desvío" (42).

Soon, however, Dolores finds herself on the same level as that of her husband and his mistress. She, as do they, becomes preoccupied with vengeance, another Romantic characteristic. Even the minor characters have their petty reasons to seek revenge. Dolores' discovery of her husband's affair is the result of her rejection of a jealous Don Juan figure who wanted to hurt her for having rejected him. Dolores soon discovers that Mercedes' motive for revenge reverts back to the days before she and Gonzalo were married, for Mercedes and Gonzalo were in love before Dolores and Gonzalo were matched by their parents. Mercedes stops at nothing to seek vengeance against Dolores, the woman who stole from her the only man she has ever loved: "ni los crímenes la arredaran ni el deshonor le da espanto" (41). The vicious cycle of vengeance continues after Dolores throws Mercedes from her home, another act of revenge, exposing her husband's dishonor. Because of the scandal this situation causes, Gonzalo ends his relationship with Mercedes. Mercedes now has another reason to take vengeance on Dolores for ruining her affair with Gonzalo; thus she tells Gonzalo about the love between Pablo and Dolores, hoping that he will assume the worst. He responds, "¡Si querías vengarte, bien te has vengado! También vengaré la afrenta si existe!" (79-80). This line summarizes the actions of all three in this sordid love triangle: Dolores, Mercedes, and Gonzalo; each has been hurt by the vengeance of another, and each vows to return the damage by seeking revenge. Pablo too takes part in seeking vengeance as he lies dying, for he knows his death will show the public Gonzalo's true identity. Rather than die indoors and out of sight of the public eye, Pablo seeks revenge by summoning up enough strength to die outside where all can witness Gonzalo's dishonor. He cries:

> ¡Morir... y en este lugar?...
> ¡No! ¡Necesito salir!
> ¡Lo que digo sé!
> ¡De hacerlo hallaré manera!
> ¡Mi cadáver aquí... fuera,
> la deshonra para usté! (95)

This final scene, full of bloodshed and violence on stage, is reminiscent of Romantic drama. Dolores' closing words emphasize the role destiny has had on their lives: "¡Cada uno recoger puede lo que el destino concede!" (96).

IDEOLOGY

Although *La mejor ley* is not a social drama, it makes several strong statements concerning the social implications of marriage. The failed union of Gonzalo and Dolores provides us with a harsh protest against arranged marriages. Both husband and wife complain about the situation that society and their parents have put upon them. In a discussion between the two, Dolores describes how she had no choice when she married Gonzalo: "Por voluntad de mis padres, acepté tu nombre..." (16). She refers to their marriage as "esta unión que acordaron sin nuestro voto" (16). Later, she sarcastically questions Gonzalo about their happiness: "¿Puede existir otra ventura mayor para dos séres honrados, que la de vivir ligados por la virtud y el honor?" (17). Mercedes, the mistress, also recognizes the suffering the arranged marriage has caused. When comparing herself to her rival Dolores, Mercedes describes how both suffer because of society's rules: "¡una, la ley que se impone: otra, el crímen que se humilla!" (48). Pablo too notes the difficulty society has imposed upon their situation: "una nota discordante en el concierto social" (52). At the end of Act I, Dicenta creates a visual image of how things would have been if society had not played a role in the marriage between Gonzalo and Dolores; as they leave the room, Gonzalo is Mercedes' escort, and Pablo escorts Dolores.

Not only does Dicenta condemn those marriages that are not based upon love, but he also criticizes those that protect wrongdoing. Gonzalo knows that he will remain respected as a married man as long as he can keep his affair a secret. He explains this to Mercedes, his lover, in order that she will understand the importance of their secrecy: "¡Por ti, por ella, por nuestro honor... que el mundo ignore este amor!" (49). He uses his marriage to Dolores as a cloak, hiding his sins from all, even his own wife. For a while, Gonzalo is quite successful in his well-meditated plan. Priding himself on his cleverness, Gonzalo encourages Mercedes to be Dolores' best friend in order that she will never suspect their impropriety:

> La virtud
> que el mundo avalora más,
> es la astucia en el pecado.
> ¡Su amiga: siempre á su lado!
> que ella no dude jamás. (49)

It is ironic that Gonzalo uses the honorable institution of marriage to camouflage his affair with Mercedes. Once the affair has been made public, Gonzalo is overcome with fear that he will live in dishonor: "¡Fuera el escándalo horrible!" (66). As Dolores throws Mercedes out of the house, Gonzalo blames his wife for having revealed his secret and for bringing dishonor to his home:

> ¡Ver mi nombre escarnecido
> ante el mundo! (*con desesperación.*)
> (*con ira*)   ¡Y es por ti... !
> ¡Qué es lo que hiciste! (70)

CONCLUSIONS

The title of the play, *La mejor ley*, reflects Dicenta's attitude about marriage; it is an institution governed by law, not love, and when two people truly love each other, that is the "mejor ley." Love is the central issue in this drama, as Dicenta seeks to open the minds of those who adhere to the "moral vieja." Prior to the arranged marriage between Dolores and Gonzalo, each of them was in love with another, Pablo and Mercedes, respectively. Due to their inability to escape society's demand upon them, Dolores and Gonzalo find themselves married to each other without the benefit of love. Dolores accepts her position as wife and dutifully completes her obligations as such, even though she knows she will never love Gonzalo. He, on the other hand, chooses to follow his heart and to ignore the sacrament of marriage by having an affair with his beloved, Mercedes. They are both victims, as are Pablo and Mercedes. Because it lacks action and is too full of rhetoric, *La mejor ley* suffered greatly on the stage. Besides its keen evaluation of the institution of marriage, its only other redeeming quality is the character Dolores, the quick-witted and honorable victim, who most certainly spoke to many in the audience who could share her pain. Dicenta does not seek to terminate or devalue the institution of marriage, nor does he necessarily argue for divorce in this play, but rather he questions those social conventions that unite two people in marriage who are not in love with each other and he condemns the sort of marriage which protects wrongdoing.

Los Irresponsables (1890)

Rafael Calvo played the leading role in the first production of *Los irresponsables* on November 27, 1890 in the Teatro Español. Like Dicenta's previous dramas, *Los irresponsables* is essentially Romantic and melodramatic. However in *Los irresponsables* Dicenta undertakes an innovative theme: a plea for the acceptance of divorce. Although H.B. Hall believes *Los irresponsables* to be "a bad play," Hall nevertheless stresses its novelty "in its approach to the institution of matrimony to cause a storm of protest" (49). *Los irresponsables* picks up where *La mejor ley* left off. As Dicenta pushes for individual freedom in the choice of a spouse in *La mejor ley*, in *Los irresponsables*, he provides a father who is willing to break tradition and allow his daughter to choose a husband who will make her happy, one she loves. The tragedy lies in the man whom she chooses to be her husband.

Plot

Felipe, a newcomer to a small town, falls in love with Margarita, the daughter of one of the district's most respected families. Margarita and her father, Don Anselmo, hold Felipe in high regard because since his arrival he has always shown himself to be an honorable man. Margarita soon falls in love with Felipe, and her father allows them to develop their relationship further, even though the local priest discourages them. To complicate matters, Margarita's cousin, Carlos, returns to the small town in order to ask for Margarita's hand in marriage. Don Anselmo, Margarita's father, tells Carlos that Margarita has his permission to choose whomever she wishes to marry. Carlos is outraged when he realizes that Margarita is in love with Felipe, an old acquaintance of his whom he knows to be married. Felipe is not living with his wife, nor does he know of her whereabouts. After having discovered his wife with a lover one night, Felipe had killed her lover while his wife had escaped. Beginning anew in the small village where Margarita lives, Felipe wishes to forget about his scandalous past. Carlos refuses to keep this information a secret, for he wants Margarita to choose him instead. After Carlos discloses Felipe's secret to Margarita's father, Don Anselmo immediately demands that Felipe leave his home, and Carlos, feeling his family's honor has been violated, challenges Felipe to a duel. Before the duel takes place, Don Anselmo realizes that his daughter had fled to Felipe's home, where she plans to live with him without the bonds of matrimony. Don Anselmo arrives at Felipe's home hoping to avenge his honor. Upon confronting the two lovers, Don Anselmo draws his gun and fires at Felipe. Tragically, Margarita intercepts the bullet as she dies defending her lover.

TECHNIQUE

Following the mediocre success of *La mejor ley*, *Los irresponsables* was well received by both critics and audiences alike. Andrés González Blanco considered *Los irresponsables* a great success and believed it to mark a turning point in Dicenta's career as a dramatist: "Fue sin duda el primer drama que contribuyó a afianzar y robustecer su personalidad literaria" (215). Dicenta's technique, although remaining true to the Echegarayan neo-Romantic *tragedia de levita* that had shaped his previous dramas, undergoes several important changes, indicating a slow progression from simple imitation towards his own personal style.

Los irresponsables, like *La mejor ley*, is a three-act, neo-Romantic play written in verse. It has many of the same Romantic characteristics present in Dicenta's previous plays, yet, unlike *La mejor ley*, *Los irresponsables* is not bound by an overabundance of rhetoric or lack of action. Dicenta solves these problems in *Los irresponsables* by adding new characters to his usual list of those who are directly affected by the two lovers and their plight. In both *El suicidio de Werther* and *La mejor ley*, Dicenta concentrates on the few main characters and their families: in *El suicidio de Werther*, Fernando, his mother Carlota, his beloved María, and María's father Don Julián; and in *La mejor ley*, Gonzalo, his wife Dolores, his lover Mercedes, and his friend Pablo. Each of the characters is important for his/her personal relationship with the protagonist. In his third play, however, Dicenta creates several new characters to add humor and to provide a different perspective of the unfolding tragedy. Even though his previous plays include the servants of wealthy families, their roles are completely insignificant in the development of the dramas. In *Los irresponsables*, however, Dicenta provides a humorous counterpart to the love affair between Felipe and Margarita in the frivolous relationship between the servants, Gaspar and Rosa. This mirror image is reminiscent of the *gracioso* of many Golden Age dramas whose love affair mimics that of his master, such as Calisto's servant, Sempronio, in *La Celestina*. The purpose for this direct reflection of the master in *La Celestina* is to indicate that there is no real difference in passions between the servants and their masters; they both suffer from the same love sickness. In the late nineteenth century, however, Dicenta uses this device simply to provide humor in the midst of a tragic story; there is no indication that he is drawing a correlation between the protagonists and their servants. Rosa and Gaspar do not have a dominating role, nor do they appear frequently throughout the drama. Their primary action occurs near the end of the first act, before the truth has been revealed about Felipe's past, as they tease each other while setting the table:

>ROSA: ¡Majadero!
>GASPAR: Es que al mirarte me embobo, y no sé qué hacer, Rosilla.
>*(Trata de cogerle una mano por debajo de la mesa.)*
>ROSA: ¡Quieto, Gaspar!
>GASPAR: Pero chica, si es en broma. (31)

Another important character addition in *Los irresponsables* is the priest, Padre Andrés. His presence serves as an opposing view to all that which Dicenta argues in this play. Unlike the anticlerical Galdós, Dicenta provides a sympathetic priest who is both well-loved and respected in his community. Padre Andrés represents tradition near the turn of the century when much that is considered sacred about tradition is being questioned.

As stated above, Dicenta carefully adheres to the neo-Romantic tendencies popular on the nineteenth-century Spanish stage. The protagonist of *Los irresponsables*, Felipe, like Fernando of *El suicidio de Werther*, successfully plays the traditional Romantic hero, albeit in a modern setting. He is, according to Padre Andrés, "un hombre desconocido," a mysterious man about whom very little is known except that he is rich (18). In a style reminiscent of the earlier Romantic plays of the nineteenth century, Felipe has much in common with Don Álvaro, who, like Felipe, arrives as a stranger in a town where he hopes to begin his life anew. Furthermore, his first exchange with the woman he loves contains a reference to his eternal fate of suffering, also reminiscent of the Romantic Don Alvaro: "sufro porque es mi castigo sufrir siempre" (18). Throughout the play both Felipe and Margarita lament their tragic situation and the fact that they can never unite as husband and wife under the law. Margarita, ignorant of the truth through most of the play, suffers because the man she loves can not explain to her why he will never marry her; Felipe also suffers as he refuses to share his secretive past because he has no desire to hurt her by revealing the truth. Their relationship is yet another example of unrequited love. This internal battle that each lover suffers is expressed best in the final scene when Margarita renounces her love for Felipe and decides to return home with her father, leaving Felipe for the last time: "¡Adiós para siempre!" (84). She knows she cannot dishonor her father, yet she soon discovers that her love for Felipe is too strong to be denied. In a sudden burst of rebellion, Margarita leaves her father's side and rushes towards Felipe, saying, "¡Dejarte! Yo no puedo abandonarte, porque te adoro y soy tuya." (84). Unfortunately, this final act of free will on her part brings her death, for before she can explain herself to her furious father, she has been mortally wounded by her father's bullet as she throws herself between her father and Felipe.

The setting of *Los irresponsables* reflects a change from Dicenta's earlier dramas as well, for rather than depicting upper-class individuals in their modern-day urban dwellings, Dicenta moves his characters to the country, far from the city. This is a significant variation from his first two dramas in that in *Los irresponsables* the protagonist, Felipe, is searching to escape from the city and all the pain that he had experienced there. Nature, for Felipe, represents a fresh start. Nature also provides the topic for a significant discussion between Don Anselmo, Margarita's father, and Padre Andrés. The two men argue about its beauty and importance, Don Anselmo praising its wonders and Padre Andrés denying its worth. This distinction proves important as Dicenta builds his argument against society's laws in favor of natural law.

IDEOLOGY

What truly contributed to *Los irresponsables*' success was not necessarily anything innovative in Dicenta's technique, but rather his approach to certain social issues that, according to González-Blanco, "dio lugar a apasionadas polémicas entre periodistas" (215). H. B. Hall agrees: "the boldness of the theme and the accompanying discussion of current social questions established Dicenta's reputation as a challenging new figure" (49). Dicenta's argument is multifaceted: he condemns an unjust society for judging an innocent man; he questions long-standing traditions that allow innocent victims to suffer needlessly; and finally, he advocates divorce and the acceptance of free love.

In *Los irresponsables*, Dicenta returns to exploring the plight of the social outcast, whom he first creates in *El suicidio de Werther*. Felipe, however, is not a typical social outcast; he is a wealthy individual of the upper class, not a poor man struggling to make a living. Felipe is not condemned by society for having been born into the wrong social class, but rather for having left his wife and for falling in love with another woman. Society is blind to details, ignoring the legitimate reasons Felipe has for not reconciling with his wife; therefore, Dicenta establishes Felipe as a warm, sympathetic character from the beginning of the play in order to prepare the audience to accept his thesis that marriage and other social traditions should be questioned when they allow innocent people to suffer. According to Dicenta, Felipe is an innocent victim of fate and law. By pushing the audience to sympathize with Felipe, Dicenta ridicules a society that condemns a person for not adhering to the social code; their disdain is viewed as harsh and unjust towards a man such as Felipe.

In a discussion between Felipe and Padre Andrés, Felipe describes that the pain he has suffered has made him come to realize that "estar solo es lo mejor" (24). Padre Andrés, who at this point in the play is ignorant of Felipe's past, questions Felipe about his views on marriage. Felipe asserts that marriage is an invention of the devil and that those who are truly in love do not need it:

> Por su cuenta
> es el santo matrimonio,
> con sus leyes inmortales,
> un semillero de males
> y una invención del demonio....
> No le sirve para nada.
> los que en la infamia se agitan
> burlan su severidad;
> los que se aman de verdad...
> esos no la necesitan. (29)

Through Felipe Dicenta questions long-standing traditions and their validity. He questions the positive attributes and permanence of the institution of marriage if it allows innocent victims to suffer. Dicenta takes this argument against marriage one step further by openly advocating divorce and free love, novel subjects for the Spanish stage. Felipe complains to Padre Andrés that once one marries, he or she "sacrifica a su consistencia todo" (26). According to Felipe, the newlywed couple "ya están ligados y eternamente amarrados, suceda lo que suceda" (26). Padre Andrés assures Felipe that one must have faith and that bad marriages are an exception to the rule. Felipe bitterly retorts:

> Y al que la excepción le toca,
> ¿qué le resta? El desgraciado
> que la sufre ¿no podrá
> libertarse nunca? Está
> para siempre condenado.
> ¿Es justo decirle a un hombre
> o a una mujer: sufre, llora
> y tus amigos tus angustias devora;
> tu dignidad y tu nombre
> a un infame están unidos;
> para redimir tu suerte
> sólo hay un medio: la muerte? (27)

Padre Andrés argues that as a sacrament of the Church, matrimony is not to be opposed or resisted, that it is each individual's duty to resign himself/herself to whatever situations arise.

Dicenta establishes an important distinction between Felipe's keen reasoning and Padre Andrés' weak support of tradition on the grounds of religion and each individual's "deber" (28). As Padre Andrés invokes the name of God in his defense of matrimony, Felipe is quick to disagree, stating that God would not allow suffering to continue in his name: "Tampoco debe en su nombre eternizar la amargura" (26). Dicenta, through Felipe, argues that it is unfair for someone to be forced to suffer in silence in order to shun public criticism, or to be humiliated if he/she chooses to ignore the proper social code.

Dicenta continues to argue against other long-held beliefs throughout the play. Taking full advantage of the viewing public's deep-felt sympathy for Dolores in *La mejor ley*, who suffered greatly in an arranged marriage, Dicenta provides a father, Don Anselmo, in *Los irresponsables* who is willing to go against established tradition and allow his daughter to choose her own husband. Again, Padre Andrés defends tradition as Don Anselmo, Margarita's father, explains to him that he is not responsible for finding his daughter a suitable husband. Throughout the play Dicenta constructs a clear division between the priest's traditional views and liberal thought, voiced through both Don Anselmo and Felipe. According to Felipe, it is natural that we, as humans, evolve, and that in our evolution, traditions evolve as well. He praises progess as "la más justa de las leyes" (35). In an ideal society, Felipe would have been allowed to divorce his adulterous wife and to marry the woman he loves; instead, he is forced to receive society's never-ending condemnation and to accept that he can never marry Margarita.

CONCLUSIONS

In *Los irresponsables*, Dicenta demonstrates significant development as he begins to break away from simple imitations of Echegary's neo-Romantic plays. Dicenta's innovative thesis, calling the audience to question long-standing traditions and accept ideas such as divorce and free love, sets the stage for his future thesis plays. Dicenta's goal in *Los irresponsables* is to draw a clear distinction between natural law and social law; he illustrates that social rules are not necessarily defined by natural law. Many social customs, in fact, are completely unrelated to the actual nature of mankind. Marriage, for example, in nineteenth-century Spain is an institution based upon economic and social standards; the natural law of love is neither a prerequisite nor a concern between the two people who are joined together in marriage. Dicenta's method of differentiating natural law and social law involves the priest, Padre Andrés, who defends tradition, and Felipe (and in a more minor way, Don Anselmo), who urges progress and change. Throughout the play, Padre Andrés argues against the liberal thoughts of the townspeople. He believes that all parents should arrange marriages for their children; he questions Don Anselmo's acceptance of Felipe, whom he accuses of lacking faith since he does not attend church; he accuses Felipe outright of not being a Christian because of his liberal views about marriage; he wholeheartedly defends marriage; he vehemently opposes divorce and free love; and finally, he supports society's unjust condemnation of Felipe. Unlike both Clarín and Galdós, who use corrupt priests to criticize religious traditions and institutions, Dicenta chooses to create a lovable priest whom the audience can accept and with whom the audience finds much in common, including his traditional beliefs. Padre Andrés blindly supports tradition, using religion to defend his reasoning, yet his blindness inhibits him from seeing the suffering that is caused by certain social codes. By characterizing Padre Andrés as a warm sympathetic individual, Dicenta validates the public's enduring loyalty towards tradition. In his characterization of Felipe, however, the audience has no other choice except to sympathize with Felipe, for Dicenta portrays him as an intelligent victim of society who clearly shows more reason in his questioning of tradition than does Padre Andrés in his defense of it. The title of the play, *Los irresponsables*, becomes ironic as the audience realizes that the two lovers are not the irresponsible ones after all, but rather those who are irresponsible are those who blindly maintain long-standing traditions that allow innocent victims to suffer.

HONRA Y VIDA (1891)

Information on Dicenta's next play, *Honra y vida*, is scarce and full of errors. Both Andrés González-Blanco (214) and Jaime Mas Ferrer (*Vida* 75) provide an incorrect date for the debut of Dicenta's first one-act historical drama based on a traditional legend; they agree that *Honra y vida* debuted in 1888 when in fact, the printed text itself indicates that it was first performed in Zaragoza's Teatro Principal on April 16, 1891. Dicenta wrote *Honra y vida* while he was working in San Sebastián as the director of *La Unión Liberal*. Dicenta found himself isolated from his contemporaries in Madrid, and he yearned to return to the capital to stage his plays. Instead, however, *Honra y vida* was first performed in Zaragoza, a tribute to the capital of his birthplace. *Honra y vida* is a simple one-act historical drama the main theme of which is honor; set in Seville during the last few years of Pedro the Cruel's reign (1350-1369), *Honra y vida* revives the traditional legend of one of Spain's most remembered monarchs.

PLOT

Don Jaime is one of King Pedro's finest soldiers who won the king's approval and praise late one night as he, a poor, homeless man, successfully defended himself from eight men who attacked him for no apparent reason. The king witnessed this impossible battle. So impressed was he with Don Jaime, the king honored and lavished him with luxurious gifts and provided him with a fine mansion and a beautiful wife who came from a well-respected, wealthy family. The story begins as Don Jaime's wife, Doña Inés, is overcome with emotion because her husband, with fifty other soldiers, left home in the middle of the night without being seen by anyone, under the order of the king. Doña Inés admits to her maid that since she has been left alone, she is frightened because of previous threats made to her by the king. Soon the king arrives, explaining to her that he must have her, that he had sent her husband away so that they could be alone. His sexual advances disgust her, and in her rejection, she constantly makes references to her honor. She falls to her knees and begs him to leave her alone, but he, more cruel that ever, tells her that she has no choice but to give in to his desires. When she threatens suicide, the king tells her he will kill her husband, Don Jaime. He gives her one hour to think about his offer, and he leaves.

Meanwhile, Doña Inés' fervent prayers to the Virgin are interrupted by her husband, who has secretly returned out of love for his wife in order to allay her fears and tell her all is well. When he turns to leave, she becomes hysterical, begging him to stay. Finally she admits to him the truth, and the two of them discuss possible options to deny the king his wishes and salvage their honor. As the king approaches, Doña Inés hides in an adjacent room, promising to do whatever her husband deems necessary. As the two men confront each other, the king reminds Don Jaime that he would have nothing if the king had not provided it all for him. Jaime tells him he is welcome to take back all of his wealth and riches, even his life, but his honor is not something that can be given away; it is truly his. The king becomes enraged and threatens to kill Don Jaime. As Don Jaime lifts his sword to defend himself he realizes he cannot disobey the king because of his deep sense of respect for the divine right of kings. He falls to the king's feet and begs him to leave his wife alone, yet the king refuses. Don Jaime then opens the door and Doña Inés falls into his arms. Left with no other choice, he stabs her in the chest, killing her while the king looks on in complete shock.

HISTORICAL BACKGROUND

Dicenta's *Honra y vida* follows a rich history of historical dramas on the Spanish stage dating back to the Renaissance when Juan de la Cueva (1550-1610?) "urged his fellow dramatists to abjure the classical sources and to draw their themes from national history" (Chandler and Schwartz 79). Miguel de Cervantes (1547-1616), one of Juan de la Cueva's contemporaries, explored the genre of the historical drama in *La Numancia* (1584?), a play which received so much attention and praise that it was revived in the nineteenth century during the siege of Zaragoza, the location of the debut of Dicenta's *Honra y vida*. The three masters of the Spanish stage during the Golden Age, Lope de Vega, Tirso de Molina, and Calderón de la Barca, each wrote historical dramas, and the first

Romantic success in Spain, *La conjuración de Venecia* (1834), was also based upon a historic event. The trend remained popular through Spanish Romanticism with dramatists such as Antonio García Gutiérrez (*El trovador* 1836), Juan Eugenio Hartzenbusch (*Los amantes de Teruel* 1837), Antonio Gil y Zarate (*Guzmán el Bueno* 1842), and José Zorrilla, who, although better known for his *Don Juan Tenorio* (1844), devoted the majority of his plays to exploring themes from national history. One of his best plays, *El zapatero y el rey* (1840), is, like *Honra y vida*, a historical drama based on a medieval legend about King Pedro the Cruel. José Echegaray later restored the popularity of historical drama in many of his neo-Romantic plays, such as *En el puño de la espada* (1875) and *En el seno de la muerte* (1879). As in Dicenta's previous dramas, Echegaray remains a major influence in the young dramatist's development. Dicenta, however, seems to have borrowed from several different forms of popular drama from the late nineteenth century. He obviously chose to continue the neo-Romantic historical drama made popular by Echegaray, yet unlike his predecessor, Dicenta limited his play to one act, placing it in the category of the popular *género chico*, generally reserved for musical, comical, or *costumbrista* pieces. Dicenta's departure from his usual full length play is no surprise given the nature of the Spanish stage at the end of the century, for, according to José María Martínez Cachero, the one-act play remained the most popular genre during the last quarter of the century:

> En la temporada teatral de 1872-73, de las 271 piezas estrenadas en los teatros madrileños, 204 lo eran de un solo acto, y con parecida abundancia continuó ocurriendo este hecho hasta, aproximadamente, los años finales de siglo. (368)

Madrid, however, remained the most popular location for the "género chico," which may explain the lack of any critical reception for *Honra y vida*, performed not in Madrid but in Zaragoza.

There is no information available regarding Dicenta's sources for *Honra y vida*, but one can assume that he was familiar with José Zorrilla's treatment of Pedro the Cruel, and possibly with the earlier playwrights, Lope de Vega (1562-1635) and Juan de la Hoz y Mota (1622-1714). The popularity of Pedro the Cruel in literature dates back to Pedro López de Ayala (1332-1407), who, as a firsthand witness of the events that occurred during Pedro's reign, recorded his cruelty in his *Crónica de don Pedro Primero*. Pedro's role in literature, however, has enjoyed a broad spectrum of interpretations and has therefore earned him two separate titles: "el justiciero" and "el cruel." In the many plays by Lope de Vega that focus on the reign of Pedro the Cruel, the monarch is characterized as a "rey justiciero" or a "galán enamorado." Lope de Vega avoids completely

Pedro's cruel side, tending more often than not to sympathize with the king. José Zorrilla also chooses to explore the positive side of the king, despite his well-known cruelty, in his *El zapatero y el rey*, based on de la Hoz y Mota's *El montañés Juan Pascual, primer asistente de Sevilla*. A truly Romantic drama, Zorrilla's *El zapatero y el rey* treats a king who is characterized by his wise and just decisions. In fact, the only similarity between this play and *Honra y vida* is an allusion to the fact that Pedro raised a common man to an exalted status; both Blas Pérez, the shoemaker's son of *El zapatero y el rey* and Don Jaime, the commoner of *Honra y vida*, are raised to a high rank in Pedro's court.

This exalting of a commoner is not historically documented. Moreover, none of the events depicted in Dicenta's *Honra y vida* has a basis in fact. There do exist, however, several legends that ring familiar. José F. Montesinos describes a king in *La corona merecida de Lope de Vega* (1923) who is so taken by Juan de la Cerda's wife that he vows to kill her husband. Before she goes to beg the king to spare her husband's life, she disfigures herself in order to avoid his advances. In a similar legend, the married woman he pursues commits suicide rather than surrender to his advances (136-146). It is not known whether Dicenta was familiar with these legends, but it should be noted that his *Honra y vida* is certainly original in both content and style.

TECHNIQUE

Honra y vida is a one-act play comprised of nine scenes, yet the final scene is numbered ten. There is no scene five, for no other apparent reason except perhaps for an error on the part of the dramatist (or his publisher). All of the scenes take place in one of Don Jaime's luxuriously decorated rooms. To aid the audience in gaining a quick perspective of the background to this short drama, Dicenta uses the servants of the household who discuss Don Jaime's fortune in having been singled out by the king. Romantic characteristics abound in *Honra y vida*, as the main theme of honor dominates all actions. Like other dramas from the Romantic period that fall under the category of *romanticismo histórico*, Dicenta's newest production contains positive Christian references (an uncommon trait among Dicenta's plays), portrays medieval themes, and is written in the eight-syllable verse common to the *romances*. The entirety of *Honra y vida* takes place at night, providing the mysterious atmosphere so prevalent in Romantic drama. Even the stage decorations (Arabic architecture and oriental furniture) reflect the Romantics' preoccupation with things from afar. *Honra y vida* lacks, however, a true Romantic hero. Instead, Dicenta focuses on the three main characters and their immediate plight. As is always the difficulty in one-act dramas, the characters often seem shallow, since there is only a limited amount of time in which to develop their personalities. In *Honra y vida*, however, Dicenta successfully creates three characters who, given their relatively limited time on stage, manage to portray three clear types: Doña Inés (the faithful wife), Don Jaime (the honorable and loyal subject), and King Pedro (the arrogant, unjust ruler).

Our first impression of Doña Inés is that of an emotionally distraught woman, and once we understand the source of her inner pain, we immediately sympathize with her situation. She resists the king's advances, and she questions his motives, noting how loyal her husband is to King Pedro: "¿Por qué siendo él tan leal sois tan infame con él?" (19). Although overly emotional, Doña Inés speaks with wisdom. She is an honest woman who believes strongly in her faith, petitioning the Virgin Mary to intercede at this most difficult moment in her life. It seems her prayers are heard, for just as she throws herself down in front of the altar to the Virgin Mary, Don Jaime arrives. Doña Inés' outstanding characteristic is her devotion to her husband, even as she willfuly dies at his hands. The unrequited sacrificial love Doña Inés feels for Don Jaime is quite Romantic; as they are not able to enjoy each other's love on earth, they are forced to wait until the hereafter.

Since we learn about Don Jaime from other individuals before his first appearance on stage, our perception of him is preconceived. We know him to be highly respected and brave because of the story told by his servants, and after hearing Doña Inés's expression of love for him, we know that Don Jaime is a man worthy of a good woman's love. More than halfway through the play at the end of scene vii, Don Jaime makes his first appearance as he comforts his weeping wife. We soon learn that one of his most outstanding characteristics is his sense of honor, which is threatened by his other most outstanding characteristic: his devotion to his king, whom he believes rules divinely. He is faced with a dilemma when he finds he cannot defend his honor for fear of insulting God by disobeying the king:

> ¡Y que, si es
> tal mi desdicha, que al verle,
> en lugar de acometerle,
> tendré que caer á sus piés!
> porque todo se lo debo;
> por que es el rey, y es sagrado,
> y debe ser respetado,
> y á quebrantar no me atrevo
> leyes que el cielo dictó. (31)

Don Jaime fears that the king, with his ultimate power, will be allowed to take advantage of Doña Inés, yet he continues to fight for his honor. Don Jaime tells the king that he can take everything away from him except his honor:

> Tomad lo que gustéis, pronto me muestro
> á dároslo; tomadlo, todo es vuestro.
> Pero mi honor es mío,
> dentro de mi alma se conserva y crece,
> mi honor me pertenece
> y á robarlo, señor, os desafío. (34)

This scene is reminiscent of Lope de Vega's *Fuenteovejuna* (1619) in which Frondoso, a commoner, threatens to kill the *Comendador* after the latter uses his power to try to take advantage of Laurencia, Frondoso's love. Unlike Frondoso, who does not hesitate to object to the commands of the *Comendador*, Don Jaime is overwhelmed by his need to obey the king; his only recourse is to kill his wife in order to defend the one thing remaining him over which he has total control: his honor.

Just as we have an idea of Don Jaime before his first appearance on stage, we also form our opinions about King Pedro before he first arrives. At first, we think he is a kind and generous king for having bestowed upon Don Jaime such honor and wealth, but soon, we learn that he is a coldhearted individual who is only interested in his self-serving needs. King Pedro's arrogance is first evident as Doña Inés explains to one of her servants that the king has threatened her to submit to his desires: "No hay quien mis designios tuerza ante un deseo empeñado; si no os entregáis de grado os rendiré por la fuerza" (15). King Pedro will resort to force if he has to in order to fulfill his desires. Once he arrives and demands that Doña Inés surrender, King Pedro explains his selfish reasoning to the distraught woman: "¿Amo? lo que amo poseo. / ¿Odio? lo que odio destruyo" (22). King Pedro's arrogance is overwhelming as he later claims (when confronted by Don Jaime) that he represents God to Don Jaime:

> Soy tu Dios: si tu Dios tiene un antojo,
> ¿qué harás tú, su vasallo, su presea,
> sino dar á tu Dios lo que desea,
> caer á sus plantas y templar su enojo? (34)

IDEOLOGY

The ideological aspect of *Honra y vida* is minimal for two reasons: first, Dicenta's choice to write a one-act drama is probably the result of his desire to please his audiences, who were flocking to the theaters that offered *teatro por horas*, and second, the inherent nature of the one-act *género chico* drama inhibits the dramatist from expressing any particular view at depth. However, in his first one-act drama, Dicenta uses an age-old tradition to force his contemporary audiences to reevaluate two issues: first, the abuse of power and its effect, and second, the reason that societies hold on to corrupt beliefs for so long if only to maintain tradition. As he has done in his previous dramas, Dicenta pushes his audiences to question the norm, the accepted, non-challenged traditional beliefs. Although nineteenth-century Spaniards, with the exceptions of the Carlists, did not believe in the divine right of kings, their ancestors did, and Dicenta shows his contemporary audiences a glimpse of how dangerous it is not to question tradition. In *El suicidio de Werther*, Dicenta condemns society's victimization of Carlota and unjust judgment of Fernando, who both suffer from not being able to improve their social status. In *La mejor ley* and *Los irresponsables*, Dicenta urges his audiences to reexamine their view of marriage and its permanence. In *Los irresponsables* especially, Dicenta uses an amicable priest who, although well liked, provides a very weak support for maintaining tradition, thus pushing the audiences towards the more astute observations made by Felipe who questions tradition. Dicenta continues this trend, although in a minor way, in *Honra y vida* by allowing the audience to be spectators of an event far removed in the past, an event in which they can more easily see the need for progress and a change of perspective, just as we, late twentieth-century readers, see the same need in Dicenta's other late nineteenth-century dramas. Dicenta's contemporary audiences would no doubt recognize the flaw in the "Divine Right of Kings" in *Honra y vida*, for Don Jaime, an honorable man who believes that the king was placed on his throne by God, is incapable of fighting for his honor because he cannot go against God.

CONCLUSIONS

Dicenta's first one-act play is fast moving and full of suspense. Accustomed to viewing comical farces or musical pieces in the playhouses that offered *teatro por horas*, Dicenta's audiences must have come away from this powerful one-act drama in a state of shock. Their senses must have been overwhelmed as they contemplated the injustice of King Pedro and the tragic sacrifice of Doña Inés. In tracing Dicenta's development as a dramatist, one cannot ignore his ongoing attempt to provoke his audiences to reevaluate common thought, especially when beliefs are based on traditions that cause innocent people to suffer.

LUCIANO (1894)

Following the premiere of *Honra y vida* (1891), Dicenta soon returned to Madrid in 1892, freeing himself from the clutches of the upper-class conservatives in San Sebastián. Returning to the big city was difficult for Dicenta, as he struggled to make a living. Although he was writing for *El Resumen*, Dicenta lived in poverty, and it was during this pivotal point in his life that Dicenta became much more aware of the conditions that affect those who are poor and marginalized by society. Having separated from his wife three years earlier shortly after their marriage in 1888, Dicenta and his lover, Amparito, now lived outside of society's approval and suffered from prejudice. Dicenta considered himself an artist, and his ultimate desire was to become a successful playwright, and like Fernando in *El suicidio de Werther*, Dicenta hoped to gain approval from society through his talent. Several years passed before the appearance of Dicenta's next play, and the change in his technique and outlook is clearly evident. *Luciano*, first performed by the company of Emilio Mario on February 25, 1894 in the Teatro de la Comedia in Madrid, is Dicenta's first venture into prose drama, and like *El suicidio de Werther* (1888), *Luciano* explores the world of the artist, allowing the audience to glimpse Dicenta's own struggle as an artist misunderstood by society. The play is largely autobiographical as the protagonist finds himself in an unhappy marriage with a wife who is incapable of supporting or understanding his ideals as an artist. The transition from verse to prose allows Dicenta to express more realistically the hardships experienced by artists like himself. González-Blanco emphasizes the importance *Luciano* has on the development of Dicenta as a playwright:

> Este drama era ya la liberación definitiva del teatro de verso, el indicador que marcaba el rumbo hacia el teatro realista. Se había emancipado ya de la tiranía del verso; ahora había de buscar nuevas formas de inspiración… en *Luciano* [Dicenta] encontró su camino, que había buscado durante tanto tiempo. (256)

Not only does Dicenta abandon the use of verse in this drama, but he also casts aside some of the Romantic features that define his previous plays. The theme is controversial as Dicenta seeks to gain acceptance for divorce in a society where divorce is not socially acceptable.

PLOT

Luciano is a sculptor whose wife, Julia, cares nothing for his talent as an artist. Julia, with the encouragement of her mother, Doña Isabel, constantly pesters Luciano about their financial situation, although they live quite comfortably. Luciano's in-laws live in his home, and their constant allusion to their higher social status serves to belittle the sculptor. Luciano comes from a rural, low-class background, and Julia's parents feel it is Luciano's duty to provide for their daughter and her family in the manner to which they are accustomed. To complicate matters, Luciano's ill mother, Doña Dolores, moves in with Luciano in order to seek medical treatment in the city that she cannot receive in the countryside where she lives. Both Julia and her mother are determined to treat Doña Dolores with disdain, for they are totally disgusted by her rural manners. Doña Dolores only wants Luciano to be happy and successful, and once she realizes that she is the cause for her son's marital strife, she insists that she must leave. Luciano, however, finds it impossible to forgive his wife for her treatment of his mother and her total lack of respect for his work.

In the meantime, Luciano has fallen in love with Angela, the Duchess of Monza, a childhood playmate of his who has returned after a ten-year absence during which she was married and widowed. Although Angela and Luciano truly love each other, they do not act upon that love, for they respect the institution of marriage. Julia soon believes that Angela and Luciano are having an affair, and Luciano tries to defend himself, but to no avail. Even though Dolores has done everything she could possibly do to keep her son's marriage from falling apart, it has all been futile. In her poor physical condition, she is unable to take such a shock. She slumps over and falls to the floor, dying of a broken heart. Luciano immediately blames his wife for her ill treatment of his mother, and he, together with Angela, begins to pray as the curtain falls.

TECHNIQUE

It is immediately obvious that *Luciano* is quite different from any other play Dicenta had yet written; however, there is evidence that he had written a short story with the same characters and theme prior to *Luciano*'s first appearance on stage. In *De la batalla* (1903), there appears an autobiographical short story ("Un divorcio") in which the protagonist, a painter, learns that his new bride, Julia, is only interested in the money he can earn from his paintings; she has no comprehension of his ideals of art. The protagonist summarizes his feelings:

> Mientras yo pensaba en la gloria, ella pensaba en el dinero... El artista solo es para ella una letra de cambio... Se acabó. Ya no tengo una mujer. Acaba de divorciarnos con una frase. (63)

In "Un divoricio" we see the origin of the spiritual separation, and in *Luciano*, we are introduced to the couple again as they continue to find each other increasingly incompatible. Edwin S. Morby points out that Dicenta "did not now rewrite 'Un divorcio' as a play, but made *Luciano* its sequel" (385). In *De la batalla*, which was not published until 1903, Dicenta includes twenty-six previously published articles and short stories that were "escritos en una de las épocas más duras que tuvo para mí hasta ahora la lucha por la vida" (5). This reference can only be attributed to the time period before the 1895 production of *Juan José*, for following its extremely successful premiere, Dicenta achieved the social status that allowed him the time and money necessary to dedicate his life to writing plays. Although there is not enough information available concerning the exact dates of the separate publications of the articles and short stories in *De la batalla*, it is very likely that the story "Un divorcio" was first written before *Luciano* premiered, especially since it acts as a prequel to the plot of *Luciano*.

The autobiographical nature of *Luciano* can not be ignored, for Dicenta, like Luciano, also discovered shortly after his wedding that his wife was not interested in his artistic talents except for materialistic reasons. José Deleito y Piñuela notes: "El autor confesaba en la intimidad que había llevado al proscenio su propio problema íntimo y su propio dolor" (199). Never forgetting the pain he experienced at such a young age, Dicenta published in 1915 a novel titled *Mi Venus* in which he explored in greater detail the same strained relationship between the artist and his wife. Luciano, Miguel (the protagonist of *Mi Venus*), and Dicenta all share similar characteristics. Dicenta, like Luciano and Miguel, also suffered from a failed marriage. All three men are artists in their own right: Miguel and Luciano are sculptors, Dicenta, an author. All consider their careers as artists as primary in importance. Each artist lives a bohemian lifestyle as he disregards conventional rules of behavior while pursuing his career as an artist. All three men find themselves attracted to women of the upper class, and they all marry to achieve a higher status. Originally, they were each attracted to their wives through their own vanity; they were seduced by the aristocratic title and beauty of their brides, and the women too were superficially fascinated by the success and fame achieved by the artists. The wives in all three marriages show very little interest or respect for the work their husbands do. In both *Luciano* and *Mi Venus*, Dicenta emphasizes the importance of choosing a life partner who is not only respectful but also understanding. All three artists realize that their marriages lack the fundamental mutual respect that is required to survive. After abandoning their failed marriages, each man reunites with a woman who understands and supports his ideals. Both the novel and the play could be considered Dicenta's treatise on the definition of true love based upon his own experience.

IDEOLOGY

There are two strands to Dicenta's thesis in *Luciano*; first, he argues for the acceptance of divorce and free love, and second, by condemning a society responsible for ostracizing those of lower birth, Dicenta shows how moral virtue has no relation to social status. Although Dicenta advocates divorce in both *La mejor ley* and *Los irresponsables*, the plea for the disruption of marriage in *Luciano* is not the result of honor offended or any other adulterous act; instead, the couple in *Luciano* suffers from complete incompatibility, an important distinction. Never before had a Spanish writer openly advocated the dissolution of marriage for any reason other than honor's sake. In *Luciano*, Dicenta, based upon his own painful experience, steps forward to argue for the acceptance of divorce for such a reason as incompatibility, especially in a time when marriages are still arranged and the couple may find they have nothing in common. Because divorce is not socially acceptable, Luciano, like Felipe in *Los irresponsables*, finds himself unable to break the bonds of matrimony without avoiding public scandal. Dicenta's argument centers on the injustice of the situation when social codes take precedence over an individual's rights to be happy. Dicenta uses Dolores, Luciano's mother, to express the dilemma faced by Luciano:

> ¿Tiene mi hijo derecho á romper los lazos que le unen con Julia, porque esos lazos son obra de los hombres, y los hombres se engañan, y los hechos pueden más que las exigencias sociales y que las imposiciones de la ley? ¿Será esto verdad?... No; leyes divinas son las que unen á Luciano y á Julia; leyes á las que no pueden sustraerse. (Con tono de duda.) Esto es lo que creo... lo que debo creer. (72)

Through Dolores, Dicenta urges us to ask ourselves the same question, and like Dolores, we too may find that we doubt the reasoning behind such laws that inhibit the pursuit of happiness. Although Dicenta does not unite Angela and Luciano on the stage, the final words of the play, following the death of Luciano's beloved mother, hint at the future union of the pair as Angela says "Ven, Luciano; vamos a rezar juntos por tu madre" (79). Deleito y Piñuela concludes: "Claro es que el auditorio vió, al través del rezo, algo menos devoto, y el drama, como *Los irresponsables*, pasó premiosamente" (199-200).

In his argument for divorce and the acceptance of free love, Dicenta uses another underdog in society, one who is oppressed by those of higher social status and by strict social codes. Luciano suffers not only from his inability to separate and obtain a divorce from an insensitive wife but also from a society that condemns him for the low-class family into which he was born. Like Fernando in *El suicidio de Werther*, Luciano is a young artist struggling to achieve success and acceptance in a society that judges him as low class. Unlike Fernando, however, Luciano marries a woman who comes from an upper-class family and he manages to obtain all the wealth and fame that he has hoped for. Luciano soon realizes, however, that his wife, although she is wealthy and accepted by society, lacks the morals and values that he expected to come naturally to those of a higher social status. Dicenta repeats this theme many times in his plays as he emphasizes the fact that one's worth can not be judged by one's place on the social ladder. Dicenta's negative tone is evident even in the stage directions: "El mueblaje será lujoso, pero de mal gusto" (7).

Luciano is best able to express his frustration through his art. One of Luciano's most recent creations is a sculpture of a young man who is struggling on a large craggy rock. He is wearied, yet he is not giving up. There is a sense of being in a state of limbo as the statue expresses the plight of a man who is not yet victorious but neither is he defeated. Luciano explains its significance to Don Rafael:

> Pues ese hombre soy yo; yo, que arrollado por enemigos crueles que se enroscan a mi alma para aniquilarla, no puedo destruirlos.... ¡Y yo, que combato sintiendo filtrarse en mi espíritu su veneno y extenderse por mi conciencia su fría odiosidad, me estremezco, no de miedo, no de horror, de hastío y de asco! (44-45)

In the same way that Fernando sees himself in his work in *El suicidio de Werther*, Luciano is able to depict his own pain in the sculpture of a man who hangs between two extremes: agony and ecstasy; Luciano is able to see what he wants (Angela) just out of his reach while he struggles in his sad existence with his uncomprehending wife (Julia). Luciano's determination, however, is only evident in his artwork. Instead of fighting for the happiness he desires, Luciano takes the passive approach of simply ignoring his wife, pretending that she is dead. By seeking support from Angela from the cruelty of his wife and her family, Luciano does nothing to solve his predicament, but rather he avoids it. Not until the end of the play do we see the possibility of happiness for Luciano as he completely rejects his wife, whom he blames for his mother's death, and joins Angela in prayer.

Dicenta continues to explore the difference between the classes in his depiction of Luciano's mother, Dolores, in comparison with Julia and her mother, Isabel. Dolores is characterized as a virtuous woman who, despite the cruel treatment she receives from Julia and Isabel, maintains an attitude of kindness and respect towards them. Before Dolores even arrives in Madrid, Julia and Isabel begin to plot her departure. Isabel whispers to Julia:

> Dentro de una hora llega la madre de tu marido. Creo que no habrás variado de opinión, y que, ya que no hemos podido impedir que venga, haremos lo posible para que se vaya inmediatamente. (14)

Julia and Isabel constantly make reference to Dolores' country manner and poverty in an attempt to belittle her in front of Luciano. Later Julia, in an argument with Luciano, demands that Dolores leave their house and return to the country because:

> Ni me agrada el carácter de tu madre, ni sus costumbres se avienen con las mías. Y luego, ¿qué voy á hacer al lado suyo, de una mujer que desconoce en absoluto los usos y costumbres de la sociedad á que pertenezco? (38)

The stark contrast between these women is clear: Dolores, the humble low-class woman, is defined by her selfless nature and extreme virtue; whereas Julia and Isabel, both of the upper class, are characterized by their cruelty, arrogance and total disregard for others. Dicenta proves the point that social status does not guarantee moral virtue.

CONCLUSIONS

H. B. Hall finds that in *Luciano* "the element of social criticism is greater and more particularised" than any of Dicenta's previous dramas (50); however, he denies Constancio Eguía Ruiz's statement that "el socialismo en bruto palpita en *Luciano*" (209). Instead, Hall claims that the ideas presented in *Luciano* simply "suggest that Dicenta is groping towards a drama of class conflict" (51). It is true that the level of "socialismo" should be questioned, but, upon a careful examination of the drama, one can not ignore Dicenta's effort to portray the differences between the classes and the suffering that the lower class endures at the hands of the upper class. The sculpture of the man on the craggy rock is an important symbol in *Luciano* as it represents the constant struggle of society's victims as they continue to try unsuccessfully to improve their social status and to obtain acceptance. Dicenta repeatedly shows that society's victims are stuck in a vicious circle; no matter how hard they try to overcome the oppression of those who are above them; both financially and socially, these victims are inevitably defeated. Just as Fernando's virtue and great skill as an artist (*El suicidio de Werther*) do nothing to erase society's unfair prejudice against him, Luciano can never overcome the cruelty of his in-laws despite his high morals and success as an artist. Dicenta attacks the upper-class society, describing it as "esa multitud semiculta, semipudiente, que se juzga lo bastante grande para no respetar nada que no comprenda, y es lo bastante pequeña para no comprender nada grande" (22).

Although Dicenta treats a realistic theme with true character types, *Luciano* suffers in its presentation as it is reduced to a series of speeches and arguments. The artistic quality is sacrificed in Dicenta's attempt to preach to the audience his views concerning marriage and class division. Despite its lack of artistic merit, *Luciano* proved to be an important play, not only in the development of Dicenta's talent, but also in Dicenta's bold thesis. Deleito y Piñuela describes the effect achieved by *Luciano*: "Frunció el ceño la crítica honesta, y quedó el autor en entredicho, como hombre que llevaba al teatro enseñanzas peligrosas" (200). Dicenta was already making a name for himself.

EL DUQUE DE GANDÍA (1894)

Dicenta's next play is a total departure from all that he had previously written, for only days following the premiere of *Luciano*, Dicenta presented his first *zarzuela*, *El duque de Gandía*, with the music of Antonio Llanos and Ruperto Chapí. *El duque de Gandía* premiered in the Teatro de la Zarzuela on March 10, 1894 (*Luciano* premiered on February 25). Its immediate success revealed Dicenta's versatile talent, and gave him more recognition as the budding young playwright became more well known.

PLOT

The lyrical story takes place in sixteenth-century Spain with members of the court of Carlos V and his Empress Isabel. The hero, Francisco de Borja, the Duke of Gandía, is rumored to have a secret passion for the queen, even though he is married. The source of this rumor is the Count of Úbeda, who once loved Leonor, Gandía's wife. Having been rejected by her, Úbeda plans to ruin Leonor's marriage to Gandía by spreading this vicious rumor about her husband. Because the king is away at war, Úbeda's scheme is successful. Upon hearing the rumor from her confidant, Friar Juan, the Empress Isabel admits that she and Gandía share a very deep love for each other but that they have never acted upon their feelings. Friar Juan advises her to exile Gandía, and she concedes to his counsel. Before he leaves, however, Gandía kills Úbeda in a duel after the latter boldly acknowledges his responsibility for the rumor.

After his departure, Gandía joins the king and fights valiantly and recklessly, feeling he no longer has a reason to live. Because of Gandía's service to the king, upon their return to the court, the Emperor Carlos asks Gandía to announce his arrival to the Empress. Gandía is shocked by her appearance. Isabel's health has drastically declined since his departure four years before, and now that she is near death, Gandía is unable to control himself and immediately pours out his love for her, decrying their earlier decision to ignore their feelings. She momentarily loses herself in her love for Gandía, but quickly recognizes that the two of them will never be able to pursue their love. Because she can no longer live tortured by her own self-repression and because she feels it absolutely necessary to maintain the honor of her position as queen, Isabel slumps to the floor and dies soon afterward. For her, death is an escape from an unforgiving world where she is forbidden to follow her true love. The epilogue contains a moving scene in which Gandía must identify the queen's body in her coffin before a large number of church and court dignitaries. His sorrowful reaction to her decaying body is quite poignant. The curtain closes on the sad scene with strains of "Miserere" fading away.

HISTORICAL BACKGROUND

El duque de Gandía is a thoroughly Romantic tragedy based on a well-known historical legend. Francisco de Borja was canonized a saint by Clement X in 1671 (St. Francis Borgia). According to the *Enciclopedia universal ilustrada,* following the death of Queen Isabel in 1539, Borja decided to become a priest because he was so moved by her horribly decomposed condition:

> Sintió Francisco de Borja aquel hondo desengaño de la vanidad del mundo,... Desengaño que... pasó todo en lo interior, obrando aquella insigne conversión no de vida pecadora en cristiana, sino de vida buena en perfecta. (24: 1040)

Borja wrote about his reaction to the Empress' death in his *Diario espiritual* in May of 1564. Since his death and subsequent canonization, the legend has been treated many times in literature and art. Both Calderón de la Barca and the Duque de Rivas write about Francisco de Borja's decision to become a priest, the former in *El gran duque de Gandía* (1671) and the latter in a *romance* entitled "El solemne desengaño." There is also a famous painting by José Moreno Carbonero in 1884 entitled "La conversión del duque de Gandía," and in the stage directions of the epilogue, Dicenta advises the director to match the stage as closely as possible to the painting: "Procúrese que la escena y los personajes representen lo más aproximadamente posible el famoso cuadro de Moreno Carbonero, La Conversión del Duque de Gandía" (86). Dicenta, who was obviously very familiar with the legend, chooses to create a fictional background to the events that lead up to this turning point in Borja's life. The picture that Dicenta paints is far from the truth, for Borja truly loved his wife and was completely devoted to her and his family of eight children. In fact, it was not until after her death in 1546 that he joined the Society of Jesus (Farmer 54). In his comprehensive study of Catholic saints, *The Lives of the Saints*, Alban Bulter describes how Leonor's death affected Borja: "when she lay ill it took all Francis's determination to pray that not his will but God's should be done in her regard" (128). The *Enciclopedia universal ilustrada* points out that on her deathbed, Leonor was "atendida con el cariño del santo duque" (24: 1041). The story Dicenta relates is purely Romantic, and it must be remembered that its purpose was to entertain, not inform. The only documented historical truth to Dicenta's *zarzuela* is the death of the Empress followed by the Duke of Gandía's responsibility to transport the coffin to Granada and his subsequent horror after identifying the body.

TECHNIQUE
MUSIC

Although *El duque de Gandía* is a *zarzuela*, it did not conform to the shorter musical pieces that filled the stage at the time; instead, it is a full three-act play with an epilogue. There is a variety of music in Dicenta's first lyrical drama ranging from the *jácara* to the solemn *Miserere*. The play begins with a fast-paced tune sung by the chorus with the refrain: "¡Viva la dicha! ¡Viva el placer! ¡A gozar; á reír; á beber; á beber!" (5). The next song is a *jácara*, a comic ballad, and due to the humorous nature of the story, it is worth repeating in its entirety:

MONT.	Iba Juana la Rabicortona
	cruzando la plaza del Zocodover...
CORO.	¡Del Zocodover!
MONT.	y un galán, atajándola el paso,
	la dijo al oído: ¡Hermosa mujer!...
	Si tú me dejases seguir á tu lado,
	Á donde tú fueses, iba yo también.
	Y ella repuso:
	—Bien puede ser
	que se cansara
	vuestra merced.
	—Yo no me canso,
	puedo probar.
	—Pues pruebe.—Pues pruebo.
	Y echaron a andar.
CORO.	Y ella repuso:
	—Bien puede ser
	que se cansara
	vuestra merced.
MONT.	Caminaron por calles y plazas,
	hablando él, y ella dejándole hablar.
CORO.	Dejándole hablar.
MONT.	Y en una calleja estrecha y obscura,
	cuando iban la esquina los dos á doblar,
	salieron dos jaques, guiñóles la moza,
	y á palos molieron al pobre galán.
	Echaron al suelo,
	le hicieron callar;
	después, le quitaron
	cuanto hay que quitar;
	y la moza, con los jaques,
	por la calle arriba echó,
	y el galán, sin novia
	ni ropa quedó.
CORO.	Ni ropa quedó.
MONT.	Desde aquel suceso, cuando ve á una moza,
	dice que se cansa, que no puede andar;

> y al ver unas faldas, venir á su encuentro,
> parece que el diablo le viene á buscar,
> según la mirada
> y el gesto de agraz
> que pone, al mirarlas,
> el pobre galán. (11-12)

The first appearance of the Duke of Gandía is in scene five, in which he sings a solo lamenting his impossible love for the queen. It is a moving piece full of emotion:

> Un crimen es amarla;
> mas ¿qué puedo hacer yo,
> si mi alma entera vive,
> del sueño de su amor?
> Ella es toda mi vida;
> ella es todo mi sér,
> mi afán, mi Dios, mi gloria,
> mi porvenir, mi fe. (18)

Towards the end of the first act there is a great crescendo of music as Leonor discovers the truth about her husband; the final two scenes are entirely in song. The song begins slowly and climaxes as the Duke of Gandía, Leonor, the Marquis of Montanilla, the Count of Úbeda, and the chorus exchange words in a dizzying whirlwind. In Act Three, Dicenta provides more detailed stage directions relating to the dancing and singing than he had previously. The setting is the Zocodover Plaza in Toledo, and the townspeople are anxiously awaiting the return of Carlos V from Flanders. The song begins with the men trying to gain the favor of the ladies; it is a dance of sorts as the women, ever flirting, move around the stage in an attempt to avoid the men. Finally, as Carlos V arrives, there is a grand parade with dancers, drummers and "dulzaineros" (66). Dicenta details the scene:

> Mientras el Coro canta, avanzan los Bailadores y Acompañamiento dando vuelta á la plaza al son de dulzainas y tambroiles [sic]; las dos filas de Bailadores, lo hacen danzando al uso del país; al llegar al tablado, se divide la multitud en dos hileras, por entre las cuales pasan, el Consejo, el Alcalde y los Alguaciles... (66)

The final scene, the epilogue, is spoken, yet is both preceded and followed by the *Miserere*. The title of the fifty-first Psalm, *Miserere*, means "have mercy," and it is sung during Holy Week. The *Miserere* is the composer Gregorio Allegri's (1582-1652) most famous piece, yet at that time it could be heard only in Rome during Holy Week performed by the papal choir. By papal decree, it was forbidden to sing the work elsewhere, and its only existing copy was strongly guarded by the papal choir. Years later, Wolfgang Amadeus Mozart, at the age of fourteen (1770), had heard the work only once during Holy Week when, returning home, he reproduced it in its entirety upon paper. The *Miserere* has a most prominent place in the Divine Office and in various ceremonies, including the burial of the dead. Its presence in the final scene of *El duque de Gandía* serves to evoke great emotion on the part of the spectators, for not only do they recognize Mesonero Carbonero's famous painting in the setting of the stage, but they also hear the *Miserere*, music they associate with Christ's crucifixion.

ROMANTIC CHARACTERISTICS

Like all but one (*Luciano*) of Dicenta's previous plays, *El duque de Gandía* reveals many Romantic qualities. Dicenta continues many of the same techniques he used in *Honra y vida*, his first historical drama: oriental furniture, positive Christian references, eight-syllable verse, night setting, and excessive emotion. The medieval setting provides the playwright with the ideal location for this Romantic tragedy, and the Duke of Gandía, like so many Romantic heroes, is plagued by unrequited love and is preoccupied with vengeance and honor. As in *La mejor ley*, there is an imbalance in the matters of love; Úbeda loves Leonor, but she is married to Borja, and Borja loves the queen, who is married to Carlos V. Also as in *La mejor ley*, vengeance is taken by one who is spurned by love; Úbeda seeks to hurt Leonor for having rejected him. Vengeance is then repaid with vengeance, again as in *La mejor ley*, when Borja kills Úbeda. The unrequited love between Borja and the queen is thoroughly Romantic as each laments the role destiny has played in their lives. Queen Isabel dies of a broken heart, and just before she dies, she expresses the pain she has suffered by being torn between her duty as the queen and her love for Borja:

> Odiarle quiero, y le adoro;
> quiero olvidarle, y me estrecha
> el corazón con sus brazos
> de sombra, y á mí se aferra,...
> No quiero verle; mis ojos,
> para no verle, se cierran,
> y su imagen, en la noche
> que yo creo se refleja.
> Contra su amor busco apoyo

en mi dignidad de reina,
y en mis deberes de esposa,
y contra su amor no encuentra,
ni orgullo la soberana,
ni la esposa fortaleza. (75)

CONCLUSIONS

Dicenta's first *zarzuela* was a great success and was much enjoyed by the theater-going public. Coming only days after *Luciano*, *El duque de Gandía* helped Dicenta prove that, although he was a journalist, he was a dramatist at heart. These two distinctly different plays indicate Dicenta's great versatility and his inventive mind. There is no apparent thesis in *El duque de Gandía*, which confirms the argument that Dicenta, the voice of the oppressed, is able to set aside his theses and write drama for entertainment purposes only. The dramatist who had made a name for himself by staging controversial topics, such as advocacy for divorce and the acceptance of free love, gained even more credibility following the premiere of *El duque de Gandía*, for Dicenta appealed to not only the lowest and least appreciated classes but also to the opera-loving multitude of the bourgeois.

OVERALL CONCLUSIONS TO CHAPTER THREE

The six plays studied thus far can be divided into three categories: drama, "leyenda dramática," and "*zarzuela*." With the exception of *Luciano*, all of Dicenta's first productions (*El suicidio de Werther*, *La mejor ley*, *Los irresponsables*, *Honra y vida*, and *El duque de Gandía*) are examples of the Echegarayan neo-Romantic school. Dicenta takes full advantage of the Romantics' techniques: unrequited love, low lighting, blood spilled on stage, inexorable fate, preoccupation with vengeance, medieval themes, strong sense of honor, Christian elements, extreme emotion, mysterious situations, and the use of verse. Although he follows Echegaray's example by portraying the upper classes with Romantic themes, Dicenta differs in his decision to depict society's victims among the low class and to explore certain social issues at depth. In *El suicidio de Werther*, Dicenta shows great compassion for those who suffer from society's unjust prejudice. Fernando, because he is the son of a prostitute, has no hope of ever becoming accepted by society despite his talent as an artist or his high moral character, and his mother, Carlota, despite the fact that society is to blame for having forced her into prostitution, will forever suffer from the community's condemnation. Both are forced to accept their inability to climb the social ladder. The same is true in *Luciano*, Dicenta's first prose drama, for both Luciano and his mother Dolores are constantly belittled by Luciano's in-laws, who, although from a higher social class, prove morally deficient in comparison to Dolores and Luciano. In these two plays Dicenta becomes the voice of society's underdogs as he strives to establish the unmistakable difference between the social classes and the great injustice those of the low class endure because of the higher classes' misguided prejudice. In this way, Dicenta's argument is twofold. He forces his audiences to reevaluate what has always been accepted by society simply because of tradition.

Dicenta's first plays, with the exception of *El duque de Gandía*, all reflect Dicenta's ongoing ideology of the injustice of certain social structures. Dicenta does not always use the underdog to build his case; in fact, in several instances, the rich suffer just as much. In *Los irresponsables*, for example, the victim of society's condemnation is a wealthy man who finds himself incapable of achieving acceptance because he no longer loves the wife who betrayed him. The same is true of Dolores in *La mejor ley*, who, having been forced into an arranged marriage, discovers her husband is unfaithful. Both deserve the option of divorce, yet because society does not approve, they must choose between society's condemnation—by abandoning the spouse and uniting with their true love—or unhappiness—by remaining with their unfaithful mate. Dicenta's call for acceptance of divorce is best seen, however, in *Luciano*, in which neither party has betrayed the other, but rather, they each suffer from complete incompatibility. Dicenta urges us to question such social traditions that prevent individuals from seeking true contentment. This same ideology is also evident in Dicenta's only "leyenda dramática," *Honra y vida*, in which Dicenta pushes his contemporary audiences to question what was long believed several hundred years earlier: the divine right of kings. A corrupt king should not be allowed to satisfy his every desire for the reason that he is divinely crowned, and had this tradition not been so prevalent at that time, Jaime would have had the right to challenge the king in a duel for having threatened his honor.

Honra y vida and *El duque de Gandía* stand apart from Dicenta's other early dramas in that he chooses to recreate history with a fictional twist. Both dramas, although accurately staged in the past, provide fabricated stories based upon ancient legends. *Honra y vida* did not enjoy success on the stage for two reasons: Dicenta's attempt to explore such a heavy theme in a limited time frame, and the fact that it premiered first in Zaragoza, not Madrid. Dicenta's first lyrical drama, *El duque de Gandía*, on the other hand, was quite successful as it proved Dicenta was a talented playwright who was not only capable of shocking audiences with "enseñanzas peligrosas," but also fully skilled in the art of pure entertainment.

With the exception of his successful lyrical drama (*El duque de Gandía*), Dicenta's first plays, besides indicating his versatile talent and inventive mind, establish his desire to be an advocate for society's victims as they set the stage for his masterpiece, *Juan José*. They are all, except for *Luciano*, overwhelmingly Romantic in theme and plot development, and although none of his first dramas are truly realistic, there is an obvious development in *Luciano*, which is entirely in prose. Unfortunately, because it is more a series of speeches, its artistic quality is significantly weakened. It is not until his next play, *Juan José*, that Dicenta perfects his technique by portraying a realistic story that truly moves the theater-going public. Dicenta was not pleased with his first contributions to the stage. In *Idos y muertos* Dicenta says that there is no need to discuss his first productions, explaining, "Útiles fueron para gimnasia de mi inspiración y para martirio de los amigos, obligados á escuchar su lectura" (143). In fact, one of his early plays, *El hijo de Sancho Alvar*, is forever lost because he decided to burn it:

> Ni de este drama, ni de otros ya estrenados y hasta aplaudidos, he de hablar. ¿Para qué? Si nadie los recuerda, no vale la pena de mentarlos. Si alguien los recuerda, tampoco mentarlos hace falta. (144)

Dicenta was far too critical of himself, for these first dramas are rich, not only in technique but also in theme as they indicate the ongoing development of Dicenta's ideology regarding the unjust social structures of his time.

4
Dicenta's First Social Dramas: *Juan José* and *El señor feudal*

JUAN JOSÉ (1895)

IN AN INTERVIEW WITH José María Carretero, Dicenta described his financial situation prior to the premiere of his masterpiece *Juan José* in 1895; when asked if his first dramas paid him well, Dicenta replied:

> No, hombre; muy poco; tanto, que cuando llegó el estreno de *Juan José* estaba en situación horrible, ¡espantosa!: en uno de los momentos más difíciles de mi vida, y conste que he tenido muchos muy difíciles... Sin ropa que vestir y sin cigarro que fumar, escribí *Juan José*, con lápiz y sobre cachos de papel de estraza que me daba un tendero conocido... No se me olvidará que pude asistir al estreno gracias a un alma caritativa que me prestó un pantalón y una americana viejos. ¡Horrible! (634)

Dicenta knew well what it was like to struggle to survive. For thirteen years he lived in extreme poverty, as he wrote plays hoping to achieve fame and success as a dramatist. It was only after the great success that his masterpiece *Juan José* achieved that he was able to escape from misery and poverty. His experience during those thirteen years manifests itself in his plays as he chooses characters that represent the poor working class of late nineteenth-century Madrid. In a letter Dicenta wrote to José de Urquía (included in the Cátedra edition of *Juan José*), Dicenta explains how living among the poorest members of society inspired him to bring their story to the stage:

> La miseria me llevó a convivir con los humildes y con los miserables. Entre ellos escogí modelos para personajes de mi obra; ellos, con sus dolores, con sus ignorancias, con la pobreza material y moral a que les reducían la codicia, el egoísmo y la crueldad de explotadores y viciosos, trajeron a mi corazón primero que a mi inteligencia el trágico poema de los desheredados, al cual quise dar vida escénica en *Juan José*. (*Juan* 65)

In *Juan José*, Dicenta explores the struggle of one honorable man who is bound by his poverty and driven by passion.

PLOT

The protagonist of *Juan José* is a poor factory worker who is characterized by honesty, jealousy, and extreme passion. The drama begins in a tavern in a poor area of Madrid where several men are drinking, talking, and playing cards. The discussion turns to their friend, Juan José, who is madly in love with Rosa, another factory worker. Paco, a rich young man who had inherited the factory from his father, has fallen in love with Rosa and decides to take every measure to win her over. There is a confrontation in the bar when Juan José arrives and realizes that Rosa is in the back room singing a *malagueña* with Paco and his friends.

By Act II both Juan José and Rosa have lost their jobs: he for his temper, and she because of factory layoffs. They have no money to buy coals for heat or food to eat. One day, while Juan José is out searching for a job, Isidra, an older woman playing the Celestina figure who encourages Rosa to leave Juan José for Paco to take advantage of his wealth, offers to help Rosa by giving her food and coals; Rosa happily accepts her offer. When Juan José arrives and notices Isidra there with food and heat, he angrily insults her and accuses her of trying to ruin his relationship with Rosa. After he commands Isidra to leave, he and Rosa argue about their situation to the point that Juan José becomes violent and strikes her. By the end of Act II, he has decided to do whatever it takes to feed Rosa, with the result that he leaves the house to search for food.

Act III begins in the jail of Madrid. The jailer and Cano, an inmate, are talking about Juan José, who has been sentenced to jail for eight years for stealing food. Juan José receives a letter from Andrés detailing all that has happened since he was imprisoned. Cano reads it aloud to Juan José since he is unable to read, revealing that Rosa immediately moved in with Paco after he was convicted and that she is living a life of luxury. In desperation, Juan José plans to escape.

The second part of Act III begins in Paco's home as Rosa is getting ready to go out for the evening with Paco, when Juan José comes in the door at the back and makes his presence known to her. As she is trembling with fear, he notices the prosperity surrounding him. He tells her he plans to kill Paco, and he locks her in her room to go find him. After killing Paco, Juan José returns, and Rosa throws the window open, screaming for help. As he struggles to silence her screams, Rosa falls limp on the floor. Horrified, Juan José realizes he is responsible for her death too. Andrés arrives and urges him to escape, yet Juan José says there is no reason to run. He claims that his life is worthless without his only reason for living, Rosa.

CRITICAL RECEPTION OF *JUAN JOSÉ*
IMMEDIATE CRITICISM

After its premiere in Madrid, *Juan José* was unanimously praised by the public and critics, and almost immediately Dicenta became for the moment the most celebrated playwright in Spain. *Juan José* remains Dicenta's best known play, and yet it perhaps would have never appeared had there not been a break in the program at the Teatro de la Comedia the week of October 29, 1895. Weeks earlier, Dicenta had taken a copy of *Juan José* to Emilio Thuillier, a renowned actor, who, although enthusiastic about Dicenta's latest play, persuaded Dicenta not to show it to Emilio Mario, the director of the company, for fear that it would immediately be rejected as a "drama de alpargata" (García Pavón 36). When the company found themselves without a play to perform, they hurriedly decided to use *Juan José* to fill the gap. The play was enthusiastically received following that first performance and ran so long that Mario was forced to form another company in order to move the production to the Alhambra, where it was performed one hundred and fifty times (Hall 55). The immediate critical reception *Juan José* received was unanimously favorable in Madrid press:

La Época, Fernández Shaw
   El señor Dicenta es, sin duda alguna, entre los autores de la nueva generación, el más inspirado, el más genial, el que con más iniciativa y con arte más extraodinario, sabe llevar a la escena las grandes luchas de la vida contemporánea, "pensando alto, sintiendo hondo y hablando claro." (qtd. in Mas Ferrer, *Vida* 121)

El Heraldo, Federico Unecha
   No ha hecho Dicenta otra obra con armazón tan sólido ni con tan vigoroso entraña … la presentación naturalista de las figuras se hace con arte y sobriedad, nada sobra y nada falta. (qtd. in Mas Ferrer, *Vida* 123)

El Resumen
   El autor de *Juan José*, por voto unánime de la opinión docta, se encuentra desde anoche en lugar preferentísimo entre los primeros cultivadores del teatro genuinamente español, del teatro nacional moderno: revolucionario, atrevido, regenerador. (qtd. in Mas Ferrer, *Vida* 124)

El Globo, Arturo Perera
   La victoria obtenida es tanto más señalada, cuanto que el argumento, el asunto y el plan de *Juan José* eran otros tantos escollos y peligros que había que sortear para llevar a buen puerto la nave, siendo como es el Teatro de

la Comedia un verdadero foso para obras de la índole del drama del señor Dicenta. (qtd. in Mas Ferrer, *Vida* 124)

El Día, Enrique Sepúlveda
Realismo de buen gusto todo y en muchos momentos de provechosa enseñanza, el que campea avalorándole en la hermosa creación de usted, a tal extremo llega, que, salvo contadas ocasiones (las precisas para que el literato diga "aquí estoy yo"), no existe apenas en *Juan José* el convencionalismo escénico. (qtd. in Mas Ferrer, *Vida* 121)

La Correspondencia, A. Pimecas
Juan José es un drama de pasiones, energías, arrogancias y caracteres nuestros, sin asomo de vida francesa, bien hablado, con diálogo sobrio, con frases hermosísimas dichas con naturalidad y sencillez, es cosa que merece ser conocida y celebrada... (qtd. in Mas Ferrer, *Vida* 121)

El País
Joaquín Dicenta es un revolucionario sempiterno, un enemigo formidable y sincero de todas las mentiras que llamó convencionales Max Nordau... Dicenta ha vencido en *Juan José* como vencen los maestros, sin retórica, sin lirisismos, sin frases de relumbrón: haciendo natural y justo. *Juan José* es un drama que tiene la hermosura y la grandeza de la verdad... con el estreno de ayer, Dicenta y la dramática española han ganado una batalla, han tenido un triunfo. (qtd. in Pérez de la Dehesa 20-21)

La Idea Libre, Ernesto Alvarez
Así son los trabajadores; así son los burgueses. Víctimas los primeros; verdugos los segundos. Así es también la justicia; condena al infeliz y absuelve al delincuente... Esto es vergonzoso para la especia y debe de concluir. O la sociedad se reforma o se hunde. Ya no huele algo a podrido: todo hiede a corrupto. (qtd. in Pérez de la Dehesa 21)

Blanco y Negro, Luis Gabaldón
El éxito alcanzado por *Juan José* ha sido tan espontáneo como justo. Aquel público tan serio, tan estirado, del teatro de la Comedia, muy atento al frac y muy solícito para cuidar el brillo de su pechera, que suele leer las cotizaciones de la bolsa en las escenas más culminantemente artísticas, ha tenido para la obra de Dicenta sinceros y legítimos aplausos, ha seguido con vivísima simpatía la figura de Juan José, y a través de las negruras y amarguras de la azarosa vida del expósito, saciada de profundas penalidades, agigantada por los quebrantos del presidio, que abren el paso

a la duda y a la mortificante desesperación y acicatan su pensamiento para el mal, ha sentido y ha sentido hondo. (qtd. in Pérez de la Dehesa 20)

Revista Contemporánea, Melchor Palau
Juan José es la obra más importante que ha pisado la escena en estos últimos tiempos; al así calificarla no me refiero a su valor literario, en lo cual está muy por bajo de otras recientes, sino algo más trascendental y temible: señalo como circunstancia agravante el haberse presentado en el teatro de la Comedia, que contra sus costumbres de antaño, está funcionando de *Teatro Libre*, *Théâtre Antoine* o *Independent Theatre*... el género Hauptmann, a que por sus personajes y tendencias claramente pertenece, había intentado en *La de San Quintín*, en *Teresa*, en *María Rosa*, y en *El pan del pobre* perforar el tradicional muro de la escena española; pero por brumoso del asunto, unas veces por escasez de claridad y precisión, otras por exceso de tonos judiciales melodramáticos, no lo había conseguido.

Dicenta se ha impuesto retrocediendo en vez de avanzar y envolverse en lo enmarañado y complejo; adoptando para seres escénicos nuevos las formas originales del teatro, con sus sencilleces, sus libertades pasionales, sus energías de resolución. (Palau 621-22)

La Ilustración Española y Americana, José Bustillo
Así acaba ese drama hermoso, legítimo, de pasión, sin tesis ni problema en su interés pasional, á no ser que la sociedad alarmada quiera buscar el problema en las mismas entrañas del conflicto dramático, tan posible en todas las esferas 0sociales. (Bustillo 277)

CRITICISM TO DATE
Since the premiere of *Juan José* in 1895, critics have often argued the social question present in the play. For a definition of "social theater," we turn to Francisco García Pavón who provides a detailed study of Spanish social drama from 1895-1962 in his *El teatro social en España (1895-1962)*. García Pavón's definition is twofold: social theater is limited first to those plays that focus their attention on class struggle and the human emotion rising from unjust social structures; and second, to dramas of which the heroes are from a working class that is conscious of both social injustice and the need for reform (18). *Juan José* certainly meets both of these requirements; the hero is a poor working-class individual who realizes the social injustice present in a society where he must steal food in order to keep from starving, and the play itself focuses on this struggle between classes. Although *Juan José* fits García Pavón's definition for "social" theater, because its central theme is not based on social injustice but

rather on a domestic tragedy, many critics often ignore the social implications or minimize their importance.

Although *Juan José* is praised as Spain's first social drama, its best qualities are not found in Dicenta's treatment of the differences between the classes, but rather in his realistic exploration of the singular tragedy of one poor man. Just over a month after the premiere of *Juan José*, Miguel de Unamuno in *La lucha de clases* on December 7, 1895 praises Dicenta's talent yet minimizes the social aspect of *Juan José*:

> El drama del señor Dicenta es bueno artísticamente por revelar la esencia de la vida social de hoy en uno de sus aspectos, por ser resplandor de la verdad, por revelarnos la honda significación de un mundo. No es bueno por tener tesis socialista, sino que tiene tesis socialista por ser bueno. (qtd. in Pérez de la Dehesa 21)

Unamuno does not deny the social question present in the play; instead, he denies that the social issue is the reason for Dicenta's success. Unamuno was reacting in part to the revolutionary youth who immediately embraced Dicenta as their leader in their fight against society's great injustices; Rafael Delorme, one of Dicenta's contemporaries, worshiped Dicenta and even called *Juan José* "la biblia" in his article "El socialismo en el teatro" published in *El País* on October 31, 1895:

> Los soldados que peleamos en las brillantes legiones de la juventud española por la igualdad y por el derecho tenemos ya el *leader* que nos conduzca en esta lucha tremenda que contra lo absurdo, lo injusto y lo irracional están librando los hombres nuevos que en esta generosa España piensan mucho y sienten hondo... El drama de Dicenta es socialista, profundamente socialista: tiende a la regeneración social, basada en el derecho uno e igual para todos. Joaquín Dicenta, pues, ha enarbolado en Juan José la bandera de la igualdad; alrededor de ella, debemos de agruparnos todos cuantos jóvenes tendamos al porvenir lleno de grandezas. "¡Adelante!", grita el autor de *Juan José* y "¡adelante!", debe gritar a su vez la juventud socialista española. (qtd. in Pérez de la Dehesa 24)

The popularity of *Juan José* among Spain's radical youth at the turn of the century is one of the reasons that not long after its premiere local authorities began to prohibit its performance throughout Spain: "El Obispo de Mallorca, por ejemplo, lo prohibió en su diócesis" (Pérez de la Dehesa 25).

Despite the attempt of Dicenta's contemporaries and the revolutionary youth of the time to herald *Juan José* as the voice of the proletariat, critics, among whom included Manuel Bueno, José Deleito y Piñuela, Gonzalo Torrente Ballester, Francisco García Pavón, and Francisco Ruiz Ramón, dispute the social issue in Spain's first "social" drama and assert that the title character is a Romantic hero obsessed with honor, reminiscent of Calderón de la Barca's and Lope de Vega's cloak and dagger plays and, more recently, José Echegaray's melodramatic bourgeois dramas. Manuel Bueno in *Teatro español contemporáneo* (1909) denies the existence of any social issue in *Juan José*, stating that the title character is "sencillamente un enamorado que roba y mata, no por necesidad y por anhelos de desquite social, sino por amor" (113). Both José Deleito y Piñuela (*Estampas del Madrid teatral fin de siglo*, 1946) and Gonzalo Torrente Ballester agree with Manuel Bueno as they emphasize the sensationalist nature of *Juan José* and its themes of homicidal jealousy and revenge for love spurned. Torrente Ballester in *Teatro español contemporáneo* (1957) claims that *Juan José* is nothing more than an honor play: "más respiraba por la herida del honor que respondía a la lucha de clases" (17). García Pavón also calls *Juan José* a "drama de celos y honra," and he denies the relevance of social issues brought up in the play with his claim that the succession of tragic events in the drama is simply accidental: "El hecho de que el paro, y por esto el hambre, condicionen el robo y doble crimen después, es todavía accidental, un determinante dramático apenas consciente de su caracterización social" (49).

Francisco Ruiz Ramón, in his *Historia del teatro español* (1967), continues García Pavón's argument against the social issues in *Juan José*; the adverse social conditions exist only for dramatic effect. According to Ruiz Ramón, although Juan José is a passionate man driven to murder, his fight is against a man who has stolen the only thing that has ever mattered to him, Rosa, not against his employer who caused him to freeze, starve, and steal. Ruiz Ramón states that *Juan José* is much less a "choque de clases" but rather a "choque de personas morales" (427). Ruiz Ramón also concurs with Manuel Bueno and Deleito y Piñuela in their assertion that Juan José is simply a Lopean protagonist transferred from the "aldea" to the city:

> Juan José es hermano del villano con conciencia de honra y de dignidad personal del teatro de Lope de Vega, sólo que vestido de proletario y habitante no de la aldea, sino de la ciudad. (428)

Ruiz Ramón believes that individual passions ("honra, amor y celos") drive the protagonist (428).

The above-mentioned critics are certainly correct in their assessment of Juan José as a man who is more driven by passion and jealousy than social misfortune, yet their denial of the existence of a social issue in *Juan José* is unconvincing. While Rafael Pérez de la Dehesa (*El grupo germinal: una clave del '98*, 1970) continues his predecesors' argument that *Juan José* is a "drama de amor y celos," he maintains that it is also a social drama: "pues Juan José es un obrero consciente de pertenecer a una clase social explotada, y que simboliza en el contratista la odiada burquesía" (18). Jaime Mas Ferrer also points out the dual nature of *Juan José* as a social drama with Romantic characteristics. In both *Vida, teatro y mito de Joaquín Dicenta* (1978) and his introduction to the Cátedra edition of *Juan José* (1992), Mas Ferrer claims that the superficial structure of *Juan José* reveals a Calderonian drama of love and jealousy. He divides the play into two separate structures: the first, a typical "drama convencional de amor, pasión y celos," and the second, the conflict between classes and the social injustices suffered by the lower class (Introducción 50). Unlike previous critics, Mas Ferrer gives great importance to the social nature of *Juan José*, stating that "ya desde la escena primera vemos una serie de implicaciones sociales que van *in crescendo* en hondura y profundidad..." (Introducción 52). Although Mas Ferrer is correct in his analysis of the structure of *Juan José*, his assertion that the social issue becomes increasingly important as the play progresses is seriously flawed. In fact, the social issue decreases substantially as Jesús Rubio Jiménez demonstrates in *Ideología y teatro en España (1890-1900)*, in which he emphasizes the great difference between the first and last scenes of *Juan José*:

> Al principio tiene primacía lo "sociológico," al mostrar documentalmente la situación del asalariado urbano—el término "proletario" me parece excesivo en este caso -. Cuando acaba el drama, es lo pasional lo que domina. (162)

Although Rubio Jiménez disputes the impact of the social issue in *Juan José*, as do the majority of Dicenta's critics, he completely disagrees with Torrente Ballester, García Pavón, and Ruiz Ramón in their evaluation of *Juan José* as a drama with a hero who is obsessed with honor. Rubio Jiménez claims that the protagonist is not defending his honor but rather "su dignidad y sus derechos de hombre igual a cualquier otro hombre" (*Ideología* 162).

The most accurate assessment of *Juan José* is H. B. Hall's 1952 article "Joaquín Dicenta and the Drama of Social Criticism." Hall points out that many critics have been too quick to judge *Juan José* as a simple adaptation of the themes and motives of the Echegarayan drama from a middle-class to a working-class setting, with "honor" being the motivation behind Juan José's criminal acts. Hall rejects this interpretation by pointing out that Juan José says the word "honra" only once (II,6) and by emphasizing that Juan José's motives are "simpler and less conventional than the 'honor hidalgo'" (56). Another point Hall makes about honor is the question of marriage. The primary characters live together, yet they are not married; therefore, "honor" in the strict conventional sense cannot be in question. Rather than "honor," Hall maintains that Juan José's motive in killing Paco and Rosa is the result of his desire to possess Rosa, "which means for him the satisfaction of two primitive wants: sexual passion and, more important, the need for maternal protection" (56). Hall explains that *Juan José* is "fundamentally a tragedy of jealousy... with certain social implications" (57). Hall asserts that Dicenta wanted to "protest against a social order which was so largely responsible for that tragedy" (58). However, Hall cannot define *Juan José* as a "social drama"; instead, he believes *Juan José* is more a drama of passion characterized by its adherence to the "cuadro de costumbres" tradition:

> the convincing naturalism of the tavern and prison scenes, the sympathetic portrayal of a range of well-defined minor characters drawn from the lower classes, the enlivening touches of the *madrileño*'s dauntless humour in adversity, and the apt, flexible, racy dialogue of the best scenes were unparalleled in the serious drama of the time. (58)

BACKGROUND

In creating Spain's first social drama, *Juan José*, Dicenta borrows minor details from his earlier short story of the same title and adds deeper social implications to emphasize the oppression of the working class by the ruling class. Seven years prior to the famous production of *Juan José*, Dicenta had published a book of social sketches, *Spoliarium* (1888), in which appears a short story entitled "Juan José." "Juan José" and the other sketches compiled in *Spoliarium* describe events that generate pity for the poor and downtrodden and scorn for society's unfair conventions. It is obvious that Dicenta borrowed freely from "Juan José" in his creation of the drama by the same name, yet the two differ greatly in the presentation of the theme of society's victimization of the low class.

In "Juan José," the protagonist's mother is a prostitute who finds herself pregnant and out of work, and unlike the drama, which contains no mention of Juan José's mother, the short story focuses as much attention on the plight of Juan José's mother as it does on him. When Juan José's mother realizes that she is pregnant with him, she immediately hates the fetus for deforming her body, her livelihood. Once Juan José is born, his mother quickly abandons him, and just as in the play, a beggar woman finds the infant Juan José and takes him in, hoping he will generate more charity on her behalf. In the play, Juan José makes a reference to this sad period in his life, without providing many details. The short story, however, describes in detail Juan José's troubled youth, the abuse he suffered at the hands of the beggar woman and her son, his discovery of the truth about his blood mother, his running away at the age of thirteen, and his growing up on the streets.

As in the play, Juan José falls in love with a woman named Rosa. In the short story, Juan José credits Rosa for saving his life: "Rosa es mi madre, mi hermana, mi querida todos los afectos en uno" (34). In both the play and the short story, Juan José is madly in love with Rosa, willing to do anything for her. The poverty in the play, however, is much more detailed, as Juan José and Rosa suffer hunger and freezing cold, and Juan José, for lack of income, is forced to steal food for Rosa. In the short story, however, Juan José wants to provide Rosa with luxurious gifts; his concern is not the simple necesities of life such as food and heat. Since Juan José's earnings are hardly enough for the two of them to eat, much less for her to have the luxuries she desires, Juan José steals money for Rosa to buy a particular coat that she has always wanted. In the short story, as in the play, Juan José is arrested for theft and placed in jail. However, in the short story, Rosa visits Juan José at first until he is sentenced to a three-year jail term; she stops visiting, and no letters arrive. After Juan José completes his sentence, he finds out that Rosa has fallen in love with another man. With vengeance in mind, Juan José goes to Rosa's new home and stabs her in the throat. He then kills her and her lover and says proudly, "Yo he sido" (40). Juan José, sentenced to death for his violent crime, is then hanged.

The key social implication in the drama revolves around Juan José's victimization and oppression by his employer who not only causes him to lose his livelihood but also his only love, Rosa. The short story contains no reference to Juan José's line of work, nor does it mention an oppressive employer. Juan José's incarceration in the drama is the direct result of having stolen bread to feed Rosa. In the short story, Juan José steals a coat in order to fulfill Rosa's selfish whim to have the latest fashion to keep warm.

TECHNIQUE
REALISM

As Unamuno indicated in his criticism of *Juan José*, the play was successful "por ser resplandor de la verdad" (qtd. in Pérez de la Dehesa 21). In *Juan José*, Dicenta has created an accurate representation of the exploitation of the working class in nineteenth-century Madrid, despite the play's occasional tendency towards the neo-Romantic. Dicenta's decision to break away from the stilted verse of his earlier dramas and to use prose to portray with authenticity the speech of the proletariat represents his continued move towards realism. The setting of the play in the slums of Madrid, depicting a worker's tavern, a prison, and the home of a poverty-stricken couple, serves to enhance the realistic elements of *Juan José*. In the tavern scene, the characters fill their conversations with petty remarks and gossip, fully drawing the spectator into the realistic situation. Later, in Juan José and Rosa's home, there is a shocking realization of their poverty; the disrepair of the furniture and the extreme cold they endure are symbolic of the emotional torture Juan José suffers. In order to bring even more realism to the scene, Dicenta uses a reference to contemporary events in the wall decorations; "La Lidia," a well-known publication in Madrid that treats bullfighting, hangs on the back wall (37)[1]. The poverty evident in their home is later contrasted with the luxurious furnishings of Paco's home. Even the prison scene, with its one wooden bench, represents a true to life scene of a late nineteenth-century Madrid jail.

Dicenta was so concerned about the realistic execution of the lines and the appearance of the set that he included explicit stage directions to both the actors and the director. Before each act, Dicenta describes how each stage property should appear, giving detailed instructions for specific locations and proximity. For example, in the bar scene at the beginning of Act I, Dicenta documents every detail, even the half-empty wineglasses that are placed on a tray near the card players: "En un taburete colocado al lado de los jugadores habrá una bandeja con varias copas de vino a medio apurar" (7-8). To help the audience further in believing the setting, Dicenta includes a trap door that gives access to the cellar where the wine is stored: "Entre el mostrador y el escaparate, una trampa practicable que da acceso a la cueva del establecimiento" (7).

Besides Dicenta's precise directions for the stage and its properties, he also explains throughout the dialogue exactly how each actor should perform his or her part. For example, the entire bar scene at the beginning of Act I is conscientiously choreographed as the characters drink and the bartender refills their glasses. Dicenta advises the actors to take special care in their portrayal of the scene: "Cuídese mucho de todo lo referente al servicio de vino, enjuague de las copas y demás detalles que se irán marcando en el curso de la representación. (7) Later, in the middle of the dialogue, Dicenta again explains exactly how he expects the actors to interpret the scene:

> El mozo llena unas copas en el mostrador; los coloca en una bandeja y las lleva adonde están los jugadores. Cada uno de éstos coge una copa. Cuando terminan de beber, el mozo coloca la bandeja en el taburete y retira la que está sobre el mismo. Llega con ella al mostrador, vacía el sobrante de los vasos en la jarra y enjuaga las copas. Todas estas operaciones las hará mientras sigue el diálogo. (8)

Dicenta also advises the actors concerning their interpretation of the colloquial

---

[1] All references to *Juan José* are taken from the sixth edition, published in Madrid in 1897.

speech of the workers: "Cuiden los actores que representen esta obra, de dar á los personajes su verdadero carácter; son obreros, no chulos, y, por consiguiente, su lenguaje no ha de tener entonación chulesca de ninguna clase" (6). The language spoken by the men in the tavern is full of colloquialisms, abbreviations, popular expressions, deformations, and proverbs. For example, among the deformations are "primáa" for "primada," "echao" for "echado," "andao" for "andado," "sacao" for "sacado," "libertá" for "libertad," "pa" for "para," "voluntá" for "voluntad," "usté" for "usted," "pa dirnos" for "para irnos," "náa" for "nada," "cansao" for "cansado," etc. (9-14). Dicenta uses the undereducated Perico, as he tries to read aloud from a newspaper, to make the spectator more aware of the lifestyle the factory workers were being forced to live as a result of their lack of education; because Perico is hardly able to read or pronounce the words, the meaning of the article is nearly lost.

Romantic Characteristics

Although Dicenta has carefully moved towards a more realistic portrayal of contemporary life, Romantic characteristics are still evident in *Juan José*. While he realistically treats the living conditions of the factory workers and the suffering caused by those of the ruling class, Dicenta makes the central character of the lower class essentially Romantic. Peak correctly charges that Juan José is a "romántico en blusa" (110). Hall too claims that Juan José, "another descendant of the romantic hero" (55), "talks more like a *señorito* than an illiterate bricklayer" (59). In comparison to the great Romantic figures of the Spanish stage, Juan José is certainly Romantic. Juan José is of unknown origin; he is a creature of extreme passion; he is dominated by love and vengeance; and he ultimately resorts to violence when overcome by what fate has bestowed upon him. The ever-present unrequited love throughout the drama leads towards the melodramatic ending in which Juan José kills both Paco and Rosa in a fit of passion.

Characters
Andrés

Juan José's closest friend, Andrés, is humorous, optimistic, and self-assured, and he often uses humor to lighten the heaviness of their situation. Andrés openly discusses his opinions about Juan José's relationship with Rosa, and he exposes intimate details about his own relationship with Toñuela. Andrés, unlike Juan José, has a mother who cares for him deeply; this love is enough to sustain him through the difficult times. In fact, Andrés shares many characteristics with Dicenta. Whenever Andrés reaches the point that he has no money for food or coal, he always has the option of returning to his mother who provides him with a meal and a warm place to sleep. Dicenta too turned to his mother when in desperate need:

> La casa de mi madre era un último asilo, donde me refugiaba cuando el hambre apretaba mucho y cuando el frío resultaba excesivo para dormir á la intemperie. (*Idos* 101)

Juan José never had this option, and his self esteem suffered greatly because of it. Andrés kindly offers to share whatever his mother has to eat with Juan José and Rosa: "no sé lo que habrá puesto la vieja; pero de lo que haya os traeremos un poco" (53).

As much as he cares for Juan José, Andrés does not understand Juan José's love for Rosa. With the exception of his mother, whom Andrés describes as "la sola mujer que no engaña" (17), Andrés finds all women to be evil, saying that Rosa is "como todas las mujeres, mala" (12). Andrés's matter-of-fact attitude differs greatly from Juan José's negative emotional outlook. When Juan José expresses his pain about the thought of losing Rosa, Andrés reprimands his friend: "Es pa empezar contigo a trastazos. Estaría bueno que un hombre se acongojase por una mujer. Todas juntas no valen una perra" (15). Andrés advises Juan José to leave Rosa, saying "no se acabó el mundo por eso" (17). After Juan José laments his lack of a mother, Andrés becomes more sympathetic towards his friend, saying "¡Sí es desgracia!" and "¡Pobre Juan José!" (18).

Domestic abuse seems to be common among the lower class, as Andrés, who believes physical punishment is necessary in order to control his live-in lover Toñuela, describes how fortunate he is:

> Toñuela se sujeta á mí; si hay dos, con dos pasa; si no los hay, pone los pucheros á la funerala; y Á esperar otro día; y si se me baja aguardiente á los déos y si se me suben los déos a la cara de ella, se aguanta y como si tal cosa... (12)

Rosa believes that Juan José should have hit her instead of causing the brawl at the tavern: "¡Hubiera estao bien que me pegase!" (41). Toñuela explains to Rosa that she has been slapped for much less: "Por menos he llevao yo muchos cachetes" (41). To this, Andrés humorously responds: "¡Y los que llevarás! ¡Más efecto os hace á las mujeres un cachete á tiempo que un sermón de Cuaresma!" (41). Refusing to step between Juan José and Rosa, Andrés tells a story to explain:

> Bajaba yo por la calle de Embajadores, y al desembocar en el barranco, me veo a uno que le estaba atizando á su mujer, ó lo que fuera, un palizón órdago. No es que yo me asuste porque se les tiente el traje á las mujeres;

pero aquel ciudadano pegaba tan fuerte y ella soltaba tales quejíos, que me dió lástima y me metí por medio, y sujeté la mano del hombre y le dije: ¡Camará, basta; ni que fuese la señora una caballería! El sujeto era razonable, y se contuvo; ¡pero ella!... ¡A ella había que verla!... Se puso en jarras, se vino pa mí, arrimó su cara á la mía, como si quisiera tragárseme, y me soltó esta rociáa: "¿A usté qué si me pega, tío morral? ... Pa eso es mi marido..." Vamos, que si me descuido me pega ella a mí.... Gritarle al otro: ¡Siga usté hasta que se canse, buen amigo! (43)

Later, after Juan José becomes violent with Rosa, Andrés points out comically: "Lo que habrá pensao Juan José: á falta de pan buenas son tortas" (53).

ROSA

Rosa, Juan José's lover, is a weak character who is only motivated by her instincts of self-preservation. She is with Juan José simply because he defended her against a group of men who were abusing her, and once Rosa realizes she no longer needs his protection, she seeks comfort from someone who can better support her, Paco. Our first impression of Rosa is from the comical Andrés:

Está hecha á otra vida. Mucha juerga, y mucho vestido de raso, y mucha bota de charol. Lo que tiene siempre una mujer cuando es guapa y tira la vergüenza á la calle. Así es que la viene muy pelo arriba agarrarse al trabajo. (12).

Although Rosa is of the same social class as Juan José, she pretends that she deserves more, and she laughs heartlessly at Juan José when Paco makes a comparison of his wealth to Juan José's poverty: "¡Qué suerte tienen algunos hombres y qué mal ganáa!" (15-16). Rosa takes full advantage of the power her beauty has over men, especially Paco, vainly boasting to Isidra:

No me gusta presumir ni echar plantas, pero, sépalo usté; así, mal vestida, y con esta facha, y sin dármelas de farolera, donde estuviera Paco y mi cuerpo se presentase, no habría más que un ama; yo. (28)

Later, in yet another display of vanity, Rosa complains that even the soap is not good enough for her: "No traiga usté más este jabón. Me pone muy ásperas las manos" (70).

Rosa is shallow, selfish, and completely lacking in strength of character; she is so impresionable que she believes everything Isidra tells her, hardly making any effort to think for herself. Both Juan José and Andres know that Rosa no longer loves Juan José (if she ever did), as Andrés relates, "va pa dos meses que quiere volar por su cuenta" (13). Rosa's faithfulness goes no further than self-gratification, and now that she has tired of what little Juan José has been able to provide for her, she finds it easy to consider leaving him for another. Rosa flirts shamelessly with Paco and agrees to sing with him, yet when Juan José arrives, she blatantly lies to him: "Yo no quería. Fué él quien se empeñó" (34). Later, when Andrés blames her for the situation at the bar which ultimately led to Juan José's losing his job, Rosa weakly defends herself:

> ¿En qué he faltao yo? ¿Porque un hombre le diga á una mujer buenos ojos tienes ya han faltao la mujer y el hombre? ¿Se ha propasao Paco conmigo? ¿Le he dejao yo que se propase? ¡Entonces!... Sólo que Juan José, y Toñuela, y tú empeñáis en echarme los cargos encima; y yo aquí pa sufrirlo todo: privaciones, desconfianzas... Y si un día me harto y tiro por la calle de enmedio me pondréis como un trapo. (42).

Perhaps Rosa's biggest flaw is her total lack of understanding of Juan José's situation or his love for her. Despite Juan José's attempts to secure employment to improve their situation, Rosa selfishly complains: "¡Aunque yo reviente, no importa!" (49). Rosa completely disregards Juan José's feelings as she blames him for their misfortune. She has neither love nor compassion for Juan José, and this is most evident in the final act when she quickly abandons Juan José in prison to become Paco's mistress. Her feigned illness to avoid seeing Juan José the day of the trial is yet another example of her selfish indifference.

As Rosa moves up the social ladder by becoming Paco's mistress, she finds that Paco loves her as much as Juan José, but the difference is that Paco can afford to spoil Rosa with material things; whereas Juan José could not even afford to feed her. Rosa proudly describes the control she has over Paco: "Paco es un Dios pa mí. Me basta decirle esto me apetece, pa que lo traiga; y en tocante á cariño... cada día me quiere más" (71).

In her final moments as she realizes that both she and Paco may be facing death, Rosa is at her weakest, pleading Juan José for mercy and forgiveness: "¡Oh! ¡Por caridá!... ¡Tenla tú de mí!... No, Juan José! ¡Te lo suplico!... ¿Quieres que te lo pida con los brazos en cruz?... ¡No lo esperes!... ¡Perdóname!" (75-76). Frightened, Rosa announces that she recognizes Paco's footsteps, to which Juan José responds bitterly: "Nunca has conocido los míos" (77). Rosa does not deserve the love and affection given her by both Juan José and Paco, and despite her newfound status on the social ladder, she remains a low-class woman of loose morals who is Juan José's inferior in all aspects.

JUAN JOSÉ
Dicenta's most famous character is compared by Unamuno to other great heroes of literature:

> Apenas hay en la obra novelesca de Galdós, una robusta y poderosa personalidad individual, uno de esos héroes que luchan contra el trágico destino y se crean un mundo para sí, para sí mismos, un Hamlet, un Segismundo, un Don Quijote, un Fausto, un Brand, un Juan José. (466)

Juan José is a good and honest man, a devoted and faithful lover, and a conscientious and honorable worker who believes everyone should adhere to his standard of conduct and is completely disillusioned when circumstances prove him wrong. Despite Juan José's positive characteristics, he finds that he is unable to overcome the social and economic oppression of the upper class that has left him little control over his own life. Juan José is further rendered powerless by his lack of education and inability to read. To make matters worse, unlike his friends, Juan José has no family to provide him support and affection, and even his live-in lover does not reciprocate his love. At the start of the drama, Juan José, although unhappy, has basically accepted his sad fate, as he seeks relief from his pain through Rosa, his only love.

Dicenta skillfully develops Juan José from a working-class citizen who is simply disappointed with his unfortunate situation into a man of action who, full of passion for an underserving woman and anger against an unfair society, becomes a thief (to satisfy Rosa's hunger more than his own) and thus is overwhelmed with guilt and the thought of never being able to redeem himself. Juan José is a man of great emotion, and as the play proceeds, the spectator traces Juan José's development from self-pity to outright anger through brief moments of hope to the final end of total despondency.

In his first appearance on stage, Juan José describes his emotional state to his friend Andrés, as he considers that Rosa may be leaving him:

> ...la sangre se me enciende en el cuerpo cuando imagino que Rosa puede dejarme de querer.... Es una idea que se me ha ido metiendo aquí dentro *(Señalando la frente.)* poco á poco, pero con fuerza; igual que si me la hubiesen claváo a martillazos; y no puedo deshacerme de ella, y me martiriza, y me azuza, y me tiene como sobre carbones encendíos. (15)

Andrés's response is an accurate assesment of the emotionally charged Juan José: "Eres un chico de la escuela" (15). Juan José continues his lament, this time insulting Paco, the one who is responsible for his suffering, by referring to him in a condescending manner: "ese mozo que no ha tenido más que hacer en el mundo que heredar la parroquia y los dineros de su padre" (15). In these two honest revelations, Juan José communicates the dual nature of his pain; the only two things that will make him happy and help him progress in this world, his lover and his ability to make a living, are both threatened by the same man. As he speaks, Juan José becomes enraged comparing himself to his rival:

> ...me fijaba en él, y á la vez que en él, en mi blusa remendáa y en su ropa nueva, en el yeso que había en mis manos y en las sortijas que había en las suyas, y sentí... No sé lo que sentía entonces; pero apreté con rabia el mango del palustre y estuve á punto de meterle por el pecho adelante aquella herramienta mancháa con la cal que nosotros amasamos pa que él se luzca... (16)

Juan José explains to Andrés that although he may be tempted to become violent with Paco, he is a good man: "Yo no soy malo, Andrés, no quiero serlo" (16). Dicenta emphasizes Juan José's positive characteristics, thus allowing the spectator to see the depth of the tragedy that befalls him. Juan José's love for Rosa is sincere, and unlike his friends, he believes love is forever: "En las cosas del querer, se firma con éste (*El corazón.*) y cuando éste dice 'quiero de veras,' firmao está pa toa la vida" (17). In the same way that Juan José deserves a faithful, affectionate lover, he is also worthy of a stable job that will enable him to make an honest living: "¿De qué sirve tener buena voluntá y buenos brazos y saber su oficio?... ¿De qué?..." (46). When asked if he plans to beg, Juan José responds: "¡Que pidan los viejos, los inútiles, los que no se pueden valer! El que, como yo, tiene fuerzas en los brazos, y no es perezoso en la faena, y sabe ganarlo, sólo debe pedir una cosa, trabajo" (57).

Throughout the play, Juan José becomes increasingly more desperate because of the lack of control he has over his life. His jealousy and anger give him the strength to confront Paco and accuse him of trying to steal Rosa away from him, resulting in his termination from the factory. Without means of income, Juan José and Rosa are both forced to starve and freeze, giving Rosa more incentive to leave him. Juan José's emotions progressively take control of him and render him completely irrational, to the point of becoming animalistic: "¡Pues el animal, cuando se mira acorralao, muerde!... ¡Yo también morderé! Si la bestia tiene ese derecho, mejor debe tenerlo el hombre, porque vale más" (56). Juan José's emotional decline is carefully documented by Dicenta in the stage directions, as he advises the actor playing Juan José how to interpret each line. In the beginning of the play while Juan José is still somewhat passive towards his unfortunate circumstances, Dicenta explains: "Con tono sombrío" (15), and "con tristeza profunda" (17). Yet, as Juan José opens his heart to his friend, Andrés, he becomes more impassioned, speaking "Con angustia y odio"

(19). In his confrontation with Paco in the tavern, Juan José changes from passive to active as he violently opens the door to the back room and grabs Rosa "por la muñeca con dureza" (34) and says forcefully: "¡Yo no busco nada; digo lo que debo decir, y me atengo á los resultaos!" (36). After demanding that Rosa leave, Juan José strategically places himself in the doorway, threatening "El que la quiera que salga por ella. ¡Pero no olvide que tiene que salir por esta puerta, y que en esta puerta estoy yo!" (36).

Juan José becomes increasingly more violent as his situation proves more hopeless. Upon the realization that Isidra has given Rosa coals in order to bribe her into leaving Juan José for Paco, Juan José reacts vehemently: "Empuja con el pie el brasero, que medio se vuelca, en forma que gran parte de la lumbre se desparrama por el suelo" (48). When Rosa accuses him of not caring about her, Juan José is overcome with emotion, as he slowly loses touch with reality:

> ¿No sabes que si alguien me diera un pedazo de pan, ese pedazo de pan llegaría a tus manos sin que yo lo tocase?... *(Con passión.)* ¿No comprendes lo que tú significas pa mí? ¿Ignoras que desde el punto de conocerte sólo en ti he pensao y de cuanto he tenido has dispuesto?... Pa mí se acabó el mundo al mirarte. Amigos, diversiones, ¡hasta el vaso de vino que tomaba en la taberna al volver de la obra!... A trabajar pa ella, me dije, y con calor, con frío; cortándome el viento la carne ó abrasándome el sol la piel, cantaba yo encima del andamio, más contento que nunca porque aquel frío, y aquel calor, y aquel dale que le das sin descanso eran mi jornal, el cuarto donde habitas, tu comida diaria, tu paseo de los domingos, el vestido de percal pa tu cuerpo, el mantón de lana pa tus hombros, ¡tú entera que vivías por mí!... ¡Qué me importaban el cansancio, y la faena, y el peligro!... ¡Calcúlate lo que iba a importarme padecer de día si me esperabas tú por la noche!... Ahí tienes lo que he hecho; lo que haría hoy mismo si pudiese; lo que deseo hacer... ¡Si hasta pediría pa ti una limosna, pa ti; pa mí, no! ¡Si no creyera que ibas a avergonzarte de esta juventud y estos brazos servían sólo pa echarse pa alante y pedir por Dios! ¡Y aún dices que no me interesas, que te abandono y te descuido!... ¡No lo digas Rosa, no lo digas!... ¡Por ti intento yo todo, todo! ¿Qué quieres que haga? (49-50)

Rosa's coldhearted response, "¿Qué voy yo a decirte?... ¿Qué sé yo?" (50), infuriates Juan José to the point that he momentarily regains his sanity, realizing her unworthiness: "Rosa, ¡tú eres mala!" (51). Juan José, in a matter of seconds, changes his speech from that of undying love to that of pure hatred: "Eres una infame, te lo repito. ¡No, tú no mereces que se te trate como te he tratao yo!... A ti hay que tratarte de otro modo; ¡como lo que eres, como lo que eras cuando te conocí! ¡Como... ! ¡Así!" (51). And with those words, Juan José raises his hand and hits Rosa.

Upon the realization that he has hurt the only one he loves, Juan José weeps, again allowing his emotions to dominate him. He approaches Rosa tenderly and returns to praising her, explaining his actions: "tú no sabes lo que es encelarse de una mujer que vale pa uno lo que la Virgen del altar" (54). As Juan José tries to console Rosa, he only manages to frighten her more by saying: "me vuelvo loco y me dan ganas de matarte" (55). Suddenly, Juan José is filled with hope, and he makes the decision that he must act in order to make a change in their lives. Juan José's final words in Act II lead the audience to believe that he may be able to take control of his sad situation and conquer the oppression that he and Rosa have been forced to endure by those of the ruling class: "¡... traeré a mi casa lo que en ella no hay; lo que tú me pides, lo traeré!" (57).

Unfortunately, Juan José's decisive action places him in jail, as he resorts to a criminal act. Juan José, although saddened by his new situation, maintains a positive attitude of hope, as is evident in Cano's description: "Anda el pobre mu entristecío con su desgracia, y se figura que achantándose y cumpliendo con formaliá podrá salir antes y volver a ser hombre de bien" (59). Juan José tells Cano, "¡Yo sólo apetezco rematar mi condena, y saber de Rosa, y volver á ser lo que he sido antes!... Un hombre honrao." (63). Upon Cano's explanation that he will never be anything more than a "licenciao de presidio" (63), Juan José becomes agitated and horrified, yet he maintains control, saying: "Aún confío, aún creo que cuando salga de presidio podré volver á ser honrao; aún espero encontrar á Rosa..." (63). All hope is lost, however, as Juan José discovers the truth about Rosa through a letter from Andrés that Cano must read to him since Juan José is illiterate. Juan José reacts "con espanto, odio y dolor" (67). Juan José sobs and immediately becomes angry with himself for weeping: "Los hombres no lloran; se desquitan.... ¡Cómo se reirán de mí! *(Con expresión de odio y acento de venganza.)* ¡No se reirán mucho; lo juro por todo el odio que les tengo!" (69).

Juan José's decision to escape from prison with Cano in order to seek vengeance for the pain Rosa and Paco have caused him is another example of his increased desire to take action. Juan José has lost all hope of returning to society as he was before, and as he confronts Rosa in her luxurious surroundings, he has also lost any semblance of love for her; he is only filled with hatred. Juan José proudly stands up to Rosa as she begs him to have mercy on Paco:

¡Claro; tan hecha estas á mandar en mí, á que nunca haya dicho "no" cuando me has suplicao, que hasta ahora mismo, en este momento, crees que te haré caso, que me iré!... Crees mal; no me voy. Espero. (76)

Juan José is now in charge of the situation, unlike the past, yet he irrationally maintains the hope that after he kills Paco, he will be able to have Rosa all to himself. After killing Paco, Juan José returns to Rosa with "alegría salvaje" (77) claiming: "Y lo he matao porque ningún hombre, ninguno, te poseéra mientras yo viva, sin que yo lo mate como á ese" (78). Juan José's moment of insane joy is cut off by Rosa's declaration that she will avenge Paco's murder. After accidentally killing Rosa as she screams for help, Juan José realizes that he has no reason to escape punishment, for he has lost the only thing in the world that mattered to him.

Juan José has transformed himself from a passive, honest, hardworking, devoted, and honorable man into an animal who causes a fight at the tavern, threatens his supervisor, physically and verbally abuses the woman he loves, resorts to criminal activity, is convicted of theft, escapes from prison, and finally, murders two people. Despite Juan José's negative actions, the spectator sympathizes with him, viewing him as a persecuted victim of society. The main difference between Juan José and the other working-class people in the play is his lack of emotional security, resulting from having been orphaned at an early age and mistreated throughout his life. Without a family to turn to for affection, Juan José irrationally clings to the first woman who pays him positive attention, Rosa. His undying love for this undeserving woman is his major character flaw. Having placed his whole reason for living in her, Juan José is destined for sadness. His situation is exacerbated by the loss of his job and the ensuing starvation and bitter cold he is forced to endure. Society has pushed Juan José into a corner from which he cannot escape. As the final curtain falls, the audience is left with a deep sense of sympathy for Juan José, a good man who was the victim of circumstances beyond his control.

IDEOLOGY

Dicenta's masterpiece, which came to be known as Spain's first "social" drama, is criticized by most scholars for its lack of social commentary, yet upon a careful reading of *Juan José*, one cannot deny that Dicenta fully intended this play to initiate a new form of theater which, as Dicenta explained in an article entitled "La verja cerrada" in *El Resumen*, would

> recoger la realidad palpitante de aquellos vicios, aquellas injusticas, aquellos problemas sobrios, que agitan y corroen a las modernas sociedades y presentarlos a los ojos del público solicitando, con el poderoso lenguaje del arte, resolución y su remedio. (qtd. in Rubio Jiménez, "Teatro" 686)

In *Juan José*, Dicenta's basic social criticism is the impossibly low salaries earned by the working class of late nineteenth-century Madrid, the complete lack of job security, and the inability to improve the situation by the legal means of voting. Dicenta's criticism, however, goes much deeper than a simple condemnation of the exploitation of the lower class; through the character of Juan José, Dicenta shows the horrible tragedy of a decent man who is deprived of human love and affection, unjustly prohibited from working for a living, and forced to either steal or beg for food and coals in order to keep from starving and freezing.

Dicenta blames society for having ignored Juan José, who as a child was orphaned and left on the street to beg. Juan José describes his painful past to his sympathetic friend, Andrés:

> ¿Padres?... Dios los dé; no sé quiénes fueron los míos, sólo sé que me tiraron á la calle, mismamente que se tira la basura al arroyo pa que la recoja el trapero. *(Con tristeza profunda.)* ... Sólo he conocido á la mujer que me recogió junto a las piedras de una cantería pa llevarme en brazos por las calles y compadecer á la gente llamándome hijo suyo. ¡Pa eso me recogieron! Y luego, cuando fui mayor y pude andar solo, pa que pidiese limosna, con los pies descalzos, y la pidiera bien, y llevase mucha, que si llevaba poca, me ponían maduro a palos. (17-18).

Juan José explains to Andrés that being an orphan made him predisposed to criminal life, yet because he is an honest man, he has spent his life resisting the temptation to commit crimes: "Y ocasiones de serlo [malo] he tenido muchas, que á quien le dejan en la calle sin otro amparo que el de Dios, más cerca le ponen del presidio que de la iglesia" (16). Dicenta shows that society is to blame for those people who are abandoned on the street who turn to crime, and although Juan José resists the life of crime, he ultimately is left with no other choice.

Orphans like Juan José are not the only victims of a corrupted society; together with his friends, Juan José suffers daily the exploitation of the ruling class. In the opening scenes of the play, Dicenta focuses the spectator's attention immediately on the complaints of the working class and the idea of class struggle as Perico, an undereducated illiterate factory worker, attempts to read a revolutionary article from the paper aloud to his companions:

> No... es... posi... ble... sopor... tar... en... si... lencio... la... con... du... ta... de... un... go... bierno... que... así... vi... vio... viola...los... sa... cra... tí... si... mos... de... re... chos... del... cui... da... dano... Hora... es... ya... de... que... el... noble... pue... blo... es... pañol... pro... tes... te... de... tan... iní... iní... iní... iní... cuos... a... ten... tados... y... salga á... la... defen... sa... de... la... libertá... y... de... la... patria... escar...

escarnecidas... por... los... se... se... secua... secuaces de la reación. (8-9)

Perico becomes excited about what he has just read, eagerly shouting to his friends: "¡Hay que echarse á la calle y acabar con el hato de granujas que nos oprime!" (9). These particular lines are crucial in Dicenta's argument, for as García Pavón noted in his definition of "social" theater, the oppressed must be conscious of the social injustice and the need for reform. The group of men in the tavern are certainly aware of the injustice, yet their reaction to Perico indicates their fatalistic attitude, as Ignacio claims scornfully: "Esas revoluciones de quita á éste pa que suba yo, las aprovechan los políticos, los señorones de levita.... ¿Son pa ellos? Que las hagan ellos" (9). Ignacio's opinion is that of the average poor working man or woman, and he assures Perico that he would fight with passion for his rights if he knew that the results would benefit those who are exploited:

> Pa luchar por nosotros, pa vengarnos de los que nos explotan, pa eso estoy pronto siempre, y te diré ¡sí! no una, cien veces que me lo preguntes. Por hacer una revolución así, nuestra, de nosotros, sí me echaría yo á la calle, y hasta perdería con gusto las dos piernas. (10)

Later, in this same scene, Dicenta provides a pessimistic perspective of the only legal recourse that the working-class citizen has in order to ameliorate his or her plight: vote. Andrés describes his first experience at the polls:

> Y lo que yo le decía la primera vez que tuve voto á un caballero que me lo compró en tres pesetas. Allá ustées; de pintor de puertas no he de pasar; conque vengan las tres pesetas y pague usté una copa, y de usté es mi voto y el de mi novia, si sirve, que quizás que sirva. (10)

Andrés's account of the corruption in late nineteenth-century voting practices in Spain is accurate. Although the Spanish people had the right to vote, the elections were notoriously corrupt: "English readers find it difficult to believe in this deliberate doctoring of election returns, but it was one of the most notorious features of Spanish life from 1876-1923" (McCabe 177). When asked which party he voted for, Andrés replies: "¡Yo qué sé!... Por el partido de las tres pesetas y una copa; maldito si me importaba aquello" (11). The working men in the tavern know that their votes mean very little and that dishonest elections are not the solution to their attempt at self-elevation. Since a revolution also seems improbable, Juan José and his friends turn to alcohol, as Ignacio says to Andrés: "A ti, en diciendo que tienes vino, no te hace falta náa" (10).

Juan José and his companions have little hope for any improvement of their situation; they are underpaid and overworked, and the future of their employment is unstable. When Juan José makes his first appearance on stage, he pessimistically answers Andrés's question, "¿Qué hay?", as he falls onto one of the bar stools: "Lo que hay cuando se trabaja desde las siete de la mañana hasta anochecío, mucho cansancio y mucho sueño" (14). Perico adds: "Y mucha hambre" (14). Juan José describes the horrible working conditions he has been forced to endure:

> De aprendiz, cachetes del maestro, y de los oficiales, y una cazuela de sobras en un rincón; después, mucho trabajo y muchas fatigas, y un jornal escaso ganáo sobre dos tablones mal unidos, tiritando de frío en invierno, abrasándome la piel en verano, afanándome desde la mañana á la noche, pa llegar por la noche á mi casa y encontrarme solo sin que nadie viniera á decirme: "¡Descansa, hombre, que bien lo mereces!" (18)

Throughout the play, hunger is a major theme as many of the characters complain about the lack of food. If the workers were paid adequately, they would be able to afford to eat, but since the proprietors are unwilling to pay the workers what they deserve, Juan José and his friends find themselves weakened, and thus not at their optimum for manual labor. Richard Barry Klein points out: "Ironically, this is part of a vicious circle which further impedes social progress because the corporate condition of the workers is too weak for any effective group action to improve their lot" (127). Dicenta draws a sharp contrast between the nearly starved men in the tavern, who complain because they have nothing to eat, and Paco, who arrives at the bar and orders a large supper for himself and his friends: "que nos arreglen un arroz con pollos y unas chuletas" (22).

After both Juan José and Rosa lose their jobs, their situation worsens as they continue to starve. Juan José actively seeks work, but is unsuccessful; Andrés explains the response he gets upon asking a contractor to hire Juan José: "Juan José es un buen oficial; pero no puedo darle ocupación. ¿Sabéis lo que hizo con Paco la otra noche? Gasta muy mal genio, y no respeta á nadie" (41). Not only is Paco responsible for Juan José's actions, which resulted in his unemployment, but Paco is also to blame for the reason that Juan José is unable to find work. Hall writes: "It is in this context that we are invited to consider the rivalry of Juan José and Paco, which appears as a symbol of the struggle of exploited against exploiters" (57). In the confrontation in the tavern, Juan José views Paco's attempts to gain Rosa's favor as an "extension of the process of exploitation" (Hall 57):

> Usté es mi maestro, el que me da el jornal con que como, y dispone de mí y de estos brazos desde que sale el sol hasta que anochece.... Sin duda por

eso, porque me paga usté, ha llegao á creerse que todo lo mío le pertenece, y no contento con lucirse á costa de mi sangre, quiere usté mandar también aquí dentro y coger lo que aquí dentro vive y llevárselo. (35)

Dicenta, through Juan José, cries out against a society that will not provide an honest, hardworking man the opportunity to work, to earn enough money to survive:

No hay trabajo; no lo encuentro en ninguna parte, ¡en ninguna!... ¡no hay más que condenar á un hombre á morirse de hambre ó á pedir por Dios! ¿Hay en esto justicia? ¿Y si no la hay, ¿por qué sucede? ¡Luego dicen que si los hombres matan y roban! ¡Qué van a hacer! (46)

Dicenta blames society for forcing good men like Juan José into a life of crime. For Juan José, begging is not an option, for he has spent the majority of his life begging for food; he refuses to return to that manner of living: "Hay algo que no me hará vender el hambre: la vergüenza" (47). Just before Juan José makes the decision to steal for Rosa, he expresses with disdain his opinion of the injustice of a society that forces a man to starve for want of work: "No es justo que un hombre trabajador se quede sin trabajo... no hacen bien en negármelo los que me lo niegan... cuando me quejo llevo razón" (56).

CONCLUSIONS

In *Juan José*, Dicenta has made a definitive step in his development as a playwright as he moves away from the neo-Romantic dramas such as *El suicidio de Werther*, *La mejor ley*, and *Los irresonsables*, which are populated with middle- or upper-class individuals, towards the modern social drama, which revolves around the lower classes. For the first time, Dicenta fills the stage with the lower classes, giving them a powerful voice against their oppressors. Paco, although a member of the upper class, is himself not far removed from the bottom of the social ladder because he was born into the lower class, and only after he inherits money does he have the opportunity to climb the social ladder. Paco represents the stereotypical *nouveau riche* who self-righteously condemns those beneath him for the sin for which he is responsible.

According to García Pavón's definition of social theater, *Juan José* is certainly a social drama, despite its Romantic hero, melodramatic ending, and traditional themes of love and jealousy. I strongly disagree with the majority of Dicenta's critics who completely deny the presence of social criticism; it is obvious that Dicenta emphasizes the inequality between worker and employer, and the unjust suffering the latter causes the former. Dicenta carefully interweaves the traditional conflict of hero versus villain with the social commentary of exploited versus exploiter. Because the source of most of the dramatic action is the conflict between Juan José and his rival, Paco, as they compete for the same woman, many critics are quick to ignore the social implications that are constantly voiced by Juan José and his companions throughout the drama. It is this conflict between Juan José and Paco as individuals which represents the larger scope of the disharmony found in society between the ruling class and the working class.

Although *Juan José* provides neither solutions for the exploitation suffered by the lower classes nor suggestions for revolution, audiences did not doubt Dicenta's thesis that a change was necessary in order to improve the conditions of the working class. Contemporary audiences heralded Dicenta as the voice of the proletariat, and *Juan José* soon became the play that represented the workers in their aspirations for revolution as the play was symbolically peformed annually on Labor Day, May 1 (Pérez de la Dehesa 33). Gies notes that *Juan José* "became a kind of socialist *Don Juan Tenorio* which, instead of being shown on All Soul's Day, was performed on 1 May each year in honor of International Workers' Day as a symbol of social protest" (327). Mas Ferrer claims that *Juan José* was, after *Don Juan Tenorio*, the most frequently performed play in the Spanish repertory:

> *Juan José* ha sido, después del *Tenorio*, quizá la obra más representada en nuestro país. El año 1937 Rafael Alberti llevaba a la escena la representación cien mil—dato recogido en la Sociedad de Autores de Madrid. (*Vida* 138)

There should be no doubt as to Dicenta's revolutionary message, as José Martínez Ruíz declares:

> *Juan José* es un drama atrevido, audaz, bárbaro... Hay en la obra la energía de un filósofo, el empuje de un revolucionario... Sí, *Juan José* no es drama, *Juan José* es el drama de nuestros días. Es la encarnación, el símbolo de esta sociedad *fin de siglo*, que se apresta a una lucha terrible.
> (qtd. in Gies 329)

EL SEÑOR FEUDAL (1896)

Dicenta's next play, *El señor feudal*, premiered December 2, 1896, over a year after the successful debut of *Juan José*. It is evident that Dicenta was becoming increasingly aware of his mission to portray the exploited working class on stage to draw attention to the suffering of the poor. As the voice of the proletariat, Dicenta studies the social question in *El señor feudal* not in the slums of Madrid, as he had with *Juan José*, but rather in a rural setting, the Andalusian countryside. In contrast to the title character of *Juan José*, the main character who seeks revenge in *El señor feudal* is much more aware of the social injustice of his situation, having gained a new perspective while living in the city for eight years. Whereas Juan José was driven by passion and rage for the loss of the one thing that defined his existence, Rosa, Jaime defends his sister's honor for the sole purpose of proving to the ruling class how unjust society truly is.

PLOT

Tío Juan's daughter, Juana, is in love with the proprietor's son Carlos, who has deliberately seduced her with no intention of marrying her. Juana fully expects to become his wife, not knowing that Carlos's father, Roque, has already made plans for his only son, Carlos, to marry María, the granddaughter of the Marqués de Atienza. Ironically, Roque used to be a servant to the Marqués de Atienza years before, and ever since that earlier point in his life, Roque has had the vindictive desire to dishonor his previous employer. In marrying his son to one of the Marqués's descendants, Roque feels he can properly humiliate the man he once served. An insult Roque received when he was the Marqués's servant fuels the evil gratification he experiences upon gaining power and property and using it to exploit everyone surrounding him. Having lost his money by squandering it all in his youth, the Marqués is now poverty-stricken and old. Roque has come to own the Marqués's estate by making loans to him over the years. In order to force María to marry Carlos, Roque threatens to foreclose a mortgage on the home in which her grandfather currently resides.

Tío Juan's son, Jaime, has been living in the city where he gained a new perspective on the relationship between proprietor and worker. He returns to the farm with a much higher sense of self-worth, and he blames wealth for the evils that the poor suffer. Once he realizes what is happening with Juana, his sister, Jaime becomes even more certain that what he has learned while away in the city is correct: the wealthy take advantage of the poor. Because he has a very strong sense of family honor, he feels it is necessary to avenge his sister's honor. In this way he can also keep María from making a choice she will regret.

Unfortunately for Roque, he is unable to see Jaime's conviction and determination, nor does he care for Juana's predicament. Juana eventually crosses the thin line between love and hate as she realizes that Carlos is never going to marry her. She stands firm behind her brother's decision to punish Carlos. The action comes to a climax when Jaime drowns Carlos in a wine vat in the storage cellar of Roque's estate. In killing Carlos, Jaime not only avenges his sister's wrong, but he also takes vengeance for the working class who have always suffered under the conditions forced upon them by the wealthy.

Background

Prior to the premiere of *El señor feudal*, Dicenta explored a similar theme in a short story entitled "El desquite," later published in *De la batalla* (1903). Narrated in the third person, "El desquite" traces the revenge of a poor working man who finds out that his employer has raped his wife. As Jaime in *El señor feudal*, Juan murders the owner of the vineyard by violently throwing him in the wine vat to drown. The short story, not nearly as developed as the drama, is a simple treatise on the abuse suffered by ten generations of farmers in Juan's family. Like Tío Juan, Juan has grown accustomed to the attitude of servitude because it has been passed down through the generations. Although he is unhappy with his hard life, it is not until his honor has been violated that Juan is transformed from an obedient, trustworthy servant into a cold-blooded murderer. Prior to his wife's rape, Juan often lamented having been born poor into a family of farmers who are forced to work their entire lives, and many times he would find himself in front of the wine vat imagining that instead of wine, the red liquid was "la sangre de todos los suyos, absorbida y utilizada por y en provecho de una raza entera de propietarios" (*Batalla* 117). Dicenta repeats this same image in *El señor feudal* as Jaime describes how the wine vat is a symbol of their hard labor:

> Me parecía que el líquido que humeaba y burbujeaba en aquel abismo articficial, líquido de color de sangre, era la sangre de todos los míos exprimida allí, estrujada allí sin compasión, en provecho de una raza entera de propietarios. (33)

Years later, in *Los bárbaros* (1912), Dicenta explores the same themes once more as he changes few details in adapting *El señor feudal* to fiction. Edwin S. Morby states:

> ...this worse of Dicenta's writings [*Los bárbaros*] is a modified and extended version of the play, of interest solely because it seems to be the only case in which Dicenta derived a work of fiction from a drama. (386)

In *El señor feudal*, Roque has deviously ruined the Marqués by taking everything he owned, with the exception of the castle, which he threatens to take if the Marqués does not marry his granddaughter to Roque's only son. In *Los bárbaros*, Anselmo and his wife, who used to be servants like Roque, achieve a higher social status by marrying their daughter into nobility. After obtaining the lands of their daughter's in-laws, they become cruel and abusive landowners. The major difference between *El señor feudal* and *Los bárbaros* is the depth of the revenge taken by the disgruntled peasants. While Jaime takes his own personal revenge by killing Carlos, the peasants in *Los bárbaros* band together, and screaming "¡Pan y justicia!" and "¡Muerte!" (213) they completely destroy the farm, burning everything, and murder Don Anselmo, his wife, and their daughter. The tortuous murder of Don Anselmo is particularly riveting:

> Atado por los pies y las manos, subiéronle a un granero que se alzaba próximo a su vivienda. Abrieron hoyo en la montaña cereal y echaron al cacique en el hoyo. Tenía el trigo el color de oro.... Los martirizadores recogieron con sus palas el trigo, y la lluvia de oro cayó despacio sobre aquel adorador del oro que todo lo había sacrificado a su acaparamiento. La lluvia de oro fué cubriéndole pies y piernas; luego se extendió por su vientre; envolvió sus manos que aun se contrajeron apretándola; desbordó por su pecho; hizo en su garganta collar. Al fin goteó por su cara. Bajaba entonces muy despacio, en hilos minúsculos, que entraron por la boca de Anselmo, y ataponaron sus narices y oídos, y cegaron sus ojos. Hubo un estremecimiento final; desapareció Anselmo bajo el amarillo sudario, y el trigo se cerró sobre él en pirámide. (*Bárbaros* 218)

TECHNIQUE

El señor feudal does little to advance Dicenta's technique, despite his attempt to move the social question from the city to the country. *El señor feudal* certainly shows evidence of realism, yet its constant melodrama and traditional themes significantly weaken the realistic effect and render the play less successful than Dicenta's previous dramas.

As in his earlier plays, Dicenta continues Echegaray's neo-Romantic technique of exaggerating emotions presented on stage, using traditional themes reminiscent of the Golden Age: honor, jealousy, and vengeance. The terrible punishment Carlos receives is a further example of the Golden Age theme of punishing the wrongdoer. Unlike Lope de Vega and Echegaray, Dicenta consciously invests *El señor feudal* with modern themes such as the idea of progress, totally contrasting with the nature of the play. Also somewhat contradictory to the social implications present throughout the play is the over emphasis on the melodramatic; the structure of *El señor feudal* is based heavily on ending each act in a climactic scene, inhibiting the play from absolute verisimilitude. Peak agrees that Dicenta relies heavily on the dramatic technique of melodrama: "With few changes this play might pass for showboat drama in the United States of the same period" (113).

Despite the neo-Romantic nature of the action, Dicenta successfully draws a realistic picture of the lifestyle of poor farmers at the turn of the century. The most realistic effect of *El señor feudal* is the detailed description of the lives of the farm workers. Dicenta pays careful attention to the setting, the dress, the speech, and the personalities of the multitude of peasants working under Roque's supervision. The first act is set on a farm, giving the spectator an accurate perspective of the daily routine of the hardworking servants. As the curtain rises, the farmers are busily harvesting wheat, one hour before sunset. Dicenta describes in detail the clothing of the workers:

> Las trabajadoras vestirán falda corta, justillo de percal y ancho sombrero de paja a la cabeza. Los trabajadores estarán en mangas de camisa con los brazos de éstas remangados por encima del codo y vestirán calzón corto, zapato de cuero y sombreros de paja. (7)

The scene is rich in details as the peasants work together while teasing each other to pass the time:

> JUAN: ¡Se paece mentira! ¡Una moza tan hacendosa enamoricarse de un gandulonazo como tú!
> BLAS: Na más propio. Eso pasa porque Dios es justo y sabe lo que hace.
> JUAN: ¡Como que va a meterse Dios en ajuntar un zángano con una hormiga! (9)

The remaining two acts are also realistic, set respectively in a poor peasant home and in Roque's wine cellar.

In yet another example of realism, Dicenta utilizes several different dialects throughout the play, making certain that the language accurately reflects the personality of the speaker. For example, there is a perceptible difference in Roque's speech and the Marqués's manner of speaking. True to his character, Roque's language is pretentious and superficial, still reflecting his years as a farmer. The Marqués, on the other hand, uses perfect grammatical constructions and always appears collected and intelligent. Even when faced with a situation that would call for an emotional reaction, the Marqués addresses Roque coolly:

> ¿Cómo has podido tú imaginar que María iba a querer a tu hijo?¡Cómo! Anda; pregúntale a ella, que ella te conteste por mí. ¡Yo no necesito oir su contestación; la sé ya! (39)

Roque is a cruel and insensitive man, who is blind to the suffering of his workers, even though he once was one of them. Roque shouts, "¡Toos los criaos son lo mismo! ¡Ladrones pagaos!" (15), as he complains that the peasants do not work hard enough. His arrogance is blatantly obvious as he orders Juana to prepare him some limonade: "Ya sabes cómo a mí me gusta. Bien escurrido el limón, y bien colao, y fresca el agua, y cargao de azúcar" (17). Roque's attempt to appear superior is weakened by the deformations, common among the peasants: "toos" for "todos," "criaos" for "criados," "pagaos" for "pagados," "colao" for "colado," and "cargao" for "cargado." Juan's first words as he supervises the harvesters in the first scene are clearly evidence of his lack of education: "¿Vas a quearte asín diquia que anochezga? ... ¡Lo menos has bebío agua trenta veces dende que se acabó la siesta!" (8).

The descriptions that Dicenta relates of the conditions of the poor peasants are detailed, realistic, and poignant. Jaime, who has been away in the city for eight years, is able to express his feelings more clearly as he has a new outsider's perspective:

> Cuando empecé a comprender lo horrible de nuestra condición, cuando en la época del pise de la uva y el trasiego del vino, veía a mi padre, a mi abuelo, a los hermanos de mi padre, a mí mismo, hombres, mujeres, niños, todos ennegrecidos por el sol, untados de mosto, sudorosos, jadeantes, con la espalda encorvada, los músculos contraídos, temblorosas las piernas y la cántara de vino sobre los lomos, llegar a aquella cuba enorme y vaciar en ella las cántaras y volver con otras y vaciarlas otra vez, sin que la cuba dijese nunca "¡basta!" (32-33)

The insatiable wine vat is one of many symbols Dicenta uses throughout the play; it symbolizes the ruling class and its constant and unfeeling demands of the lower class. This symbol is especially effective in the last scenes of the drama as the vat is finally filled to capacity with the sacrifice of Carlos; the vat no longer demands the labor of the peasants. The scene in which the peasants return time and time again to fill the vat with wine and the crescendo towards the final murder scene are reminiscent of Echegaray's melodramatic technique, as Peak notes: "There is enough here to appeal to the sensation-seekers and pack them into the theater for nights to come" (114). Another symbol Dicenta uses is the key to the wine cellar. After throwing Carlos in the wine vat to drown, Jaime locks the door and hurls the key at Roque's feet, knowing that it is too late to save Carlos's life. Symbolically, the key represents the possibility for a better future for the farmers; with it they can unlock the door to a new life.

Dicenta also uses symbols in his creation of the main characters. Unlike *Juan José*, none of the characters in *El señor feudal* is delineated as thoroughly as they are in Dicenta's masterpiece. Instead, the characters are symbolic of the different social classes. The Marqués represents the nobility of the past who, while bearing a title, finds it difficult to cope with living in the present. Of particular interest is Dicenta's treatment of the Marqués, for he is dignified, kind, and respected by the farmers. For this reason, Klein believes *El señor feudal* represents an "early stage in Dicenta's social ideas.... Ten years later,

Dicenta would never have written a play with such a favorable treatment of a member of the upper classes" (130). Roque and Carlos represent the *nouveau riche* who rise to power by crooked means and who abuse those beneath them, forgetting their own humble origins as peasants; their complete moral deficiency is emphasized by Dicenta to make the plight of the peasants even more tragic. Juan and Juana represent the "obrero masa," as defined by García Pavón: "Hombre indeciso, que conoce perfectamente la crueldad del amo, pero incapaz de rebelión alguna sin cabecilla que le anime" (57). Although they are opposed to the exploitation they endure, Juan and Juana have accepted their situation, knowing that they are enduring the same suffering, as did their ancestors through many generations. Finally, Jaime represents progress and education. Unlike his father and sister, Jaime takes action instead of simply complaining passively and accepting the past.

Torrente Ballester describes the construction of *El señor feudal* as a pyramid "cuya cúspide ocupa el pobre marqués de Atienza, y a cuyos lados se agrupan, en correlación, el Tío Roque y el Tío Juan; Jaime, hijo de Juan, y Carlos, hijo de Roque; Juana, hermana de Jaime, y María, la marquesita" (62).

Tío Juan's subservient relationship to Roque is documented throughout the drama to indicate the tragic injustice of an honorable man who is forced to serve a corrupt new member of the bourgeois. As Carlos's lover, Juana too is victimized, having been seduced and dishonored by the son of her employer. Jaime, as Juana's sister, seeks vengeance against Carlos, thus establishing his relationship to Carlos. To Juana, María is competition for Carlos, as María is being forced to marry Carlos against her will. Finally, there is some hint of a relationship of mutual trust and friendship between María and Jaime. It is likely that Jaime is in love with María, which would make his vengeance even more necessary.

IDEOLOGY

The three social classes represented in *El señor feudal* enable Dicenta to identify the class struggles existing in late nineteenth-century Spain; the aristocracy is ousted by the bourgeoisie, which in turn, is vanquished by the working class. This double conflict is clearly documented throughout the drama, as Dicenta carefully portrays the personal antagonisms of Roque and Jaime.

Roque represents the class that Dicenta attacks most strongly in the play, the newly rich who conveniently forgets the suffering of his past when he was a poor farmer in order to focus his undivided attention on gaining more power and wealth. Although he has already achieved the financial security he once envied, Roque still has the desire to rise one step higher on the social ladder; his plan to force the Marqués to have his granddaughter marry Roque's only son will ensure his success. However, his inability to recognize the strong bond of family among the working class, from whence he came, brings about his downfall. Ironically, although Roque has always had lofty ambitions, he condemns any such thought from his workers, as he tells Juana:

> Esa es la obligación del criao y de tóo el que sirve y pende de otro; respetarle y obedecerle y conformarse con su suerte y con lo que al amo se le antoje darle; esa, y no hacerse ilusiones y tirar las patas por el alto y las intenciones por las nubes. (24)

Roque constantly insults his workers, demands the highest respect, overworks and underpays them, and shows no concern for their wellbeing. The farmers know about Roque's past and are disgusted that Roque seems to have forgotten that he used to be one of them; one farmer comments: "¡Anda, y qué mala memoria tié el señor Roque! ¡No se acuerda que ha sío criao tamién!" (15).

It is important to establish the history of Roque's vendetta against the Marqués. In a conversation with his son, Roque reveals a glimpse of his poor past:

> Aun no había cumplido los veinte años cuando entré en la casa del Marqués. Entré de mozo de caballos, con tres duros de soldá.... Yo abajo entre las bestias y ellos arriba entre los príncipes y los reyes.... dende que entré en casa del Marqués, y ví aquel lujo, aquella manificencia y aquel tener a mano las satisfacciones toas de la vida, sentí un... un no sé explicártelo... sentí así, como un mareo, con un apetito muy grande en la cabeza; ganas de igualarme con aquella gente que apenas sabía mi nombre; ansia de que lo suyo fuese mío; de que estuviesen a merce mía: de ser el único amo yo, que era el último criao.... Un día, el señorito... me reprendió por no sé que falta; le contesté yo mal, y él levantando un junco que llevaba en la mano, y que tenía grabada la corona de Marqués en el puño, me lo hizo cachos en las costillas. (19-21)

This scene is reminiscent of the scene from *Juan José* in which the protagonist compares himself to his wealthy rival, Paco. Both Juan José and Roque find it difficult to express how they feel; Juan José attempts, but fails: "sentí... No sé lo que sentía entonces..." (*Juan* 16). Juan José, who is characterized by his extreme passion, immediately feels the urge to stab Paco with the trowel, thus murdering him. Roque, on the other hand, is not an emotional man; instead, he is able to think intelligently about plotting revenge against the Marqués. Although both Roque and Juan José are from the lowest income class and are both embittered by their experiences with poverty, Roque's intelligence and lack of compassion contrast greatly with Juan José's Romantic nature and lack of self control.

Dicenta's strongest argument in *El señor feudal* is that of the peasant, made audible by Jaime, who, after having spent eight years in the city, has gained a new perspective of the oppression suffered by his family and the other farmers employed by Roque. Jaime is certainly part of the working class, but the knowledge and self esteem he acquired in Madrid have empowered him to refuse to accept the conditions of the lowly peasant. The common farmer, such as Juan or Juana, on the other hand, is resigned to his or her low social status, repeating the same actions of his or her ancestors: working in every weather condition from fifteen to eighteen hours a day without question. There is also an unwritten rule of respect that the worker is required to pay to those of a higher class. For example, Juana, upon serving Roque and Carlos limonade, humbly states: "yo estoy satisfecha; que en servir y en verlos contentos gozo yo" (24). Roque is pleased with her attitude of servitude as he responds "Y yo en verte servicial y humilde, porque siendo servicial y humilde pruebas que conoces tu condición" (24). Jaime, on the other hand, would never lower himself to that level. In his first encounter with Carlos, Jaime indicates his nonconformist attitude by not removing his hat, as is customary among the peasants in the presence of someone of a higher class. When his father rebukes him for his defiance, Jaime retorts: "Como este caballero no se ha quitado el suyo, no creo que tengo obligación de quitármelo yo" (29). After Juan reminds Jaime that Carlos is the "amo," Jaime says: "El de usté, no el mío. Yo no tengo amos" (29). Later, however, Jaime graciously removes his hat while in the presence of the Marqués, stating: "me lo quito porque este es viejo y pobre y es honrado" (35).

The distinction Jaime makes between the Marqués and Carlos is further evidence of his newfound perspective attained in the city where he witnessed opportunity and progress. Jaime represents the "'proletario consciente,' formado en la ciudad, que veremos como agitador más o menos utópico en los dramas sociales del montón" (García Pavón 52). Upon returning to the country, Jaime expresses bitterness to his father about the situation of the peasants, fully illustrating the attitude of acceptance and servitude common among the working class:

> ¡Qué vida la suya! Trabajando sin tregua a todas horas, en verano, en invierno, a campo abierto, con el sol, con el frío, con la lluvia, con la nieve! Y esto un día y otro, ¿y para quién? ¿para él? ¿para sus hijos? No; para el amo, para el señor Roque. ¡Hala, tío Juan,... haz lo que hizo tu padre, lo que hizo tu abuelo; labra la tierra ajena, esa tierra de la que nunca poseerás un grano! (31)

Just as both Juan José and Roque describe the strong emotion that overcame them when they realized the injustice of their social position, so does Jaime feel this bitter hostility:

> Lo que yo sentía era odio hacia esta vida, hacia esta ignorancia, hacia esta condición desdichada nuestra, hacia esta tierra misma, que debia ser sustento de todos y se ha convertido por la codicia de unos pocos, en el más aborrecible de los verdugos. (32)

Despite his bitterness, Jaime makes no attempt at revolutionary action, and in fact, until he learns about his sister's dishonor, he had dreamed of his future life:

> Y mientras yo en la fábrica soñaba con la redención posible, con mi padre rescatado al terruño, muriendo, cuando muriese, a mi lado, tranquilo, como un hombre que acaba y no como un hombre que agoniza, con mi hermana junto a mí, obrera honrada, compañera digna de otro obrero. (65)

With Carlos's dishonorable treatment of Jaime's sister, however, Jaime is moved to action in order to take revenge, not only for Juana's dishonor, but also for all the abuse suffered by the workers for generations. Like Juan José, Jaime chooses violence as the solution, throwing Carlos into the wine vat. In murdering Carlos, Jaime strikes out against all who abuse and exploit the working class. Although the ending is melodramatic and without any solution to the plight of the peasant, it is effective in its symbolism, as Peak explains: "The least perspicacious of the audience must have recognized Dicenta's attack on oppression and exploitation of the peasant farmer" (114). Dicenta argues that progress, represented by Jaime, is only possible through violent action.

In *El señor feudal*, Dicenta continues the idea of the impossibility of love between classes that he explored in *El suicidio de Werther* and *Luciano*. Fernando (*El suicidio de Werther*) realized that he would never be able to marry María because he was an orphan of low birth; Luciano, on the other hand, succeeded in marrying a woman of a higher class, but the marriage failed, and his wife and her family never ceased in their condemnation of his rural upbringing. In *El señor feudal*, Juana naively believes she will some day become Carlos's wife, yet Carlos has no intention of marrying a lowly peasant woman. Ironically, when told he must marry María, Carlos does not protest, even though she is a member of the aristocracy. Carlos's marriage to her is designed to break boundaries, to bring more power to Roque and insult to the Marqués; this marriage between classes would never occur without Roque's threat to foreclose on the home in which the Marqués lives. Jaime too sees the impossibility of love between classes, even though he is in love with María. Juana innocently asks her brother: "¿Tamién crees tú que el mundo pué hacer que las gentes ejen de quererse?" (34). Jaime replies pessimistically: "Hace más, hace que no piensen en quererse" (34).

CONCLUSIONS

Although *El señor feudal* certainly entertained the average theatergoer, the play greatly dissapointed Dicenta's radical contemporaries who, following *Juan José*, expected Dicenta to endorse a new revolutionary style of drama. *El señor feudal* is not revolutionary, despite Dicenta's attack on the exploitation and oppression of the working class. Pérez de la Dehesa believes *El señor feudal* to be a drama that is "muy inferior a *Juan José*" (27). He continues: "Fue desengaño para todos los jóvenes revolucionarios agrupados alrededor de Dicenta" (Pérez de la Dehesa 27). García Pavón agrees: "se pierde el encanto que la espontaneidad dio a la obra anterior" (50). Immediately following the premiere of *El señor feudal*, Aureliano J. Pereira, a theater critic of *El País*, wrote a scathing review of the play:

> Es una cochinada lo que ha hecho Dicenta. Ha dado un paso atrás; se le ha visto el juego, que no es, ni más ni menos, que el de contemporizar con los abondados de la Comedia e ir *haciendo taquilla*. Por eso se habla de Dios, *que es el amo* y se saca una especie de ídolo aristócrata, señorón de rancia y noble cepa... y se pinta un socialista, Jaime, que es un sacristán disfrazado.... ¡Cochinadas! (qtd. in Martínez Ruiz, *Charivari* 249-50)

Azorín (José Martínez Ruíz) accuses Dicenta of borrowing the plot of *El señor feudal* from Georges Ohnet's *La Grande Marnière* (*Charivari* 250). Although there are similarities, the ending is completely original.

El señor feudal represents one of Dicenta's weakest plays, yet it remains important in his development as a dramatist. Despite the realism of the setting and the language, as a realistic play it is a failure, due to the following factors: the structure relies on traditional climaxes at the end of each act; the primary themes are love, vengeance, and honor; the characters are representatives of their class and not individuals; and there is an excessive use of emotion and symbolism. Dicenta also fails at "social" drama in *El señor feudal*, despite his obvious attempts to argue for the proletariat by attacking the oppressor. Ruiz Ramón argues: "El drama social se queda a mitad de camino entre la nueva mentalidad de carácter social y la vieja mentalidad tradicional de carácter moral e individual" (430).

Hall discredits Dicenta's realistic depiction of the rural Andalusia: "He [Dicenta] was less familiar with the countryside than with Madrid... and these *cuadros de costumbres* do not convince" (59). One only has to make a comparison to the rural dramas of Felíu y Codina, Angel Guimerá, and Vicente

Medina to see the difference in quality in the descriptions of rural Spain. Their dramas are far more accurate and realistic than *El señor feudal*, which comes across as overworked and unnatural. Dicenta's attempts to invest *El señor feudal* with social implications cannot be ignored, despite its poor quality, for he continues to argue for the proletariat by attacking the oppresor.

OVERALL CONCLUSIONS TO CHAPTER FOUR

In just over one year, Dicenta received from the public and critics two opposing reactions: extreme praise and adulation, and bitter hatred and disdain. *Juan José* is certainly a far superior drama to *El señor feudal*, but it is not necessarily the quality of the plays that so moved Dicenta's contemporaries, but rather, the message. *Juan José* came at just the right time to inspire Spain's radical youth with hopes for revolution, and in the year before *El señor feudal* appeared, Dicenta became their unofficial leader in their fight against social injustice.

El señor feudal failed to impress Dicenta's followers, despite its obvious social implications, for two reasons: first, because it is an inferior play based more on the traditional themes of honor and vengeance, and second, there is not enough character development to allow the audience to connect with the suffering experienced by the farmers. *Juan José*, despite what critics say, is not an honor play; Juan José kills Paco not to avenge any honor lost, but rather because he is directly responsible for Juan José's misfortunes. It is far easier for the revolutionary youth to attach themselves to Juan José rather than Jaime, for Juan José better expresses the pain and suffering and loss of control forced on him by the ruling class. Jaime, on the other hand, talks of the suffering more from a bystander's point of view; those who suffer, Juan, Juana, and the other peasants, accept their fate and fear revolution of any type. Jaime's speeches against the oppression of the lower class most surely moved Dicenta's audiences to applaud, yet the sympathetic treatment of the Marqués (aristocracy) and the lack of any plans for revolution prove the play weak in Dicenta's attempt at social criticism. In this way, *Juan José* is the more successful play, in Dicenta's excellent and deep characterization of one poor man who is pushed beyond his limits by society's great injustice.

El señor feudal is similar to *Juan José*, however, in its attack on the newly rich (Paco and Roque), but *El señor feudal* does so more overtly. Dicenta moves one step further in his social criticism in *El señor feudal*. Whereas Juan José seeks revenge against Paco for personal reasons, not for social injustice, Jaime murders Carlos not only to avenge his sister's loss of honor but also to make a stand against all oppression suffered by generations of farmers. Jaime repeatedly strikes out against Roque and Carlos by name in his condemnation of their exploitation of the working class, but Juan José's complaints are general, not directed at Paco for his oppression, but instead at society. Neither play is a full-fleged social drama, because of their neo-Romantic tendencies and traditional themes. According to Mas Ferrer, following the premiere of *El señor feudal*, no one was satisfied: "la juventud radical... le volvió las espaldas, se vio frustrada, los sectores conservadores la calificaron de subversiva y a su autor de enajenado mental" (*Vida* 146).

The disappointment expressed by those who expected more out of Dicenta as Spain's voice of the proletariat is an indication of Dicenta's inability to grasp fully the idea of socialism. Mas Ferrer defends Dicenta, explaining that philosophical socialism had yet to be clearly defined at the end of the nineteenth century and that Dicenta was largely unfamiliar with it: "Dicenta es un socialista por intuición, por instinto, no por razonamiento" (*Vida* 141). Torrente Ballester agrees: "Dicenta no era, propiamente hablando, un socialista, sino un tipo, muy español y muy ibérico, de liberal socializante" (63). Hall explains the reason for Dicenta's seemingly socialist view:

> He was not well educated, nor was he of a philosophical cast of mind, and his discussion of social problems is almost invariably superficial. However, his lack of subtlety makes him all the more effective as a sounding board for the more clamorous issues of the time, and what he lacks in perception he makes up in passion. (45-46)

Hall's illuminating explanation is true, for Dicenta is passionate, as is Juan José, and, in both *Juan José* and *El señor feudal*, Dicenta sincerely desires to bring to the stage the social injustice he has both witnessed and experienced.

5
The Productive Years: 1898-1907

CURRO VARGAS (1898)
FOLLOWING THE DISAPPOINTING PREMIERE of *El señor feudal*, Dicenta dedicated his efforts to journalism and lyrical dramas. His next drama, *Curro Vargas*, premiered exactly two years after *El señor feudal* on December 10, 1898 in the Teatro de Parish with the music of the famous composer, Ruperto Chapí. Dicenta's second *zarzuela*, *Curro Vargas* proved immensely successful, yet with its debut, Dicenta was immediately accused of plagiarism because of the similarity of *Curro Vargas* to Pedro de Alarcón's novel, *El niño de la bola* (1880). Its theme is purely Romantic, placed in modern times rather than the medieval setting typical of the Romantic dramas.

Curro Vargas is Dicenta's first play written in collaboration with another dramatist, Manuel Paso (1864-1901). In *Idos y muertos* (1911), Dicenta presents an illuminating account of his relationship with Paso, who died young after years of heavy drinking. Dicenta calls him a talented artist with a lot of potential, who, rather than facing the difficulties of living, drowned his sorrows with alcohol, seldom pursuing artistic endeavors. The two men were good friends, and following the fame and wealth Dicenta received for *Juan José*, he and Paso enjoyed traveling together as often as possible. One summer in Mallorca, Paso was overcome with his desire to fight his afflictions, to live, and to recover from his alcoholism. Paso begs Dicenta: "Ayúdame a renacer. Tú escribes para el teatro. Escribiré contigo. ¿Quieres que escriba contigo, Joaquín?" (*Idos* 119). Dicenta, full of compassion for his friend, describes his reaction: "Abrí los brazos y estreché contra mi corazón al poeta, que revivía al pie de su tumba" (*Idos* 119). The two friends wrote two plays together, both *zarzuelas*: *Curro Vargas* (1898) and *La cortijera* (1900). Both plays were well received by audiences and critics, but with the premature death of Paso in 1901, Dicenta found himself alone again in his art.

PLOT
Curro and Soledad plan to be married, but Curro decides to travel overseas to search for wealth to make himself more worthy in the eyes of Soledad's father. In his absence, Soledad gives up waiting for him to return and marries

Mariano. Mariano truly loves Soledad, yet she only respects him. It is at this moment that the play opens, and soon it is learned that Curro has returned home, wealthy as he had hoped. Once he finds out about Soledad's marriage to Mariano, he vows to seek vengeance for her betrayal; to him, their promise to marry each other before he left was as binding as marriage. Curro is well respected by everyone, especially Soledad's mother, Doña Angustias, and the priest, Padre Antonio, who reared Curro as his foster son. Both try to comfort Curro in his pain and discourage his plans of revenge, but he ignores them and remains determined.

At an annual party in honor of the Virgin Mary, Soledad and Mariano finally make a public appearance. Mariano, who has heard of Curro's threats, is anxious to confront his rival, not realizing that Soledad still loves Curro. As Soledad is singing a hymn at the closing of the ceremonies of the first day, Curro interrupts her, chastizing her hypocrisy. Curro draws his dagger to stab her, but Mariano intercedes. The two men are pulled apart by others. Padre Antonio begs Curro to renounce his vow of vengeance, and out of respect for his foster father, Curro reluctantly agrees.

The second day of the party, Curro learns that Soledad still loves him. Curro asks Soledad to dance with him, and since it is a religious event, Mariano must consent. While they dance, Soledad confirms her love for him. He is so overcome by anger at the thought of her belonging to another man that he suffocates her in the traditional embrace that ends the dance. Letting her fall to the floor, Curro is immediately stabbed by Mariano, readily accepting death, since life means little to him without Soledad.

SOURCE

Dicenta based his successful lyrical drama, *Curro Vargas*, on Pedro de Alarcón's *El niño de la bola* (1880). Although Dicenta changed the title and the names of all the characters except for Soledad, the plot is nearly identical to Alarcón's novel. Besides the obvious difference of format with the inclusion of music and dancing, what makes Dicenta's *zarzuela* different from Alarcon's novel is his addition of farcical scenes for comic relief and his characterization of Soledad. In Dicenta's *Curro Vargas*, prior to Curro Vargas's departure, Curro and Soledad loved each other deeply and planned to marry. Manuel, the protagonist of *El niño de la bola*, had only managed to speak to Soledad once before he was denied the opportunity to dance with her at the annual *fiesta*, and there is no indication that his love for her was returned. In *Curro Vargas*, Soledad marries Mariano of her own free will; however, in *El niño de la bola*, Soledad is forced to marry by her bitter father, who had made it his mission to destroy Manuel. Soledad's character is well developed in *Curro Vargas*, but as Cyrus DeCoster notes: "She [Soledad] does not open her mouth during the course of the whole novel" (112). Although Dicenta's adaptation of Alarcón's well-known novel caused a controversy among Alarcón's family and the press, "Valera, Jacinto Octavio Picón, Eugenio Sellés, and Bretón, among others, defended Dicenta" (DeCoster 117).

TECHNIQUE

In *Curro Vargas*, Dicenta successfully resuscitates the Romantic themes and techniques reminiscent of the Duque de Rivas' *Don Alvaro* or José Zorrilla's *Don Juan Tenorio*, and as Echegaray in many of his neo-Romantic plays, Dicenta replaces the legendary and the exotic with ordinary modern society. However, in contrast to Echegaray's dramas, *Curro Vargas* does not show evidence of any thesis; instead, its sole purpose is to entertain the audience with traditional themes and an abundance of music and dancing.

SETTING

Curro Vargas takes place in the same region as *El señor feudal*, Andalusia, at the beginning of the nineteenth century. The setting in the first act is an olive grove, and upon the rising of the curtain, there is an immediate contrast with Dicenta's previous rural drama; instead of workers complaining bitterly about their pain and suffering, *Curro Vargas* presents a joyous scene, full of dancing, singing, and flirting. The peasants sing happily as they beat the olive trees, gathering the olives in woven baskets. The realism of *El señor feudal* is replaced in *Curro Vargas* with song and dance. The second act takes place in the main street of the village of Alpujarra, as the *fiesta* in honor of the Virgin Mary is about to take place. Again, the men and women flirt shamelessly with each other, as the scene revolves around one particular "moza" who has climbed a ladder next to a balcony in order to finish decorating it for the celebration. As she reaches the top, the "mozos" arrive, anxiously trying to look up her skirt:

> ¡Ja, ja, ja, ja!
> Sube, sube, no te asustes;
> súbete un poquito más;
> no nos dejes con las ganas.
> ¡Ja, ja, ja, ja! (55)

Towards the end of the second act, just at the moment of climax when Curro rushes to kill Soledad but is detained by onlookers, Dicenta, for the first time, provides a sketch of the correct stage blocking of the characters. The plaza is crowded with people, and combined with the excessive emotional tone, the scene is effective in Dicenta's attempt to appeal to the senses of his audience.

ROMANTIC CHARACTERISTICS

Set in the first half of the nineteenth century, the height of the Romantic period in Spain, *Curro Vargas*, Dicenta's best lyrical drama, is dominated by Romantic characteristics: it is written entirely in verse; there is an overabundance of characters; much attention is paid to the heightened dramatic expression and the repeated use of "¡Ay!"; the extreme passions of love and hate represent the popular Romantic antithesis; violence, murder, and death all occur on stage; the hero is mysterious and passionate; nighttime scenes are prevalent, with only the moon for illumination; the themes of honor and vengeance dominate the action; the characters suffer from unrequited love; Christianity is used as a positive force; and there is a strong appeal to the senses through music and dancing. Curro exhibits many of the traits common to the Romantic hero: there is a sense of mystery surrounding his journey to a far away land; he is honorable and passionate, he suffers from unrequited love; he is prepared to follow his heart against the opposition of authority; and finally, he welcomes death upon realizing that he will never have Soledad while living. Nearly every speech is a passionate outburst, as each of the primary characters (Padre Antonio, Doña Angustias, Mariano, Soledad, and Curro) expresses his or her own personal pain regarding the lost love between Soledad and Curro.

RELIGIOUS ASPECTS

While there is no suggestion of a thesis present in the play, religion plays a major role, unlike any of Dicenta's prior dramas. The religious *fiesta* dedicated to the Virgin Mary allows for many scenes with songs and dance of worship and reverence. In many of the scenes, there is a cross, which, at one point, provides comfort to Soledad:

> ...al pie de esta bendita
> cruz, me parece que mi alma
> halla el consuelo y la calma
> y la paz que necesita. (20)

In Padre Antonio, Dicenta creates an honorable sympathetic priest who often finds himself pulled between church doctrine and his natural desire to see Curro happy. Although his first response is to condemn Curro for his decision to seek vengeance, Padre Antonio soon defends his foster son to Doña Angustias, saying: "Disculpa no tiene [Curro], pero tiene explicación" (63). As Doña Angustias questions Padre Antonio, she suddenly accuses him of believing that Curro has made the right decision. His response, "¡Quién! ¿Yo?," is further evidence of his inner struggle (63). Padre Antonio is a sensitive man, who although bound by his religious convictions, is able to see the human side of

Curro's cause.

HUMOROUS ASPECTS

Dicenta makes great use of humor throughout the lyrical *zarzuela*, as the men and women sing and dance flirtatiously across the stage. In one scene, an elegant young woman from the city, Rosina, is bitten by a bug, and the ensuing mayhem that follows is nothing short of hilarious. She sings:

> ¡Ay, ay, ay, ay, ay! no sé qué me pasa
> pensando que un bicho me puede picar,
> y al sentirlo subir por la media
> ¡ay, ay, ay, ay, ay! no sé qué me da. (22)

A young "petimetre del pueblo" responds in song:

> De su pecho, palacio de nieve,
> quisiera ser dueño, rendido galán,
> y al saber la fortuna del bicho
> ¡ay, ay, ay, ay, ay! no sé qué me da. (22)

These refrains are repeated several times before Soledad, who is disgusted by Rosina's sensitive nature, joins in: "No es poco sensible esta petimetra / nerviosa me pone con tanto ¡ay, ay, ay, ay!" (23). These lines are only examples of the genius of Dicenta's lyrics, present throughout the drama.

Another example of the humor Dicenta brings to the play is his reinvention of the Trotaconventos character from *El libro de buen amor* (1330-1347): Tía Emplastos. She is a humorous character who acts as a go-between for Soledad and Curro, and unlike Isidra from *Juan José*, Tía Emplastos is viewed as a clown, not a threat. Her presence in the drama helps lighten the mood, as so many conflicting emotions pour onto the stage. Upon Tía Emplastos' first entrance onto the stage, Dicenta first utilizes the local dialect that was dominant in *El señor feudal*. In order to make the scene more comical, rather than realistic as in *El señor feudal*, Dicenta fills the mouths of the mule drivers, Tía Emplastos, and the Mayor with words such as: "güeno" for "bueno," "orvidado" for "olvidado," "argo" for "algo," and many more (33-34).

CONCLUSIONS

In *Curro Vargas*, Dicenta redeems himself from the great failure of *El señor feudal*, yet he chooses to avoid the "social" drama for which he once campaigned so strongly. Instead, Dicenta returns to the lyrical drama which he first attempted, and successfully, with *El duque de Gandía* (1894). Perhaps reminded of the triumph upon the premiere of *El duque de Gandía*, Dicenta decided to take another "paso en el camino de la ópera española" (González-Blanco 218). In comparison to his previous plays, with the exception of *Juan José*, *Curro Vargas* is superior in all aspects. It is no surprise, as Mas Ferrer notes, that "junto con el *Juan José*, [*Curro Vargas*] fue la que más beneficios económicos dio a nuestro autor" (*Vida* 101).

LA CORTIJERA (1900)

Dicenta's next drama, *La cortijera* (March 2, 1900), is very similar to *Curro Vargas*; again, Dicenta collaborates with both Manuel Paso and Ruperto Chapí, and the same actors that performed *Curro Vargas* presented *La cortijera* in the same theater, the Teatro de Parish. Unfortunately, *La cortijera*, although entertaining, was not nearly as successful as *Curro Vargas*. It treats a similar theme of one woman loved by two men, but the religious festivities that dominated *Curro Vargas* are replaced by Spain's rich tradition of bullfighting.

PLOT

Prudencia and José are a well respected couple in a small village in Andalusia. They own a large farm, and they have two grown children, Carmela and Manuel. While Carmela is their natural child, Manuel is adopted. Manuel was found abandoned as an infant, and the kindly couple rescued him and reared him with as much love as if he were their own child. Manuel has become one of Spain's most famous bullfighters, and much of the play centers on this theme.

Manuel has fallen in love with Rosario, José and Prudencia's niece, but Rosario is engaged to be married to Rafael. Rosario does not love Rafael, finding herself more and more attracted to the glory of the famed bullfighter Manuel. Rafael, on the other hand, loves Rosario with all of his heart, and suspects that his fiancée does not feel the same. Manuel shows no respect for Rafael, as he actively pursues Rosario. To make matters worse, years before Rafael had saved Manuel's life in an incident with an angry bull; thus, Manuel's disloyalty to his friend is doubly pernicious.

Manuel and Rosario soon express their deep love for each other, as they completely disregard Rafael's feelings. After learning from one of his friends, Garrocha, that Rosario loves another, Rafael, overcome with anger, tries to stab Rosario during a dance at a party. At this point, the entire community learns of Rosario's infidelity to Rafael, with the result that Rosario is completely alienated by everyone. Even Prudencia and José blame her entirely for Rafael's pain, putting no blame on their beloved son, Manuel, who is equally at fault.

Manuel is scheduled to leave town to travel across Spain as a bullfighter. Rosario, who finds herself completely alone, implores Manuel not to leave; instead, he devises a plan in which Rosario can sneak away with him in the middle of the night. Garrocha, who has been eavesdropping, informs Rafael of

Rosario and Manuel's plans, and at the designated time of Manuel's departure, Rafael places himself boldly before the famous bullfighter. Rosario pleads with Rafael to spare Manuel's life, and when ignored, she chokes herself until she faints. When she regains consciousness moments later, Rafael has fatally stabbed Manuel, condemning Rosario to a life of suffering without her true love.

Technique
Setting

Although the first act takes place in an inn just outside of Madrid, the rest of the play, like *El señor feudal* and *Curro Vargas*, is set in Andalusia. Dicenta uses the local dialect throughout the drama, and not one of the characters is exempt from its usage. The drama is set in the years 1829-1830, and the stage decorations are elaborate and entertaining. In the second act, Dicenta recreates a typical Andalusian farmhouse scene. His stage directions call for five rope swings, which play a major part in the opening scenes. The men and women take turns on the swings, all the while singing, dancing, and flirting. The final act, still at the farmhouse, is set in a *plazoleta* named "Fuente de los naranjos," (34) and takes place entirely at night. Of particular interest is Dicenta's recreation of a live *encierro* towards the end of the second act; he uses a garden wall to create the effect, as a throng of people trample over each other running across the stage (26). Dicenta makes us imagine that there are horses on stage, as the *vaqueros* pass behind the garden wall, seemingly on horseback (27).

Structure

Dicenta creates a parallel structure in each act, as the action reaches a climax just before the curtain falls. In the final scenes of Act I, everyone is preparing for the bullfight. Prudencia and José, the parents of the famous bullfighter Manuel, do not plan to go, for they cannot bear to see their son in a dangerous situation. While they are waiting for news from the bullfight, a messenger tells them that Manuel has been gored. As Manuel attempts to prove to his parents that he is not seriously injured, he collapses into a chair and faints. The curtain falls as everyone sings: "¡Sálvele el Señor!" (17).

Just as Manuel nearly dies at the close of Act I, his lover, Rosario, faces death in the final scene of Act II. The scene is very similar to the scene in *Curro Vargas* in which Soledad is asked to sing a solo for the Virgin Mary. Although she declines, Soledad finally agrees, realizing that she must not break tradition, since she has been the one to sing the song in the past. Similarly, in *La cortijera*, Rosario reluctantly agrees to dance her traditional *copla*. Just as Soledad is nearly killed by Curro as he rushes towards her with a dagger, Rosario too escapes death at the end of her performance. As Rosario falls breathless into Manuel's arms, Rafael becomes furious at her outward display of affection for Manuel, and grabbing his sword, Rafael attempts to kill Rosario. Like Manuel, Rosario does not die, but the parallel structure of their near death experiences is effective in its foreshadowing of the final scene in Act III, in which Rafael kills Manuel, and Rosario, forced to live without Manuel, dies inwardly.

Another parallel structure is the love affair between Carmela and Varillas. Although minor in importance to the plot, their love affair is significant when contrasted to that of Manuel and Rosario. The relationship between Carmela and Varillas is one in which there are no obstacles to inhibit the couple from sharing their love completely. Manuel and Rosario, on the other hand, have initiated their affair in secret because Rosario is engaged to be married to Rafael. The difference between the two couples is most obvious in Act II as the four join together in a musical round, each singing a short rhythmical verse:

<pre>
ROSARIO: (A Manuel, por Carmela y Varillas)
            Míalos, son dichosos;
            ni temen ni dúan;
            pasarán entera
            su vía felís.
            Si tú me abandonas,
            si tú no me quieres
            Manuel de mi alma,
            ¿qué va a ser de mí?
MANUEL: Si no te abandono,
            si estarás conmigo,
            si tú eres la gloria
            entera para mí.
            Riquezas y lujos
            y galas y fiestas,
            Rosario de mi alma,
            serán para ti.
CARMELA: ¡Qué vía la nuestra!
            Yo, con los chiquillos,
            saldré a la ventana
            a verte llegar,
            y si con bien llegas,
            te daré un abraso;
            y si con mal llegas,
            me echaré a llorar.
VARILLAS: ¡Qué vía la nuestra!
            Yo, por la escalera;
            los chicos, a gatas,
            subiendo detrás.
            Y una vez en casa,
            tú, dándome besos,
</pre>

> y ellos, con la mona,
> dale que le das. (24)

ROMANTIC CHARACTERISTICS

In *La cortijera*, Dicenta continues the Romantic themes set forth in *Curro Vargas*, unrequited love, honor, and vengeance; however, he does so with much less success. The Romantic hero, Rafael, is far less convincing than Curro, and although he is filled with the unbridled passion, he is not well developed enough to appeal to the audiences' sympathy. Vengeance plays a double role in *La cortijera*, unlike its predecessor *Curro Vargas*, in that Rafael, just as Roque from *El señor feudal*, not only seeks revenge but also is the object of someone else's vengeance. Garrocha, who pretends to be Rafael's friend, means to bring harm to Rafael for having stolen the position of foreman away from him. Garrocha believes that he deserved to be named foreman years ago by the Marqués, but that Rafael pushed him aside and made sure he was chosen. Garrocha, like Iago in *Othello*, plants seeds of jealousy, hoping to provoke Rafael, and once he is successful, Garrocha feels evil satisfaction in bringing Rafael pain.

Another Romantic aspect of *La cortijera* is the special attention paid to the lighting in the final act. Dicenta uses simulated bonfires for illumination: "La luz de estas hogueras aumentará, disminuirá y se extinguirá a medida que las exigencias escénicas lo reclamen" (34). After describing in detail the method that should be used to achieve this seemingly impossible effect, Dicenta addresses the stage artists: "Se ruega a los pintores escenógrafos que no descuiden ninguno de los detalles apuntados, por ser ellos, no sólo precisos a la acción dramática, sino en ocasiones parte integrante de la misma" (34). The bonfires form an integral part of the dance between the men and the women in celebration of the night of St. John.

Unrequited love is a dominant theme throughout the drama as Rosario and Rafael both lament their unfortunate situations. Rosario, in particular, plays the forlorn Romantic heroine, as she finds herself completely abandoned by all except Manuel, who is leaving home the following day:

> Luego, mi pecho obligao
> a un insesante martirio,
> ese hombre con el delirio
> de sus selos a mi lao,
> tus padres con sus enojos,
> la gente con su desdén...
> Y, para que nunca estén
> secos de llanto mis ojos,
> tú, lejos; yo, sola y triste
> y, en mi soleá, pensando

> que otra me pué estar robando
> el cariño que me diste;
> que te has olviao de mí,
> que ya pasó tu deseo...
> ¡Ay, Manuel múio, no pueo,
> no pueo vivir así! (38)

Rosario's attempt to kill herself in the final scene, however weak, is further evidence of her Romantic nature, yet unlike Curro and Soledad who may have the opportunity to reunite after death, Rosario survives and is condemned to live the rest of her life without Manuel.

CHARACTERS

Throughout the play there are several descriptions that call for a comparison between Rosario and Manuel and the tragic couple in *Juan José*, Rosa and Juan José. The love shared between Manuel and his foster parents is something Juan José never had the opportunity to enjoy, and Manuel, having been orphaned just as Juan José, is deeply appreciative of the love and support his parents provide him. Manuel's speech, in which he describes his past, is the exact opposite of Juan José's narration of the pain and suffering he endured after having been abandoned as an infant:

> En la mitá del arroyo,
> desamparao, medio muerto
> de hambre, de frío y miseria
> sus brazos me recogieron;
> como a un hijo me cuidaron,
> por mí pasaron desvelos
> y privaciones, y angustias,
> y sustos; su pan me dieron...
> ¡Qué su pan! Me dieron algo
> mejor, me dieron sus besos,
> su cariño... lo que naide [sic]
> pué comprar con el dinero;
> lo que no encontré en el mundo,
> diquiá que encontré con ellos. (4)

Manuel, despite his great fortune, proves to be an inferior man to the honorable Juan José. Juan José loves Rosa with all his heart, whereas Manuel, who can choose from any number of women, views Rosario as an object, and nothing more. Carmela attempts to explain Manuel's nature to Rosario: "Qué pintas pa él?... Una más. / Pa el otro [Rafael] serás too! / ¡too, Rosario!" (28). Rafael agrees: "[Manuel] te quiso por presunsión, / pa lusirte, pa feriarte" (30). Manuel's lack of morals is further displayed as he seduces Rosario without any concern for Rafael. Varillas confronts Manuel, pleading with him to respect Rafael, especially since Rafael saved Manuel's life. Manuel responds remorselessly: "Sierto. ¿Y qué?... Me la salvó, / Otras he salvao yo, / y no lo he dicho entavía" (13).

There is also a direct correlation between Rosario and Rosa (*Juan José*). Just as Rosa shamelessly flirts with Paco and ignores Toñuela's advice, Rosario freely expresses her love to Manuel, and when confronted by Carmela, Rosario becomes angry and refuses to listen (28). In the final scene, there is an eerie similarity as Rafael (who represents Juan José) vows to kill Rosario's lover. Rosario, like Rosa, pleads for mercy: "¡No! ¡De rodillas os lo suplico! ¡Ser compasivos! ¡Tener piedad!" (45). Rafael's response echoes that of Juan José: "Tú, la causante de mi tormento, ¿ahora me vienes a suplicar? No, no supliques, porque es inútil. Naa tus ruegos te servirán" (45).

HUMOROUS ASPECTS

La cortijera is rich with comedy, interspersing some of the most serious moments with laughter. The aforementioned lament by Rosario in which she pours her heart out to Manuel is soon followed by a group of men and women, recklessly running into each other, as they hurry across the stage in their screaming fits of laughter (38-39). The most humorous character is Varillas, the comical *picador* who suffers from alcoholism. From the beginning of the play, it is obvious that everyone is accustomed to Varillas and his excessive drinking habits. In Act I, his drunken adventures from the previous night have left him with no costume for the bullfight, as he has pawned it for more money to drink. As Varillas confesses his indiscretion to Prudencia, who loves him as a son, she finds it difficult to keep from laughing:

> Estaba yo antianoche
> de buen humor,
> y me bebí el vestío
> de picaor.
> Me gasté los dineros
> con cuatro piyos,
> y tengo por toa ropa
> los calzoncillos;
> y me da presentarme
> mucha cortedá
> con su vestío... tan claro
> ante Su Majestá. (7)

In moments of seriousness, Varillas seems totally out of place with his comical mannerisms and expressions. As he is about to tell Carmela the depth of his love for her, he stands still and stares at her with a "gesto picaresco" (22). Varillas promises his love to Carmela using ridiculous words: "Créelo, pa ti serán / mis pensares, mis suores; / pa ti, reina de las flores, / que eres más buena que el pan" (22). Varillas's profession of love is far different from that of the charismatic bullfighter, Manuel, yet in comparison, it is also more sincere. The most amusing scene is Varillas's attempt to ask José for his daughter's hand in marriage. The two men as they banter back and forth are boisterously entertaining. José knows fully Varillas's purpose, and uses this knowledge for his own amusement, as Varillas maintains such a seriousness combined with nerviousness that one cannot help laughing out loud.

CONCLUSIONS

Although an inferior play to *Curro Vargas* in every aspect, *La cortijera* has its redeeming moments. The constant singing and dancing help to move the play along, since the action is mostly insubstantial, and even though the characters are not deeply drawn, Varillas's character is certainly captivating. Unlike *Curro Vargas*, religion does not have a major role in *La cortijera*; however, it is not entirely absent. The fervent prayers of Manuel's family upon his injury in the bullfight are evidence of the positive force of Christianity in their lives. The recurrent theme of the orphan (Fernando, *El suicidio de Werther*, Juan José, *Juan José*; Curro, *Curro Vargas*; and Manuel, *La cortijera*) reflects a deep concern Dicenta had for society's helpless victims. In all but *Juan José*, however, Dicenta explores the positive side, praising the honorable characters who are willing to adopt an abandoned orphan, such as José and Prudencia. Like *Curro Vargas*, *La cortijera* has no thesis; its sole purpose was to entertain, yet its weak plot and even weaker character development make it one of Dicenta's poorest contributions to the stage.

EL TÍO GERVASIO (1900)

In just less than three weeks (March 21, 1900) following the mediocre premiere of *La cortijera*, Dicenta's first monologue, *El tío Gervasio*, was performed by the famous Miguel Soler, for whom the one-act drama was written. Soler had previously played the role of Padre Antonio in *Curro Vargas* (1898). A moving piece, *El tío Gervasio* returns Dicenta to portraying one of society's many victims.

PLOT

Tío Gervasio is a lonely sixty-five-year-old man who, like most men his age, talks often of the past as he reflects on his long life. The curtain rises in Gervasio's tiny apartment, as he struggles to unlock the door, having just arrived home from work. Talking to himself, Gervasio complains about the one hundred and fourteen steps that he has to climb to his apartment, claiming that they are to blame for his bad cough. After lighting a gas lamp, Gervasio counts his money out on the table, having received forty-eight *reales* for six days work. He divides the money to pay the bills, and he is left with only three *reales* for "tabaco y pa vicios" (89). Suddenly realizing that he is hungry, Gervasio goes to the window that opens into a corridor and shouts for Eufrasia, who, without being seen or heard, brings him a piece of bread and some soup through the window. As he sits down to eat, Gervasio laments his lonely dinner, reflecting on the family he used to have.

Years before, Gervasio had a wife, two sons, and a daughter. Upon the birth of their third child, a son, Gervasio's wife became deathly sick. After much suffering, she died of tuberculosis, and the infant, without a mother to nurse, gradually grew so weak that he too passed away. His surviving son, Juan, became a bricklayer, and Petra, his daughter, began to work in the factory. There were happy times, as Gervasio remembers the many Sundays he and his two children would spend together enjoying picnics in the park. Soon after that, however, Gervasio was left completely alone. Juan left for Cuba to fight in the war, and Petra left with a *señorito*, never to return. While in Cuba, Juan wrote his father letters, and the last one Gervasio received was from the hospital in Havana. Juan had been injured in battle. After many months passed without another letter, Gervasio learned that Juan had died. Despondent in his loneliness, Gervasio claims he has nothing left to do but wait for death to remove him from his painful life and pray for those already dead. The curtain falls as Gervasio begins to recite the Lord's Prayer.

TECHNIQUE / IDEOLOGY

In *El tío Gervasio*, Dicenta returns to his condemnation of a society that not only allows Spain's older generation to live in such poverty but also accepts it as normal. Dicenta's first monologue is rich in details that enable the audience to sympathize with Tío Gervasio, despite the short amount of time given to plot or character development. Depending upon the actor, the length of pauses, and the speed of his speech, *El tío Gervasio* may last from fifteen to twenty-five minutes. Dicenta successfully aids his spectators in their understanding of the drama in such a short period of time by providing clues prior to Tío Gervasio's entrance, as the audience gathers important background information from the setting. The one-room apartment is tiny and sparsely furnished with a cot, a dilapidated wooden chest, and a tiny table with four chairs. The cot is covered with a "sábana y una manta llena de agujeros" (87). It is immediately obvious that the short drama will provide a brief glimpse into the life of someone who is very poor. As the curtain rises, the apartment is empty, and while the audience takes in the scene of poverty, it can hear an older man coughing heavily on the other side of the apartment door. As Tío Gervasio struggles with the key, he continues to cough, and after he enters the apartment, the audience is unable to shake the feeling that it is inside this man's apartment with him.

Tío Gervasio is dressed in a white shirt, white pants, a long patched coat made of rough material, canvas sandals, and an old silk hat. His beard looks as if he has not shaved in at least a week. Tío Gervasio's destitute appearance, together with his meager surroundings, imply that he is of the lower class. This idea is confirmed as Tío Gervasio, although complaining about the cold, explains out loud that he hopes it continues to be cold rather than rainy, because when it rains, his livelihood is threatened, and he would rather be sick with a horrible cough than hungry: "vale más que apriete la tos; duele menos" (88). Because Tío Gervasio never removes his long tattered coat, it can be assumed that his apartment is as cold as it is outdoors. Tío Gervasio's clothes are in such bad shape that, after unsuccessfully attempting to strike a match on the table, he succeeds in igniting it on his pant leg. Using the match to light the one oil lamp, Tío Gervasio explains sarcastically to himself the reason he does not have electric lighting: "Como se le ha olvidao el amo poner luz elétrica en mi palacio, hay que encender el mechero de gas" (88). Tío Gervasio's use of the word "palacio" to describe his loft apartment indicates his awareness of the injustice of his situation. Knowing that there are people who live in palaces equipped with electric lighting only makes Tío Gervasio's poverty that much more painful for him to bear. Later in the same manner, Tío Gervasio refers to his meager dinner as a "banquete" (89).

Throughout the monologue, Dicenta blames society for Tío Gervasio's sad plight. As Tío Gervasio counts his money on the table, he describes the pay scale of the workers:

> En nuestro oficio, va uno pa atrás como el cangrejo. De oficial con cuatro pesetas, á peón con dos; de peón con dos, 'a guardavallas con una; de guardavallas con una, á pedir limosna y de pedir limosna, al hospital... (88)

Tío Gervasio explains that he used to be higher on the pay scale, but that now that he is old, he is just one step above becoming a beggar. He complains about the lack of support for the elderly, comparing himself to useless horses: "¡Qué remedio! Cuando el hombre no sirve pa el trabajo se le barre y caiga ande caiga. Lo mesmo hacen con los caballos; cuando se quean inútiles á la plaza é toros" (89).

As Tío Gervasio begins to talk about his past, we learn the reason why he is alone. First, he lost his wife and youngest son. Because he was out of work, neither he nor his family had enough to eat, as he says with resignation: "¿Qué iban á hacer más que morirse?" (89). Tío Gervasio's description of the death of his wife and his infant son is poignant, as he relates the details of their suffering:

Ella encima de ese jergón, con la cara amarilla.... y los ojos que la echaban lumbre... elentando como pa ahogarse, y sujetando contra su cuerpo al chiquillo que talmente parecía de cera en la color, y de trapo en lo flojo... agarrao al pecho... tirando de él... la madre cá vez más pálida.... De pronto, el chico soltó el pecho y rodó por el jergón, como un pájaro que cae muerto dende la rama que lo sostiene; la madre se llevó las manos á la garganta; abrió los ojos mucho... se incorporó sobre la cama... quiso hablar... y después ná. (90)

Like Juan José, Tío Gervasio and his family suffered from starvation, as he, a willing and able worker, was unable to find a job. Again, Dicenta emphasizes the injustice in a society that, in not giving an honest hard-working man like Tío Gervasio a way to make a living, is ultimately responsible for the deaths of his wife and infant son.

Tío Gervasio remembers that he and his two surviving children did enjoy happy times together when all three of them were working and there was enough money left over to enjoy life more. His description of their mutual love and affection for each other only makes their later abandonment of him that much more tragic. Unfortunately, this period of so-called prosperity was short-lived, as jobs became more scarce. While his son was at war, Tío Gervasio's daughter, who looked just like her mother with the exception that "¡Su madre era güena!" (91), left with a young man, as Tío Gervasio describes: "Vendió su cara, su cuerpo" (93). After learning that his son had died, Tío Gervasio realizes that he is completely alone. Even though his daughter is still alive, she might as well be dead in his opinion: "Esa está más muerta que el otro. El otro vive aquí. *(El corazón)*." (93). Dicenta again blames society for the "death" of Tío Gervasio's son and daughter. If Juan had not gone off to fight a losing battle in the Spanish-American War, he would still be alive. In the same way, if his daughter had not been forced to sell herself because of their poverty, she would still be with her father.

CONCLUSIONS

Not a single critic mentions the existence of Dicenta's first monologue. It is difficult to assume that *El tío Gervasio* was undiscovered, especially since later more important dramas, such as *Daniel*, list *El tío Gervasio* on the final page as one of Dicenta's previously published plays (*Daniel* 91). Perhaps its length kept critics from paying any attention to *El tío Gervasio*. Whatever the reason, it is certainly important in the development of Dicenta's dramatic technique and ideology, especially following a play as week as *La cortijera*. Most of Dicenta's critics describe the period between *El señor feudal* and *Aurora* (1896-1902) as completely lacking in "social" drama of any nature. As is obvious in *El tío Gervasio*, this is not the case. Although it is a short drama, what it lacks in length it makes up for in style and content. In *El tío Gervasio*, Dicenta successfully portrays, through the experience of one man, the horrible economic conditions suffered by the older generation of the working class at the turn of the century. It is unfortunate Dicenta did not turn this play into a full-length feature including the other family members mentioned by Tío Gervasio, for had he done so, it most surely would have received much acclaim for his successful return to the social criticism for which he became so famous with Juan José.

EL LEÓN DE BRONCE (1900)

Dicenta's next play, another monologue, premiered one month after *Tío Gervasio* on April 30, 1900. Dicenta wrote *El león de bronce* for Emilio Thuillier, an actor whom Dicenta credited for having brought his most famous character to life, Juan José. Besides the great success he achieved for *Juan José*, Thuillier also played the roles of Luciano (*Luciano*, 1894) and Jaime (*El señor feudal*, 1896) in their respective premieres. In *El león de bronce*, Thuillier portrays a mentally ill young man in an insane asylum.

PLOT

As the curtain rises, Carlos, a man between the ages of twenty-three and twenty-eight, is yelling at the nurse who has just left him alone in his cell. Full of irrational fury, Carlos claims that the nurse will never find out the secret that he hides. The thought of this secret frightens Carlos, as he decides to tell the secret to an imaginary listener with the hope that he will be comforted and pitied.

Carlos begins by explaining that he is not really insane; he claims that the doctors and nurses are lying. Carlos describes how one day a strange idea occurred to him, an idea that he tried unsuccessfully to forget. Just as soon as Carlos believed the idea was forever gone, he would remember it. Eventually, the idea divided into two voices that began to argue with each other. Carlos explains that he was very poor and unloved, and that one of the voices, "uno de mis yo," began to complain about his financial situation, wishing that he were wealthy. As the other "yo" asked the first "yo" how he could achieve his goal, the first "yo" revealed the original "idea" that had held Carlos prisoner.

Carlos's first "yo" had a plan to steal money from the wealthy old miser who lived directly beneath him on the third floor. In order to take the money, Carlos would have to lower himself from his window to the window below, and upon entering the man's apartment, he would have to murder him while he was sleeping. Carlos's second "yo" vehemently disagreed to commit such a horrible crime, yet the idea would not leave him alone. The more he thought about it, the more Carlos realized that it was the perfect crime. He would be able to silence the old man before he screamed, and after taking everything he could, he would leave through the door, locking it behind him. Filled with the courage that he would never be caught, Carlos planned for the night that he would become a criminal.

At two o'clock in the morning, Carlos lowered himself down to his neighbor's apartment window and silently entered. As he made his way over to the bed where the victim was sleeping soundly, Carlos withdrew a fancy letter opener, the handle of which was decorated with a tiny "león de bronce" (11). Raising his arms high, Carlos plunged his weapon deep into the throat of the victim, who woke up with a look of surprise and immediately died.

As Carlos was thinking about how rich he would be, all of a sudden he felt a sharp pain in the hand that was still holding the weapon. Turning to look, Carlos was filled with terror upon recognizing the "león de bronce" that used to be on the handle of the letter opener. The animal had come to life and was digging its claws deep into his skin. Carlos stops his narration and begs his listener to stop laughing at him. Returning to his story, Carlos describes how he completely forgot about his mission, only thinking about escaping the wild beast about to attack him. As Carlos ran towards the window, the lion grabbed his legs, turning him back around. Carlos then ran towards the bed, where the old man was lying dead, but the lion beat him to it, jumping up on the victim's chest, ready to pounce. Realizing that he could not escape without killing the tiny lion, Carlos grabbed the letter opener and began fighting with all of his strength. The "fiera" fought back viciously, biting Carlos on his neck, his chest, and his arms. The lion successfully dodged every blow, as Carlos wildly stabbed everything in sight, opening new wounds in the corpse on the bed. Gritting his teeth and regaining his composure, Carlos determined to kill the lion. This time, his blow hit the beast, yet the lion remained uninjured. Certain of his death, Carlos stepped back and opened his mouth in shock as he realized that the lion was immortal. The lion jumped into Carlos's mouth, and after scratching his way down Carlos's throat, the lion began to chew his way towards Carlos's heart. Returning to the present, Carlos claims that the lion is still there, feeding off his heart, and that when he dies, the lion will remain with him, because the lion is attached to his soul, and the soul never dies.

SOURCE / TECHNIQUE

Prior to the premiere of *El león de bronce*, Dicenta had written a short story with the same name, later published in *De la batalla* (1903). Placing the drama and short story side by side, the only differences between the two are the stage directions added to the play and the opening and closing words of Carlos. The short story is written in the first person, as is the drama, making it a simple project to convert into a performable monologue. Morby describes the motive for Dicenta's decision to turn a short story into a play:

In need of a short piece for Emilio Thuillier... he [Dicenta] drew on *El león de bronce* for a monologue of the same name. The transformation was easily accomplished. The story is in monologue form, and, but for a few excisions, the stage version required little modification. (387)

This was not the first time Dicenta borrowed from the stories that would later be published in *De la batalla* in 1903, nor would it be his last. *Luciano* (1894) was roughly based on "Un divorcio," and *El señor feudal* (1896) shares much with "El desquite." It is, however, the first time Dicenta wrote a play that was entirely taken, nearly word for word, from one of his previously written short stories.

The changes Dicenta made in the dramatic version are, of course, stage related. He provided the actor with detailed instructions on how to deliver certain lines, something that was unnecessary in the short story. Also, the additions of the opening and closing lines of the play were included for dramatic effect and to ensure that the audience viewed Carlos as a mentally ill man. As the curtain rises, Carlos exhibits irrational behavior in his verbal attack on the exiting nurse: "¡Anda, vete! ¡Es inútil que te empeñes: no lo sabrás!" (7). The nurse does not exist in the short story. Dicenta includes him in the play to aid the spectator in understanding the mental condition of the protagonist.

The stage directions serve the same purpose, as our perception of Carlos is such that we easily believe him to be insane. Throughout the monologue, Thuillier, under Dicenta's direction, is careful to deliver his lines as if he were insane. After his senseless screaming at the nurse, Carlos directs his attention to an imaginary companion, as noted by Dicenta: "*(Después de otra pausa y como hablando con un personaje imaginario.)*" (8). Later, as he describes the two voices fighting in his head, Carlos indicates the strong hold the voices had over him: "*(Oprimiéndose la garganta con gesto angustioso.)*" (9).

Not only is Carlos's insanity established by the manner in which he speaks, but also by the content of his speech. What Carlos says (present in both the play and the short story) is crucial in providing evidence of his dementia. Besides describing the two identities battling inside his brain, there are times when Carlos seems overcome by irrational fears. As he describes how he lowered himself to the window below his apartment, Carlos remembers how afraid he was: "Hubo un instante en que, presa de horrible alucinación, creí que la cuerda se convertía en el cordel de una horca y buscaba mi cuello para extrangularlo..." (11). Despite his attempts to convince his listener (and thus his audience) that he is not insane, Carlos's defense only makes us more certain that he is mentally ill:

> No te sonrías... no me contemples con la lástima burlona conque se contempla á los locos... ¡No fue un delirio!... ¡Te juro que es verdad! El león estaba vivo... ¡vivo!, desgarrando mis músculos con sus uñas de hierro, dispuesto á hundir sus dientes en mi carne. (12)

Carlos also constantly refers to the dead man as if the old miser were making fun of him: "parecía burlarse de mí con sus ojos mates y su boca desdentada y satánica" (13). Carlos's final description of the lion living inside his body chewing away at his heart is inconceivable, with the result that the spectator neither questions nor doubts Carlos's insanity.

The one final change Dicenta made to the play in transforming it from short story to the stage is the addition of the closing lines. Had the play ended with the final words of the short story, there would have been a sense of incompletion:

> Ese es mi castigo… La fiera mordiéndome en el corazón y el avaro delante de mí, con el cuerpo lleno de sangre, la boca contraída y los ojos desmesuradamente abiertos. ("León" 7)

Thus ends the short story, to which Dicenta adds the following to close the play:

> ¿Lo ves?… ¿Lo ves allí? ¡Y se ríe…se ríe…! *(Con desesperación.)* ¡No quiero mirarte! ¡No quiero oirte!… *(Ocultando el rostro con las manos.)* ¡Perdón!… ¡Dios mío!… ¡Dios mío!… *(Contempla el espacio con ojos espantados; luego rompe en una carcajada siniestra y cae de golpe contra el suelo.)* (*León* 14)

IDEOLOGY

Whatever ideological implications exist in the play (or the short story) are veiled beneath the rantings of an insane man. Only once does Carlos make a reference to the outside world's perspective of him prior to commiting the horrible crime:

> Soy joven, decía uno de mis *yo*, y mi juventud se pierde entre los girones de mi traje. Las mujeres no me miran, los hombres me desprecian, mis ambiciones se agostan, mis anhelos de placer no se cumplen. ¡Si yo fuera rico… inmensamente rico… tendría cuanto mi deseo apetece! ¡Y esto es imposible! (9)

Carlos's complaint is that of many lower class citizens, as he struggles to achieve satisfaction in a world that severely limits one's abilities to do so. It is his desire for money, which is not viewed as insane, that pushes him to commit the crime. Although morally wrong, Carlos's decision to murder his miserly neighbor is not evidence alone to prove him insane. This is not to deny that indications of his ill mental state were present prior to the murder, for they were; Carlos carefully describes the two voices in his head that argued back and forth nonstop. It is the murder, however, that pushes this desperate young man over the edge.

The symbol of the lion is of particular interest, for it indicates a connection between Dicenta and another group that used new techniques to express their opinions of Spain: the Generation of 1898. Like Dicenta, the members of the Generation of '98 criticize the misery suffered by Spain's lower classes and the blindness of the upper class, among many other aspects of society not necessarily criticized by Dicenta. These particular authors experimented with both the form and the content of their literary contributions by inventing new styles and using a detailed prose to paint a picture for their readers or spectators. They were also very preoccuopied with all themes Spanish. Viewed in this light, it is possible to attach more meaning to the "león de bronce" that attacked poor Carlos. The lion has long been a symbol of Spain, as it represents the province in northwest Spain that once was a kingdom. Spain's current coat of arms has the symbol of a lion, together with a castle, to represent León and Castile. Symbolically, the immortal lion that attacks Carlos, enters his mouth, and begins to feed on his heart, represents Spain as a parasite, slowly draining the life away from her poor, underprivileged classes. Just as the lower class individuals are condemned to remain at the bottom of the social ladder, Carlos cannot escape the pain and suffering caused by the lion, who constantly gnaws on his heart, his soul.

CONCLUSIONS

Again, just as Dicenta's critics ignored *El tío Gervasio*, *El león de bronce* is mentioned only by one scholar, Edwin S. Morby, who refers to it as an example of Dicenta's tendency to plagiarize his own work. It has long been confirmed that Dicenta's fiction is of substantially lower quality than his drama, and the fact that he had already written *El león de bronce* in short story form that was easily transformed to fit the stage only proves that, above all, Dicenta was a dramatist at heart. *El león de bronce* in no way loses its value because it existed previously in the form of a short story; instead, its earlier existence simply indicates Dicenta's desire to redevelop a story for the stage in such a way that his argument against social injustice be heard. Dicenta's weakest play (*La cortijera*) and these two obscure monologues, performed within a few months of each other in the spring of 1900 suggest a period of deep soul-searching on the part of Dicenta as he struggled to recapture the magnitude of success he had with *Juan José* just five years earlier. It is obvious by the lack of attention given to these three plays that Dicenta was slowly losing favor in Madrid's theaters; perhaps for that reason he took a two-year break and returned to the stage with a dynamic historical drama.

RAIMUNDO LULIO (1902)

Dicenta's next play, *Raimundo Lulio*, premiered in May of 1902 in the Teatro Lírico. With three acts and an epilogue, *Raimundo Lulio* represents Dicenta's return to the full-length drama, and as in *Curro Vargas* and *La cortijera*, in *Raimundo Lulio* Dicenta continues the popular tradition of the Spanish *zarzuela*. With the music of Ricardo Villa, *Raimundo Lulio* is a lyrical drama based on the legendary historical figure of the same name (Ramón Lull in Catalan). Set in medieval Majorca, *Raimundo Lulio* is a Romantic tragedy full of suspense and action.

PLOT

Raimundo is a Don Juan figure who is well known for having seduced many women in his life, yet he has never fallen in love. Catalina's beauty and grace, however, prove to be more than he can resist, and soon Raimundo surrenders his whole soul to Catalina. Isabel, Catalina's sister, is one of Raimundo's many victims, having lost her honor to him with the hope of one day becoming his wife. Roger has always loved Isabel, and upon learning of her dishonor, he plans to seek vengeance against Raimundo.

Thus is the situation as the play opens. Although Catalina rejects Raimundo's advances, privately, she mysteriously vacillates between admissions of love for him and complete indifference towards him, leading the audience to wonder what secret she possesses. Having not ever been rejected before, Raimundo stops at nothing to succeed in seducing Catalina. He pursues her publicly, privately, hopefully, and arrogantly, despite her continued indifference. Isabel is overcome with jealousy and approaches Catalina to find out her intentions. Isabel, and thus the specator, is further confused by Catalina's answer: "A Lulio no puedo amar. ¿Qué te importa la razón?" (23).

Raimundo refuses to accept Catalina's rejection, believing that he is certain to succeed in his seduction of her. To further humiliate Catalina, Raimundo makes a public vow that he will have her "por voluntad o por fuerza" (19). He makes good his oath by sensational means. While Catalina passes through the streets on her way to church *en litera*, Raimundo approaches her, undaunted by her many attendants. Raimundo is distracted as he fights with her protectors, allowing Catalina to escape to attend mass. Upon learning that Catalina is in the church, Raimundo wastes no time in pursuing her there. With his sword drawn, Raimundo rides directly to the altar where Catalina is praying. The priests and the public are horrified at Raimundo's blasphemy. Raimundo refuses to leave the church until she promises to see him that night at her window. In order to make him leave, Catalina desperately agrees.

In the meantime, Roger has informed Berenguer, Isabel and Catalina's brother, of the dishonor already placed upon the family by Raimundo in his seduction of Isabel. The two men, Roger and Berenguer, wait for Raimundo to arrive by boat on the shore at Catalina's room. Berenguer asks Roger to allow him to approach Raimundo alone. Upon Raimundo's arrival, he and Berenguer duel, with the result that Berenguer is killed. Raimundo quickly overcomes a brief moment of regret and goes to meet Catalina.

As they meet, Catalina admits to loving Raimundo, with guarded sadness. Raimundo demands that he be allowed to come closer to her, with the result that she opens the door for him to come inside her room. Raimundo is overcome with passion, while Catalina expresses unexplained anguish. As Raimundo pulls her close to kiss her, Catalina violently pushes him away. After he insists that she give him not only her soul but also her body, Catalina removes her clothing, revealing her disgusting gangrenous body underneath her robes. Raimundo, who is horrified at the sight, turns and flees. The epilogue that follows describes Raimundo's conversion to Christianity, as he recognizes his sin and seeks solace in a monastery.

SOURCES

The *Enciclopedia universal ilustrada* describes Raimundo Lulio as a double figure, the historical and the legendary. A Catalan philosopher, mystic, poet, theologian, and missionary, Raimundo Lulio (Doctor Illuminatus) was born in Palma, Majorca between 1232 and 1236 and died at Tunis in 1315. The popular legend surrounding the figure of Raimundo Lulio is the story that Dicenta treats in his lyrical drama *Raimundio Lulio*. According to the *Enciclopedia universal ilustrada*, the legend follows thus:

> ...se le supuso enamorado de una dama, cuyo nombre y condición social se ignoran,... Dícese que este amor absorbía todas las facultades y momentos de Raimundo Lulio y que dió varios escándalos públicos con ocasión del mismo, como lo fué el haber entrado dentro de un templo montado á caballo, un día en que perseguía por las calles á la dama de sus pensamientos, la que para evitar el encuentro con el galán, penetró en el templo a la hora de la Misa.... [La dama] Dióle una cita, en lugar retirado, y allí, antes de que el enamorado prócer diese expansión á sus afectos, la dama, desnudando su cintura, le mostró su propio pecho, que un hediondo cáncer carcomía hacía tiempo. Ante tal horrible visión, Raimundo Lulio, curado de su pasión insana, despidióse de la dama, y tocado de la gracia divina, determinó consagrarse desde entonces al apostolado entre los infieles y fundar los colegios y conventos que el histórico Ramón Lull fundó en realidad. (412)

As is obvious, Dicenta freely based his drama on the legend of Raimundo Lulio, adding his own ideas for dramatic effect. The legend does not include any mention of the young lady's sister, Isabel, in the drama, and for that reason the entire motive of vengeance sought by both Roger and Berenguer is absent as well. Dicenta includes the subplot concerning Isabel not only to enhance the well-known legend, but also to provide the typical Romantic theme of vengeance.

The legend of Raimundo Lulio had been a popular subject in Spanish literature long before Dicenta wrote the lyrical drama of the same name, and even during his lifetime there was a renewed interest in the medieval Majorcan hero. Gaspar Núñez de Arce (1834-1903), one of Spain's most talented historical dramatists, published a poem entitled "Raimundo Lulio" in his collection of poetry *Gritos del Combate* in 1875. In his poem, Núñez de Arce uses the name "Blanca" for the young woman who has such a profound effect on Raimundo. Written entirely in the first person, "Raimundo Lulio" provides a singular perspective from the hero's point of view of the horrible tragedy. Two Catalan poets also treat the popular legend in poetry: Francisco Ubach y Vinyeta in *Romancer Català* (Barcelona, 1878) and Eusebio Anglora in *Calendari Català* (Barcelona, 1895) (*Enciclopedia* 412).

TECHNIQUE

Dicenta's *Raimundo Lulio* has a lot in common with José Zorrilla's *Don Juan Tenorio* (1844). Don Juan Tenorio is an arrogant womanizer who has a reputation for being able to seduce any woman he chooses; so too is Raimundo Lulio, who, until Catalina, has never failed in his constant conquest of beatiful women. Both men, Don Juan and Raimundo, take sensational measures to guarantee their success: Don Juan kidnaps Doña Inés and kills her father and Don Luis, and Raimundo kills Catalina's brother and follows Catalina into church, where, during Mass, he draws his sword and demands that she surrender to his advances. And finally, both men are dramatically transformed at the close of the drama as they each confess their sins and repent: Don Juan's conversion culminates in his death and ascencion into heaven; whereas Raimundo enters the monastery to dedicate the rest of his life to serving God.

One cannot ignore the obvious connection between Dicenta's first successful *zarzuela*, *El duque de Gandía* (1894), and *Raimundo Lulio*, as they are both founded substantially on historical fact. Both title characters were venerated religious leaders and important figures in the Catholic church: The Duke of Gandía was canonized a saint (St. Francis de Borgia), and Raimundo Lulio (Ramón Lull) was beatified following his death. Both men share a similar legend in their decision to devote their lives to Christian pursuits. Just as Raimundo's terror upon viewing his beloved's cancered body moved him to join a monastery, St. Francis, who was supposedly in love with Queen Isabel, was so horrified by the state of the queen's decomposed body shortly after her death that he turned immediately to the priesthood. Both legends provide Dicenta with the proper material for a thoroughly Romantic tragedy written in the popular form of the *zarzuela*.

ROMANTIC CHARACTERISTICS
Romantic elements abound in *Raimundo Lulio*, as Dicenta treats the typical Romantic themes of unrequited love, jealousy, honor, and vengeance. Raimundo is most certainly a Romantic hero. He is dominated by his unbridled passion, he suffers from unrequited love, and he reflects the typical Romantic motto of "yo ante el mundo." The medieval setting of the lyrical drama is Romantic and helps to recreate images of chivalry, especially as Catalina's attendants and brother fight for her honor through elaborate swordplay. Another Romantic characteristic is the positive force of Christianity. Also, Catalina's constant enigmatic allusions to her inability to surrender to her feelings for Raimundo create a Romantic air of mystery and anticipation throughout the drama, further adding to the melodramatic nature of the play. The Romantic tryst at midnight, following the ominous twelve tolls of the church bell, is purely Romantic as Raimundo and Catalina meet by the light of the moon. The element of vengeance is minor to the action of the play, yet it is certainly Romantic as Roger and Isabel's brother each seek revenge for her lost honor. Their revenge, however, is not secured through their own efforts; instead, Raimundo, just as his Romantic counterparts, is dealt his punishment by fate.

CONCLUSIONS
There is no apparent thesis in *Raimundo Lulio*, as Dicenta returns to the popular *zarzuela* to entertain his audiences. *Raimundo Lulio* is a moving lyrical drama full of suspense and action. Although music is present throughout the drama, it does not perform the same light-hearted entertaining role as it did in Dicenta's *Curro Vargas* and *La cortijera*; instead, it creates a somber mood, building a sense of dread as the drama unfolds. Fittingly, as in *El duque de Gandía*, the curtain falls as sounds of the *Miserere* fade off into the distance. Together with Dicenta's other lyrical dramas, *Raimundo Lulio* is essential in the study of the Spanish *zarzuela* at the turn of the century and most certainly deserves further study. It is also important as one traces Dicenta's continuing development, as he exhibits his versatile talent in the form of Spanish opera, a sharp contrast from the "social" drama for which he was most well known.

AURORA (1902)
In the years since *El señor feudal* (1896) in two-year intervals, Dicenta wrote three lyrical dramas: *Curro Vargas* (1898), *La cortijera* (1900), and *Raimundo Lulio* (1902). With the exception of his one-act monologues from the spring of 1900, *El tío Gervasio* and *El león de bronce*, Dicenta avoided both the social question and the realistic approach on the stage. In his journalistic endeavors, however, Dicenta continued to express his deep desire to

revolutionize the stage by portraying contemporary issues in a realistic manner. In *Crónicas* (1898), a collection of articles compiled from Dicenta's column in the republican newspaper *El Liberal* in 1897, Dicenta defends the use of realism on the stage in the chapter entitled "La verdad en el teatro":

> ¿De dónde vamos á sacar los dramas nosotros? ¿De la vida real que ante nuestros ojos palpita, ó de una vida imaginaria cortada á patrón, sentida á capricho de pudibundos cursis y falseada en beneficio de cuatro mozuelas insubstanciales y de una docena de caballeros bien alimentados? (*Crónicas* 148)

Ironically, in the years following the publication of this article, Dicenta continued to thrill his audiences with entertaining dramas depicting the imaginary lives he condemned so harshly. Although both *El tío Gervasio* and *El león de bronce* are realistic, Dicenta does not return to portraying realistic events in a full-length drama on the stage until the premiere of *Aurora* in June of 1902 in Barcelona by Emilio Thuillier's company, presented again in November of that year in Madrid's Teatro de la Alhambra by García Ortega's company. *Aurora* was praised by audiences in both Barcelona and Madrid, and Dicenta again received the acclaim he had enjoyed prior to the failure of *El señor feudal*:

> Dicenta volvió de nuevo a los periódicos, siendo ensalzado por Pereira en *El Liberal*, y recobró en parte el prestigio que había perdido con el estreno de *El señor feudal*. (Mas Ferrer, *Vida* 162)

PLOT

Manuel is a rising young surgeon who has been abroad for several years. Upon his return, he is to marry his cousin, Matilde. This entire scheme has been arranged by Remedios, Manuel's aunt, and Matilde because upon the marriage of Matilde and Manuel, the newlyweds are to receive jointly a large inheritance that was left by an uncle who specified that condition (the marriage) in his will. Aurora, who is a seamstress working for Remedios, overhears Remedios and Matilde as they discuss their plan to take full advantage of young Manuel. Aurora finds out that Matilde does not love Manuel, and that the only reason she is willing to marry him is because of the money. Aurora also learns that Matilde has a lover, Enrique, whom she intends to keep seeing even after marrying Manuel.

Aurora soon realizes that she and Manuel have met before. Because of the extreme poverty in which Aurora was raised, her health was nearly ruined, and at one point in her life she was a patient in a hospital where Manuel was an intern. When she was a child, she had worked in a factory where she was treated very badly, and these early injuries had plagued her throughout her life. The hospital took her in as a charity case, and she soon fell in love with Manuel, and he with her. He was able to help her on her way to recovery, not only physically but also spiritually. Unfortunately, the two could never hope for a future together because of the social prejudice that separated them.

Armed with her rekindled love for Manuel, Aurora confronts Matilde face to face, threatening to tell everyone of Matilde's affair with Enrique. Matilde, although shocked by Aurora's courage for a woman of her low class, ignores Aurora's threat, believing that no one would trust a poor working-class girl. Aurora is soon faced with an opportunity to prove to Manuel Matilde's dishonor. Having learned of a secret meeting scheduled between Enrique and Matilde, Aurora convinces Manuel to witness the scene. Manuel is disturbed about the situation because he believes that Aurora is purposefully attempting to sully Matilde's character for her own benefit; however, because he has already had feelings of unrest about the impending marriage, he fears Aurora is telling the truth.

Manuel overhears exactly what Aurora had hoped he would, and he is completely convinced of Matilde's guilt. Aurora is vindicated, and Matilde is enraged. Manuel disowns his family and praises Aurora's courage and honor. The curtain closes as Manuel takes Aurora's hand with the intent to marry her.

TECHNIQUE

Aurora is one of Dicenta's most important plays, as it marks his return to the realistic social drama that brought him fame with *Juan José* seven years earlier. Although *Aurora* is "un drama convencional de honor" (Mas Ferrer, *Vida* 151), Dicenta invests it with enough realistic elements to make it a first-rate modern play. *Aurora* is Dicenta's first full-length play written entirely in prose since *El señor feudal* (1896), and it represents a more accurate perspective of contemporary life than Dicenta's popular *zarzuelas* of the past five years.

Dicenta's portrayal of the class struggle in *Aurora* is enhanced by his skillful and realistic imitation of the speech of the two protagonists, Manuel and Aurora, as he depicts the background of each in their conversations. Manuel, who is well traveled and educated, uses complex descriptions and the urbane speech typical of the wealthy, as is evident in his first words on stage:

> Sí, Matilde, aquí estoy: aquí tienes al sabio, como me llamabas
> irónicamente en tus cartas: á este hombre que ha querido estudiar mucho y
> quiere valer mucho para hacerse digno de tu belleza, de tu bondad y de tu
> cariño. (29)

Manuel's speech also reflects his idealistic and naïve personality. Aurora's conversation, unlike Manuel's refined manner of speaking, lacks sophistication, reflecting her low-class upbringing. However, Dicenta is careful not to portray

Aurora as completely rustic since Manuel had taken it upon himself to teach Aurora how to read and write while she was in the hospital years before. Aurora's intelligence is clearly obvious in her ability to understand Manuel's scientific ruminations. Aurora does, however, revert to her popular dialect in scenes of great emotion, which further adds to the total realistic effect of the drama. Petra, on the other hand, who has not had the same opportunity to learn to read and write as did Aurora, uses much more dialect in her conversation than does Aurora.

The realistic setting of the play is important in the understanding of the financial situation of Remedios and her family, as most of the scenes take place inside a hotel and in its adjacent garden. As Remedios and her family eagerly await the young doctor's return, they hope to impress him with their wealth, despite the fact that Remedios is suffering extreme financial hardship. Dicenta moves Remedios and her family into a hotel where they can more successfully portray a condition of artificial opulence rather than leaving them in her modest home where Manuel might be less than impressed.

There are other touches of realism throughout the play that, because of their effectiveness, mostly go unnoticed. The characterization of Petra, the flippant servant, allows Dicenta the opportunity to interject facts that reflect his contemporary audiences. For example, Petra describes Matilde's complete lack of domestic talent, common among women of Matilde's social status: "El otro día tardó hora y media en pegar la manga de una blusa... y la pegó al revés" (11).

INFLUENCES

Aurora is a well constructed drama greatly influenced by Benito Pérez Galdós, who one year earlier had received great praise for his groundbreaking *Electra* (1901). Specifically, the hypocritical and fanatically religious Don Homobono and the young progressive Manuel remind one of Pantoja and Máximo of Galdós's *Electra*. As in many of Galdós's novels and plays, Dicenta links a successful regeneration of Spain with an education obtained abroad. Also, the theme of the possible amalgamation of the upper and lower social classes, which was popular among other European dramatists such as Strindberg, was central to Galdós's *La loca de casa* (1892) and *La de San Quintín* (1894). Even Dicenta's portrayal of the moral difference between classes, virtue belonging to the poor and hypocrisy and decadence reflecting the upper class, is reminiscent of the same themes in many of Galdós's novels and plays, particularly in *Marianela* (1878) and *Misericordia* (1897).

As he had in previous dramas, Dicenta continues the style of Echegaray, building a thesis around a typical honor drama and utilizing melodramatic turns of plot. As Hall notes: "There are points of similarity between this play [*Aurora*] and Echegaray's *Mancha que limpia*, in addition to the general influence of the

Echegarayan manner" (61). The question of honor and jealousy that is portayed in the love triangle created by Matilde as she loves one man, Enrique, and plans to marry another, Manuel, is also typical of Echegaray.

Aurora also shows some influence of Ibsen, especially in the non-tragic ending. Maryellen Bieder, in her article entitled "The Modern Woman on the Spanish Stage: The Contributions of Gaspar and Dicenta," describes the similarities between the two Spanish dramtists and Ibsen:

> As when Ibsen had Nora shut the door to the Helmer home at the end of *A Doll's House*, Gaspar and Dicenta resolve their dramatic conflicts with the grand gestures of an ideal couple who seem to promise more than themselves. (28)

Bieder refers to Enrique Gaspar's *La huelga de hijos* (1893), which explores the rights of a young woman to choose her husband, even if it means going against her parents' wishes.

IDEOLOGY

Following the premiere of *Aurora*, many critics compared Dicenta's newest social drama to his masterpiece, *Juan José*, as is related in the following excerpt from *Revista Blanca*:

> Decididamente el mundo marcha. *Aurora*, observada desde el punto de vista de mis ideas sociales, es superior a *Juan José*; dramática y artísticamente juzgada, le es bastante inferior. Sin embargo, la crítica que podríamos llamar burguesía, celebra con menos rodeos el estreno de *Aurora* que antaño celebró el de *Juan José*. (qtd. in Rubio Jiménez, *Ideología* 116)

Mas Ferrer explains his reasoning for considering *Aurora* a social drama: "por su realismo, por la visión crítica de la sociedad contemporánea y por mantener una tesis atrevida y reformista" (*Vida* 150). Dicenta conscientemente invests *Aurora* with social implications, feeling it his mission to bring to the stage the ills of society. Dicenta expresses this goal in his prologue to *Aurora*:

> Yo sólo procuro, desde mi humildísima esfera de acción, colaborar al triunfo de las nuevas ideas, de los que tienen por objeto convertir esta sociedad de oprimidos y opresores, de opulentos y de mendigos, de verdugos y víctimas, en dichoso y amplísimo hogar de hermanos, de compañeros, de seres iguales, aleccionados en el bien y regidos por la justicia, ni necesita hacer profesiones de fe, ni explicar qué móviles le hacen escribir obras del género al que pertenece mi *Aurora*. *Aurora* no significa,

para mí, una obra literaria, significa el cumplimento de una obligación, de un deber de conciencia. Sí, amigo mío: hay que HACER HUMANIDAD NUEVA—a este fin, justo y noble, debemos contribuir todos. (*Aurora* 1)

In his argument for a "humanidad nueva," Dicenta attacks many issues, including arranged marriages, the hypocrisy and decadence of the upper class, religion, child abuse, the exploitation of the female working class, and the lack of social progress in Spain. In order to portray the sharp separation of classes in Spanish society, Dicenta expresses his social message through allegory. Each character represents a different level of society: Aurora represents the honorable working class; Manuel, the enlightened thinker, represents progress; Matilde and her family represent the corrupt ruling class, driven by calculated ambition; and Homobono represents the greedy Church, which, not satisfied with poisoning minds with fanatical thought, seeks financial support through any means possible.

The injustice of arranged marriages had already been argued some hundred years earlier by Fernández de Moratín in *El sí de las niñas* (1801), *El viejo y la niña* (1790) and *El Barón* (1803), yet Dicenta felt it necessary to return to the problem in *Aurora* to show how little society had progressed. Unlike the earlier dramas, however, the arranged marriage in *Aurora* is forced upon the couple by means of a will left by a wealthy uncle, who promised a large sum of money to the newlywed couple upon their marriage. Manuel and Matilde do have the choice not to marry, yet Matilde's greed and Manuel's innocence, together with the persuasion of Matilde's financially burdened family, bring the couple to plan a wedding.

In his portrayal of Matilde and her family, Dicenta condemns the hypocrisy and decadence of the upper class through a consistent comparison of Aurora and Matilde, the former being virtuous and the latter greedy and selfish. This is best portrayed in the scene in which Matilde and Enrique express their love to each other while Aurora, hidden from their view, listens with disgust. In the stage directions, Dicenta makes it clear that Aurora's actions are paramount in the audiences's understanding of the stark contrast between her and Matilde:

Aurora seguirá toda la escena con atención creciente, interrumpiendo su labor para manifestar con sus gestos la impresión de vergüenza y asco que el diálago entablado entre Matilde y Enrique le produce.... Escena durante la cual deben reflejarse en el rostro de aquella obrera envilecida por la miseria y por el abandono, pero honrada de condición y leal de caracter, múltiples sentimientos, entre los cuales predominarán dos: el de irse encontrando superior poco á poco á los dos miserables que tiene enfrente, y el del asombro y la repugnancia que maldades, de las que ella no es capaz, le producen. (25)

The dissimilarity between the arrogant rich Matilde and the poor humble seamstress is most evident when Aurora confronts Matilde with her dishonor. Matilde, who is at first disdainful and arrogant, becomes desperate as she tries to persuade Aurora not to interfere with the wedding by reminding her how wealthy she will be, but Aurora, disgusted by Matilde's greed, interrupts her with a comment that reveals the discrepancy between their moral character and their social status:

> ¿Quiere usted comprarme? *(Con ironía.)* Yo no soy de las que se venden. *(Con altivez.)* No. Ni vendo el querer como usted, ni la conciencia como su amante.... Sí, le quiero;... solo que yo le quiero sin esperar que él pueda quererme; y tú finges quererle, con la esperanza de ser rica; yo puse los ojos en él para adorarle, tú para deshonrarle; yo para hacerle con mi cariño un paraíso, tú para hacerle con tus maldades un infierno. ¡Calcula si hay diferencia entre nosotras! (47)

Like Jaime in *El señor feudal* as he refuses to remove his hat as a sign of respect in the presence of Carlos, Aurora sees no need to maintain respect for someone who does not deserve it, despite the differences in social status. Dicenta often illustrates the fact that there is no correlation between social class and morality.

Through the hypocritical religious figure of Homobono, Dicenta continues what Galdós started in *Electra* one year earlier by portraying the corruption of those who use religion to manipulate others. Homobono is the only one, besides Aurora, who is opposed to the marriage of Manuel and Matilde, not because he knows of Matilde's dishonor and the lack of affection she has for Manuel, but because of the second stipulation of the will left by Manuel's wealthy uncle. As the administrator for a religious community, Homobono seeks to prevent the wedding, knowing that if he is successful, the money Manuel and Matilde were to receive will be given to the religious community. Homobono suspects that Matilde does not love Manuel, and he uses this suspicion as a front for his ulterior motives in confronting Remedios about the impending wedding: "si ella no le ama, y por no amarle, se hace infeliz, la boda significaría un peligro para ella y acaso un crimen para quienes le aconsejen y la permitan" (39). However, when Aurora reveals to him her knowledge about Matilde's affair with Enrique, Homobono hypocritically tells Aurora that she is alone in her decision of how to handle the situation:

> Pero la culpa, si existiera, tú eres quien la sabe, tú quien lo has visto; yo no sé nada, no he visto nada, no puedo mezclarme, por consiguiente, en nada. Eso es cosa tuya.... Haz lo que juzgues más conveniente; y para tí el pecado, si es que hay pecado, y la gloria si hay gloria. (44)

Aurora, Dicenta's first female protagonist, is a virtuous, well-meaning victim of society who, although recognizing her lowly state and accepting her fate, longs for a better life and laments her sad past. There is a scene between Aurora and Petra, Aurora's fellow servant who was born and reared in the same poor neighborhood, that represents Dicenta's most vivid and bitter description of the life of the lower classes. Through the conversation between the two servants, Dicenta attacks the exploitation of the female worker. Aurora's account of their painful past is especially poignant:

> Descalzas, vestidas de andrajos; solas en medio de la calle desde pequeñas. Solas y sin calor de nadie; ni aun el de nustros padres, ni el del sol. Nuestros padres en la obra ó en la fábrica; el sol sin acercarse nunca á nosotros, porque la calle era tan estrecha que no lo dejaba pasar, y nosotras... Nosotras á la merced de Dios, haciendo juguetes con la basura del arroyo. (20)

Aurora continues to describe how she hated the weekends because her parents would spend all of their money on alcohol, as she and her siblings starved. After the death of both of her parents, Aurora and her siblings were orphaned, like so many of Dicenta's protagonists, and they were forced to separate in their attempt to survive: "como los pájaros pequeños, cuando un tiro mata á los grandes" (22).

Both Aurora and Petra were only ten-years-old when they began to work at the factory where they suffered "el humo de los fósforos y la humedad negra del taller" (21). Aurora, wracked with sobs, explains the power the *amo* had over her:

> ...á obedecer al amo, que es quien dispone de tu jornal y de tu comida; quien puede echarte de la fábrica á puntapiés y hacer que revientes de hambre en medio del arroyo. El amo es tu Dios: dispone de tí, manda en tí... Esta idea es la que le meten á una en los sesos, y una, claro, á cumplir con el amo, á sudar para él, á trabajar para él, á hacerse tiras la carne y polvo los huesos para él. ¡Qué remedio! Es la obligación. Y si el sudor te ahoga, y el fósforo te asfixia, y el trabajo te mata, y tu carne se rompe á cachos, y tus huesos se parten á crujidos, ¡no importa! (21)

The *amo* inflicts this abuse on both men and women who work for him, but Aurora expresses an even deeper pain in her description of the abuse suffered by the women. In her case, the *amo* raped her when she was only fourteen years old: "Tan acostumbrada estaba á obedecerle, que hasta, para deshonrarme le obedecí.... ¡Qué afortunadas son las obreras feas! ¡A esas no les piden más que trabajo!" (21-22). The suffering Aurora and Petra endured is horrific, not only because they were abused and exploited by their employer, but also because they were only children at the time. Dicenta's message is revolutionary in that Manuel will marry the dishonored Aurora at the close of the drama.

In broader terms, *Aurora* is an example of the Spanish dilemma of *las dos Españas*, a problem explored by Galdós in *La Fontana de Oro* (1870). On one side there are Manuel and Aurora, who in their fight for progress, represent freedom and democracy, encourage scientific discovery, and look to the future for the new Spain, extricated from the clutches of her past. On the other side, there are those like Remedios and her family who, in their rejection of progress and education as a road to Spain's future, represent tyranny and oppression in their defense of the past, their support of tradition, and their religious fanaticism. This idea of *las dos Españas* is made clear by the conversation between Homobono and Manuel upon the latter's return from studying abroad:

HOM: ¡Picarón! Cinco añitos por esos mundos de Dios, es decir, del diablo, porque Inglaterra y Alemania son protestantes; y Francia peor todavía, porque es republicana. ¡Lástima que esos pueblos estén por sus costumbres y por sus creencias fuera de nuestra santa religión y lástima que los jóvenes vayan á ellos con achaque de aprender ciencia!

MAN: ¡Qué remedio, don Homobono! En la España católica la enseñan pocos, y á esos pocos ó no les hacen caso ó les dejan morirse de hambre en un rincón.... Además, poco importa que sean católicos ó protestantes los pueblos donde la ciencia vive y se dignifica y adelanta.... La ciencia se cuida poco de religiones. Como sólo tiene dos enemigos irreconciliables: el fanatismo y la intolerancia. (29-30)

Dicenta argues for a new Spain in which social status is not based upon blood lines or defunct traditional views; instead, all will have the opportunity to enjoy success and happiness based upon merit of character. Aurora and Manuel, both of high moral character, break violently from Spain's past in order to create a "humanidad nueva." Manuel's final words to Matilde and her family summarize Dicenta's argument for a new Spain:

En ella [Aurora], aún hay vida, y donde hay vida puede haber salud. En vosotros, no; vosotros no podéis acompañarme; los muertos no andan, y vosotros sois muertos sin enterrar. Quedáos ahí solos; pudríos ahí solos con vuestras pequeñeces y vuestros crímenes. Ven tú (a Aurora). En tí hay sangre joven, sentimientos puros, conciencia virgen; en mí hay inteligencia y hay voluntad. ¡Ven, Aurora! Más cerca, más cerca aún. Siempre juntos. De nosotros puede brotar algo fecundo. Deja a esos. Vamos a hacer humanidad nueva. (32)

CONCLUSIONS

Aurora shows significant development for Dicenta as he returns to exploring the problems of class struggle by deliberately incorporating allegory into the play's structure. Immediately following its premeire in Madrid, a critic from *Revista Blanca* praises Dicenta's revolutionary theme in *Aurora*, yet criticizes the artistic value of the play:

> Como obra literaria, *Aurora* es brava, ruda, vibrante, naturalista. Como obra revolucionaria, es de lo más valiente y atrevido que se ha escrito para el teatro español. Como obra dramática, su construcción es anticuada, según demuestran las siguientes señas particulares: monólogos, discursos, intervención de cartas, visitas de amigos, medios artísticos y dramáticos en desuso entre los dramaturgos extranjeros que buscan la realidad y la imitan lo más que pueden. Los caracteres está [sic] bastante mal definidos; la obra parece escrita deprisa. (qtd. in Rubio Jiménez, *Ideología* 116)

Del Valle Ruiz, in his critical review of *Aurora*, also admires its sentiments while discrediting Dicenta's skill:

> Pero a falta de estas artimañas poco honestas, el Sr. Dicenta ha epelado, en cambio, a otro recurso no menos eficaz, aunque nada estético ni de buena ley, explotando con ansias de avaro la ignorancia popular y el gran filón de envidias, odios y rencores que tan revuelta y fuera de sí traen a la gente obrera más exaltada y revolucionaria. (561)

Manuel Bueno disagrees, claiming that Dicenta's attempt to incorporate symbolism into the play's structure in no way diminishes the value of the drama: "Creo que el Sr. Dicenta ha hecho una tentativa simbolista, sin abdicar de sus procedimientos dramáticos" (117). Contrary to Manuel Bueno's statement, *Aurora* is not a symbolist drama reminiscent of the symbolism movement that originated in France in the last half of the nineteenth century; instead, *Aurora* is a simple allegorical approach to the conflict between classes. Unfortunately, Dicenta's use of allegory undermines his social message, as Hall claims that even Dicenta recognized the weaknesses of *Aurora*:

> Dicenta must have realised that such an attempt to give social significance to Echegarayan melodrama by means of an almost mediaeval allegorical scheme did not meet the needs of the hour, for he turned to other dramatic forms during the next five years. (62)

It is difficult to assume that Dicenta avoided social drama for that reason alone, yet it is certain that the social aspects of the play are somewhat sacrificed by

Dicenta's use of allegory. *Aurora* treats many of the same issues from Dicenta's earlier social dramas, but from an entirely different perspective. In the creation of his first female protagonist, Dicenta explores the themes of child abuse, rape, and class struggle through the feminine perspective of the exploitation of the working class. Yet, instead of leaving Aurora in her lowly state of unhappiness and oppression, Dicenta allows fate to help Aurora escape and seek a life that corresponds to her high moral character. Although Dicenta's experiment of combining allegory and a social theme is not as well received by audiences as he would have hoped, his vision to explore contemporary social issues is realized as he introduces Spain's theater-going public to a female protagonist who voices the injustices that weigh so heavily upon his heart.

DE TREN A TREN (1902)

A few weeks following the Madrid premiere of *Aurora*, Dicenta's next play, *De tren a tren*, a one-act *comedia*, premiered on November 29, 1902 in the Teatro de la Alhambra, and according to González-Blanco, it received a "clamoroso éxito" (219). Presented by the same acting company, García Ortega, *De tren a tren* is a lighthearted humorous piece, reminiscent of Cervantes' *entremeses*.

PLOT

Aurelia, twenty-four years old, and her fifty-year old husband, Tadeo, have recently moved to a small town outside of Madrid. They are a wealthy couple, and they have brought with them from Madrid their maid, Escolástica, who has been with Aurelia her whole life. Aurelia and Tadeo argue incessantly, as she complains about having to move away from the city. Tadeo's jealousy and spendthrift nature is the motive behind his decision to move away from Madrid, for in the city, Aurelia was always busy with guests, parties, and going to plays while Tadeo was working. Tadeo, by moving, hoped to save money and to keep Aurelia home.

The play opens in a *hotelito* that they have rented, and the home is in an obvious state of dissarray. Tadeo is preparing to take a train into the city for business, as he tells Aurelia that they will be having a guest for dinner, a childhood friend of his whom he has not seen in twenty years. Aurelia is insistent that it is impossible to arrange the furniture, unpack, and have dinner ready before the train arrives at eight o'clock with Froilán, Tadeo's friend. Tadeo, however, ignores his wife, demanding that dinner be ready when he returns.

After Tadeo leaves, Aurelia sends Escolástica for food while she daydreams at the window. Across the street is another hotel where another couple is living, and Aurelia, during the long lonely days, has been spying on their activities. She has noticed that the lady is as young as she is, and the husband is older, like

Tadeo. Aurelia describes what she saw on the day she and Tadeo arrived and every day since. First, she noticed her neighbor hanging over the balcony, waving goodbye to her husband. Soon after, the lady entered her room and returned with a bright colored handkerchief, which she tied to one of the balcony railings. Since Aurelia's neighbor's curtains are nearly transparent, Aurelia was able to see shadows through them; one was the young lady, and the other was a young man. The young lovers embraced and made love while Aurelia lamented her loveless relationship with Tadeo.

After Escolástica leaves, Aurelia returns to the window, as she longs for a man her age, someone who would love her and understand her. She realizes that her neighbor has just put the signal out to her lover that her husband is gone. Aurelia describes what she sees, as the couple across the street embrace and kiss. Soon however, the couple seems to be nervous, as if frightened. The young man disappears, and Aurelia leaves the window. As she returns to her housework, she hears a gunshot. She assures herself that it must be a hunter since she is in the country.

Just at that moment, a young man enters her home through the window through which she was just staring. Horrified, Aurelia commands him to leave, yet he assures her that he is not there to hurt her, asking her for help. He is the young lady's lover from across the street, and after realizing that her husband had returned early, he was forced to escape and seek a hiding place in Aurelia's home. Carlos is his name, and as he begs Aurelia for help, she, full of jealousy, denies him, telling him that he must leave. Escolástica arrives home and convinces Aurelia to help the young gentleman.

Aurelia tells Carlos to hide in the bedroom, as she answers the door. The mayor and the young lady's husband from across the street march into Aurelia's home without explanation. Aurelia demands to know their purpose as they begin to search every room. Just as they are about to enter the room where Carlos is hidden, the bedroom door opens, and Carlos appears there, dressed in Tadeo's robe, slippers, and cap. He pretends to be Aurelia's husband, and angrily asks why he has been disturbed from his *siesta*. The two men claim that they are looking for a thief, yet after being questioned by Carlos about the details, they realize that they have no idea who they are looking for. They did not even see the man they call a thief, and since there is nothing missing, Carlos encourages them to drop the search.

As they are arguing, Tadeo returns home, much to the surprise of everyone there. Carlos continues to pretend to be Aurelia's husband, as he descredits Tadeo's claim to be the master of the house. Carlos discovers Tadeo's wallet in his robe pocket, and he uses it for identification to convince the mayor and the man from across the street. Aurelia, overcome with emotion, faints. The police arrive and arrest Tadeo, dragging him off as he screams at his wife. When Aurelia regains consciousness, she immediately plans to go to the jail to rescue

Tadeo, but Carlos detains her, begging her to wait just a little longer. At that moment, someone knocks on the door, and Carlos goes to answer it. It is Froilán, the expected dinner guest, who, upon seeing Carlos, is totally shocked, for Carlos is his son. After Carlos takes his father aside and explains the situation to him, Froilán leaves to get Tadeo. Upon their return, Tadeo lovingly chastizes Carlos, claiming that if he had known, he would have gone along with the act. The curtain closes as they prepare for dinner.

TECHNIQUE / IDEOLOGY

De tren a tren is unlike any of Dicenta's previous one-act dramas. *De tren a tren* is a short comical skit, designed to tempt audiences to uncontrollable laughter. The humorous elements are present throughout the dialogue, even in serious moments. For example, as Aurelia complains to Tadeo about her loneliness, expressing the suffering she endures living far from the city, Tadeo sarcastically replies: "¿Que no tienes con qué entretenerte?... ¡Será injusta! ¿Y las doce gallinas? ¿y el gallo? ¿y la cabra? ¿y el cerdo? ¿y yo? ¿Te parece poco?" (7). Aurelia responds, "No, hijo, demasiado. Estoy por decirte que todos esos animales me sobran" (7). Aurelia claims that she would be happier if Tadeo had allowed her mother to move with them, to keep her company. Tadeo scoffs at the idea: "¿Tu madre?... ¡Cá! De ninguna manera. Tu madre tiene un genio imposible. Cuando las personas llegan á cierta edad se hacen insoportables" (8). Aurelia answers: "Mi madre te lleva dos años" (8). Escolástica is especially humorous, in her insolent behavior towards Tadeo. After she brings Tadeo hot water for him to shave, he burns himself, screaming at Escolástica: "¡Condenada agua! ¡Cómo está!" (8). She responds mockingly: "A gusto del señor, hirviendo" (8). Later, Tadeo compares himself to his childhood friend, who he says has changed a lot over the years: "Está muy viejo el pobre; con todo el pelo blanco. Yo en cambio, ya ves. *(Con ademán presuntuoso.)*" (13). Escolástica responds "*Con seriedad cómica*": "¡Usted lo tiene más negro cada día!" (13).

Although full of humor, *De tren a tren* is not without the social commentary typical of Dicenta. As in *Aurora*, Dicenta continues to argue against arranged marriages. Although she is unhappy with Tadeo, Aurelia explains to Escolástica her great fortune in having married a man so wealthy: "Todas las mujeres soñamos con un querubín que nos lleve á la Vicaria. Menos mal, si las que nacen pobres, como yo, alcanzan la suerte de despertarse al lado de un tadeo cualquiera" (9). Later, however, Aurelia, overcome with self-pity as she watches the young couple in love across the street, blames her mother for her unhappiness:

> ¡Felicidad! Para las madres, cuando se trata de sus hijas, ¡qué fácil resulta encontrarla! "Ahí tienes un hombre viejo, pero rico; insoportable, pero trabajador; sin ninguna delicadeza en el alma, pero con algunas acciones del

Banco en la cartera" dicen las madres. "Con él disfrutarás comodidades, rentas, buena mesa, buena casa, buenos vestidos... ¿Qué más necesitas para ser feliz?" Nada; podía contestarles una, la felicidad. ¡La felicidad! No la que me ha proporiconado mi madre; la otra, la que olvidan las madres cuando se hacen viejas. (16)

Carlos, not knowing that Aurelia has married an older man, guesses that Aurelia is married to someone like himself:

Casada con un hombre joven, amante, lleno de pasión, de ilusiones y de ventura.... Lo contrario sería una imbecilidad de la suerte.... Usted que goza la dicha de un matrimonio, *matrimonio*, compadézcase de una mujer infortunada, sometida á las impertinencias y malos tratos de un viejo ridículo. (21)

Carlos is refering to his lover, who, like Aurelia, is married to a much older man.

Dicenta indicates that many women who suffer the same fate as Aurelia have no choice but to seek their happiness elsewhere, perhaps in affairs with young men like Carlos. Carlos truly loves the unfortunate young woman from across the street, and when informed by his father, Froilán, that his lover is promiscuous, Carlos begs Aurelia to forgive him for having placed her in such a compromising position for someone as unworthy as Angelita, his lover: "¡Conque Angelita ha pasado el Guadalquivir muchas veces! ¡Y por una dama tan... fluvial he comprometido yo á usted, Aurelia!" (38). Aurelia laughs at him, and soon, Carlos, who seems to have recovered completely from his broken heart, flirts shamelessly with Aurelia. The final words of the drama insinuate a possible affair between Aurelia and Carlos:

CARLOS:	*(A Aurelia.)* ¿Me perdona usted?
AURELIA:	Sí.
CARLOS:	¿De veras?
AURELIA:	De veras.
CARLOS:	*(Cogiendo la mano de Aurelia y besándola.)* ¡Gracias, muchas gracias!
ESCOLÁSTICA:	¡Cuidado! ¡Pueden verse las sombras desde el hotel de enfrente! (40)

CONCLUSIONS

De tren a tren is one of Dicenta's most unique dramas. It is full of humor, yet it still maintains a slight thesis without compromising the comical value. The title warns husbands that a lot can happen from train to train, and that perhaps husbands should make a stronger effort to make their young wives happy.

Unfortunately, those who have studied Dicenta's plays have consistently ignored *De tren a tren*, not only missing a truly entertaining drama but also failing to recognize the depth of Dicenta's versatility on the stage as he successfully includes a thesis in a lighthearted drama.

PA MÍ QUE NIEVA (1904)

Two years passed before Dicenta's next play, ¡*Pa mí que nieva!*, another original contribution to the *teatro por horas*, premiered in the Teatro Moderno on December 12, 1904. Dicenta describes it as a *modismo* written in two *cuadros*, "trazados sin los acres rasgos de los madrileñistas de oficio" (González-Blanco 220). González-Blanco describes the origin of the style utilized in ¡*Pa mí que nieva!*:

> ¡*Pa mí que nieva!* podría llamarse proverbio dramático, si en nuestro país hubiera gozado de mucha boga ese género que en Francia nació en la dulzona ñoñería del pensionado de Saint-Cyr bajo el patrocinio de Mdme. Maintenon, la gran educadora, por los años de 1750; modificóse con Carmontel de 1768 a 1781, perfeccionóse gracias al talento de Theodore Heclerc [sic], que escribió hacia 1823 a 30, juguetes muy lindos y llegó a su definitiva cumbre de exquisitez con el gran poeta Alfredo de Musset, autor de tan lindos proverbios como *On ne badine pas avec l'amour*... (261)

PLOT

Pepiya and Pepiya, teenagers in love in the slums of Madrid, lead difficult lives; they are always hungry and cold, and their families abuse them rather than love them. The first *cuadro* depicts the pair cuddling close together to fight the cold as they share a cup of coffee and express little hope for the future. At the beginning of the second *cuadro*, twenty years have passed since the end of the first *cuadro*. Pepiya, who is now Doña Josefa, is a wealthy prostitute, and Pepiyo, now Don José, has returned from abroad where he made a fortune. They immediately recognize each other and tell what has transpired since they saw each other last.

TECHNIQUE / IDEOLOGY

¡*Pa mí que nieva!* is virtually without any action, yet there are many small realistic details that reflect the situation of the poor people living in Madrid's *barrios bajos*. Of particular interest, is the opening scene of an authentic *cuadro de costumbres*, in which an old waiter from the nearby café comes onto the stage screaming: "¡Calienteee!... ¡Moka puro!... ¡Calienteee!" (5). Dicenta describes the Tío's appearance in the stage directions: "con la cesta al brazo y la cafetera de metal en una de sus manos. Será hombre viejo y mal vestido, abrigado con una bufanda" (5). The spectator witnesses a snowy café scene, complete with a beggar, in the poorest neighborhood of Madrid.

Pepiya's description of her daily life is reminiscent of Aurora's narration of her sad past. After earning very little money, Pepiya returns home to her cruel father and hardhearted stepmother to give them what she has earned. Like Aurora, Pepiya, who is only fourteen years old, is forced to work because her family cannot survive on the meager income of her parents. Through Pepiya's description of her parents' cruel treatment of her, Dicenta condemns the child abuse that is common among the lower classes:

> A las once he *acabao* la venta del papel—cuatro pesetas entre *tó*—y he *tirao pa* casa. Mi padre estaba en la esquina, unto á la *tasca* del Mellizo, borracho como una cuba y con ganas de *soplar entoavía*. M'aguardaba, y, claro: ¿qué dineros traes? Vamos, padre, tome usté un perro grande *pa moniaco* y váyase a dormir.—¡Dormir!... ¡Dormir!... ¿Qué dinero traes?—Pero...—¡Pero que vengan!—¡Que no!—¡Que si! Y ¡zas! ¡zas! dos leñazos. Y yo a soltar las cuatro pesetas y él á meterse en *cá* del Mellizo, sonando los *parnés* y llamándome... casi *toas* las letras de la cartilla.... Mejor que la otra. Porque al fin mi padre *quié* el dinero que gano yo *pa* beber vino él; y la otra lo *quié pa* que beba vino otro... que no es mi padre.... Mi *madastra*, cuando se enteró de que yo llegaba de vacío, me cogió por un brazo, me empujó por la escalera *alante*; me gritó: "Aquí, bribona, como en las *posás*, el que no paga no entra." Y cerró la puerta; y se *metió pa* dentro llamándome *toas* las letras que se había *dejao* mi padre en el tintero. (9-10)

As is obvious in Pepiya's speech, Dicenta uses dialogue to full advantage, reflecting the uneducated manner of speaking of both Pepiya and Pepiyo. Pepiyo complains to the waiter that he is not able to get work, explaining:

> *D'oficio* no *m'han enseñao*; *pa* servir no tengo yo *carater*... ni ropa; *pa* entrar en la Villa hacen falta recomendaciones; y a mí, ¡como no me *recominde usté* que es la única *presona* con tienda abierta que conozco! (7)

Dicenta concentrates on the very real social problem of poverty, and the inability of those who suffer from it to overcome their fate without resorting to exteme measures. Charles E. Chapman comments on this aspect of early twentieth-century Spanish society:

> Spaniards do not expect to rise from poverty to great wealth, as men do in America, for so few of them rarely can, under the existing system, that there is not the stimulus of other men's successes to spur them on. The more

ambitious of the poor and moderately well-to-do, therefore, make their way to the Americas. (523)

Pepiyo, who has obtained his wealth abroad after much hard work, and Pepiya, who prostituted herself in order to survive, both lament the manner in which they have risen to their current status. Pepiya (Doña Josefa) complains about having to "devolver caricias que asquean y abrazar cuerpos que repugnan" (25), yet there is no real attack on prostitution.

Neither of the two, after succesfully achieving financial stability, has lost the goodness that characterized them both when they were of an inferior economic class. The fact that neither Pepiyo nor Pepiya changes significantly in over twenty years adds to the dramatic unity. Although their speech has changed to match their new economic status, when they sit down to reminisce about the past, they both revert to their earlier manner of speaking:

> JOSEFA: Ahora hablemos.
> JOSÉ: ¿Como hablamos ahora ó como hablábamos entonces?
> JOSEFA: Como entonces.
> JOSÉ: Pues entonces oye, Pepiya. ¡Estás más *salá* que la Virgen! (24)

The characters' awareness of their dialect represents a new dimension for Dicenta, unlike Aurora, who did not realize that her speech was affected by her emotions and her present company. Further adding to the dramatic unity of the static nature of the protagonists' personalities is the snow swirling on the two lovers at the end of each *cuadro*. The snow shows that very little has changed over the twenty years that separated Pepiyo and Pepiya.

CONCLUSIONS

¡Pa mí que nieva! is a pleasant, entertaining, well-unified play with realistic elements that demonstrates an important fact about the mobility of Spanish society during Dicenta's lifetime. This is not the first time that Dicenta has condemned poverty and the abuse suffered by those who are poor, yet in this short two-*cuadro* drama Dicenta pushes a new theme, that of self-acceptance. As in *De tren a tren*, *¡Pa mí que nieva!* continues to indcate Dicenta's development as a dramatist in his great skill and versatility in his attempt to embrace other styles of theater besides the social drama for which he became so famous.

JUAN FRANCISCO (1904)

Three weeks following the premiere of *¡Pa mí que nieva!*, Dicenta's next play, *Juan Francisco*, premiered in the Teatro Price on December 22, 1904. *Juan Francisco*, performed with the music of Ruperto Chapí, is a lyrical drama that combines elements of Romanticism with a thesis. Set in a small fishing village on the *costa de Levante*, Dicenta's newest *zarzuela* revolves around the traditional Romantic themes of unrequited love, vengeance, and honor.

PLOT

Juan Francisco is in love with Anita, Pedro's daughter, but because he killed Anita's brother years earlier in self-defense, the two lovers are kept apart. Pedro is an older well-respected citizen of the community, a retired fisherman who now owns a fleet of small boats that are manned regularly by the men of the village. Juan Francisco, like many of the fishermen, spends his life on the sea because he cannot bear to be home knowing that he will never have Anita for his wife. Pedro is unforgiving in the murder of his son, and Anita is torn between her duty to her father and her love for Juan Francisco.

Gaspar, another man who owns a fleet of boats, is a ruthless and calculating person who is determined to have Anita for his wife. After being rejected by Anita, Gaspar resolves to seek vengeance against her and her family. When he learns that Pedro has approved an increase in his fishermen's shares in the catch, Gaspar tries to make Pedro change his mind, without success. Infuriated, Gaspar decides to ruin Pedro financially.

When the boats come in the next day, Gaspar offers the fishermen double what Pedro offers them, knowing that Pedro can not match his offer. His purpose is thwarted when Juan Francisco arrives and discovers what has happened. Juan Francisco explains Gaspar's intent to the fishermen and asks them whom they will support. They unananimously support Pedro, for he has always been kind to them. Since Gaspar failed at this attempt to ruin Pedro, he turns his attentions again to Anita. Gaspar threatens Pedro by claiming his intentions are no longer to marry Anita, but rather, to dishonor her. Pedro, too old and weak to challenge Gaspar, laments his son's death, for he feels that if his son were alive, he would punish Gaspar. Juan Francisco, passing by, hears Pedro's lament, and without hesitation, he attacks Gaspar and kills him. Pedro, in gratitude to Juan Francisco for his protection, considers the debt of honor to his family erased. Pedro encourages Juan Francisco to marry Anita. The play closes as Juan Francisco goes back to the sea, promising to return for Anita very soon.

TECHNIQUE
ROMANTIC CHARACTERISTICS

The Romantic influences that pervaded Dicenta's early productions and especially his *zarzuelas* remain dominant in *Juan Francisco*. It is written entirely in verse; the unrequited love between Anita and Juan Francisco is the primary theme; the overexagerated and melodramatic is paramount; blood is spilled on the stage; the hero is mysterious and passionate; more than one-third of the drama takes place under moonlight; and the themes of honor and vengeance dominate the action.

Anita and Juan Francisco constantly express their great suffering, typical of Romantic heroes. Anita's first words are purely Romantic:

> ¡Ay de mí, que ya nunca mis penas
> pueden esperanza, ni alivio tener!
> ¡Ay de mí, que perdí en este mundo
> amor y ventura, perdiéndole á él!
> Juan Francisco, alma de mis sentidos,
> mi sola gloria, mi sola fe,
> ¡Nunca dichosa caeré en tus brazos!
> ¡Nunca en mis brazos te estrecharé!
> Esta vida, Dios mío, no es vida.
> Sin él, ¿qué me resta? sufrir y llorar;
> dejar que en silencio mis lágrimas corran,
> Sin que él con sus labios las venga á besar. (13)

The impossibility of the consummation of their love is the dominant theme throughout the play, as both Anita and Juan Francisco lament their unrequited love. Anita has accepted her fate, although unhappily: "yo tampoco espero en nada, ni nada quiero de nadie" (20). The *coro* often reflects the sad situation of the two lovers in song:

> El se aleja y ella llora.
> ¡Qué infelices son los dos!
> Adorándose imposibles
> para siempre con su amor. (33)

Juan Francisco, like Anita, has accepted his fate and chooses to suffer far away from his beloved:

> Dejadme sólo
> con mi amargura.
> Con mi angustia y mis dolores
> mi alma quiere estar á solas.
> Con el mar y con las olas
> sobre mi alma quiero estar.
> Mis ojos nunca podrán mirarla,
> dejadme sólo con mi pesar. (34)

Unlike other Romantic dramas in which the couple only attains freedom to love in the hereafter, *Juan Francisco* ends on a positive note with Anita and Juan

Francisco free to pursue their love.

Also adding to the Romantic nature of *Juan Francisco* is the theme of vengeance. Gaspar is constantly plotting his method of revenge, manipulating anyone he can in order to bring dishonor and financial ruin to Pedro and Anita, claiming: "que ya basta / de permitir que me hieran / esa moza y ese viejo / en el querer y en la hacienda" (50). Even after failing several times, Gaspar does not give up: "juro que he de vengarme" (76). His final attempt to dishonor Anita forces Juan Francisco to act with vengeance to protect Anita's honor: "¿Por mi culpa vengar / no puede á su padre aquél? / Pues yo hago las veces de él / y me pongo en su lugar" (86).

HUMOROUS ASPECTS

Although a moving lyrical drama full of Romantic characteristics, *Juan Francisco* provides much comic relief in the minor subplots that revolve around the main action. Like Varillas in *La cortijera*, Pascual, who is only sixteen years old, is characterized by his clownish nature. When he first appears on stage, Pascual mocks the young ladies who have been singing about their beloved fishermen; the scene is extremely comical:

> PASCUAL: *(Cantando con la mayor desafinación posible.)*
> Mi amante es marinero
> y me ha *ofrecío*
> ayer tarde un *pescao*
> que no he *querío*.
> No lo he *querío*.
> *(Pescadora 1.ª coge la cuchara llena de arroz y se la mete en la boca á Pascual.)*
> *(Con voz atragantada.)*
> ¿Qué haces?
> PESC. 1.ª ¡Ponerte un bozal
> *Pa* que calle, sinvergüenza!
> PASCUAL: ¡Ya ha *pasao*!
> *(Luego de hacer el movimento de un pavo que se traga una nuez.)*

Pascual's father died years earlier, and his mother, Curra, hopes to train him to be just like his father, who was a smuggler. In order to do so, she teaches Pascual how to use a gun. What follows is a hilarious scene in which the two clownish characters practice loading a gun while Curra sings the instructions to her son:

> Por este boquete
> se mete el cartucho,

> se aprieta unas miajas,
> se vuelve á cerrar;
> se monta el gatillo,
> se da gusto al dedo,
> y ya ves qué fácil
> resulta tirar. (26)

After Pascual repeats the chorus, he accidentally pulls the trigger, and both he and his mother fall to the floor. Everyone believes them both to be dead until they are examined and no injuries are found. Pascual raises his head slightly and with a "voz doliente," he asks: "Diga usté, ¿quién es el muerto, Sargento, mi madre ó yo?" (28). Sargento answers sarcastically: "De miedo, tú" (28).

As the day approaches when Pascual must begin his new life as a smuggler, he becomes increasingly more melodramatic about his fate. He is in love with María, and he fears that he will die before he returns. Pascual asks María to add six *padre nuestros* to her prayers because he leaves in the morning. Pascual's speech is melodramatic and overexagerated, as he tells his young girlfriend that he may die before he returns:

> Ya *toíco* está dispuesto:
> la escopeta, los cartuchos...
> el falucho... y el entierro....
> Vas á ser viuda
> in *pártibus in fidelium*. (38)

Although they are not married, Pascual refers to her as a "viuda," further adding to the comic nature of the story.

Pascual's mother, Curra, constantly rejects Sargento's advances, allowing for more humorous scenes between the two of them. Sargento, like Pascual, overexaggerates his emotions, expressing repeatedly the Romantic "¡Ay!" (10). Curra, who is not impressed, asks Sargento: "¿Le duele á *osté argo*?" (10). Sargento explains to Curra that his soul aches because she will not pay attention to him. Later, after the incident where both Curra and Pascual think they have been shot, Sargento grabs the cup from which Curra has taken a sip of water and drinks it, saying: "También estoy / *asustao*. Si usté se muere, / ¿con quién me casaba yo?" (28). Sargento continues to flirt with Curra whenever possible, and although totally unimportant to the plot, the teasing relationship between Curra and Sargento adds humor to an otherwise heavy theme.

IDEOLOGY

Unlike any of his previous *zarzuelas*, *Juan Francisco* represents a new approach for Dicenta. He combines humor and Romantic elements with an obvious thesis, an odd combination for a lyrical drama. The thesis is very similar to the one in *El señor feudal* in which Dicenta condemns those who have gained power and who use that power to harm others beneath them. Gaspar, who is exactly like Roque from *El señor feudal*, is heartless, cruel, and selfish. Pedro, however, is the opposite. Although he used to be a poor fisherman, now that he is in charge of a fleet of boats, Pedro does not use his new power to exploit those who work for him. Pedro represents the honorable middle class, and unlike Roque and Gaspar, Pedro remembers his lowly heritage and treats the fishermen fairly, even offering to raise their pay. When Gaspar tries to outbid Pedro's offer to the fishermen for their catch, the fishermen, although tempted by the higher pay, choose to accept Pedro's lower offer because of their great respect for Pedro:

> *(A Gaspar.)*
> El tío Pedro para nosotros
> siempre fué un padre, siempre alivió
> con su cariño, con su dinero
> las desventuras del pescador....
> *(Al tío Pedro.)*
> De nuestra pesca tome la parte
> que necesite; toda es de usté....
> ¡Tómela! Los marineros
> no apetecen los dineros
> que por venganza se dan.
> No quedará abandonado
> quien nunca nos ha dejado
> sin consuelos y sin pan. (76)

The fishermen represent the opposite attitude to that of Jaime (*El señor feudal*), who, filled with hatred for both Roque and Carlos for having abused his family and dishonored his sister, reacts with extreme violence, murdering Carlos. The fishermen love and respect Pedro. If Roque and Carlos had remembered their lowly heritage and treated their workers more fairly, perhaps Jaime and the other farmers would have honored them in the same way the fishermen honor Pedro.

CONCLUSIONS

Juan Francisco is one of Dicenta's weakest dramas, most likely because of his attempt to incorporate a thesis into the plot of a musical piece. As a *zarzuela*, *Juan Francisco* is lyrical and captivating, especially in the humorous scenes, but the unnaturalness of insinuating a social commentary into a drama intended solely for entertainment proves *Juan Francisco* inferior to Dicenta's other *zarzuelas*.[1] The only critic to mention its existence is González-Blanco, who simply states that it premiered with "escaso éxito" (260).

LA CONVERSIÓN DE MAÑARA (1905)

Another year passed before Dicenta's next drama, a *comedia*, premiered in Málaga. On December 2, 1905, *La conversión de Mañara* was first presented at the Teatro Cervantes de Málaga by the Miguel Muñoz company. It is genuinely Romantic in its new treatment of the Don Juan legend, and as noted by González-Blanco: "parece como que Dicenta vuelve a su viejo cauce de drama romántico" (220).

PLOT

It is the night before Inés is to be forced into marriage to a coldhearted older man, Don Rodrigo, who is also her guardian as well. Don Rodrigo has threatened to send Inés to live in a convent if she disobeys his wish to marry her. Don Juan, Inés's lover, plans to rescue her, but he is confronted by Don Rodrigo's servant, Anselmo. Anselmo, who was put in charge of guarding Inés, is stabbed and killed by Don Juan. Don Rodrigo rushes to the scene, and he too is murdered by Inés's young lover. By killing Don Rodrigo, Don Juan avenges two wrongs: first, the cruelty to Inés, and second, an incident from the past. Don Juan has recently learned that before he was born, Don Rodrigo played a part in the seduction of his mother, which resulted in his conception. Don Rodrigo pretended to be a priest and performed a false marriage for Don Juan's mother and Don Miguel de Mañara, who is Don Juan's father. Don Miguel soon abandoned his false bride and newborn son, leaving her dishonored and denying her and his only son his name.

After Don Rodrigo's murder, Inés seeks refuge in Seville, a city Don Juan selected for a specific purpose. He knows that Don Miguel lives in Seville, and he hopes to confront his father and demand that he give him his name, so that Don Juan can in turn give it to Inés in marriage. When Inés arrives in Seville, however, Don Miguel, who is forty-three years old, falls in love with her charm and beauty. Don Miguel attempts to seduce Inés, and when she rejects him, he is shocked. He is unaccustomed to failure in matters of love, and he resolves to force her to be his.

At midnight, under Inés's balcony, father and son come face to face, yet both are hidden behind masks. Don Juan challenges Don Miguel, and just before they begin to duel, Don Miguel suggests that they remove their masks. Don

---

[1] Dicenta reworks *Juan Francisco* four years later in *Entre rocas* (1908), in which he successfully eliminates the heavy thesis and minimizes the Romantic elements as he shortens the length from three acts to one act. See page 215.

Miguel is overcome with both pride and shame, for he recognizes that his son is a better man than he. Don Juan is also deeply affected upon recognizing his father. Don Miguel begs Inés and his son to forgive him, and he graciously gives Don Juan his name, telling his son to give it to the honorable Inés in marriage.

SOURCES

The story of a libertine who, after many years of seducing women, comes to terms with his misconduct and is made to atone for his sins is a central theme in Christian tradition as well as Spanish literature. Tirso de Molina's *El burlador de Sevilla* (1630) is the first formal literary treatment of the story, bringing the legendary hero, Don Juan, to world-wide attention. Since Tirso de Molina's famous Don Juan first appeared on stage, the legend has been the subject of endless treatments in many countries and in many forms of art: Molière, *Don Juan; ou, Le festine de pierre* (1665); Sir Aston Cokayne, *The Tragedy of Ovid* (1669); Thomas Shadwell, *The Libertine* (1676); Wolfgang Amadeus Mozart, *Don Giovanni* (1787); Lord Byron, *Don Juan* (1819-1824); Prosper Mérimée, *Les âmes du purgatoire* (1834); Alexandre Dumas, *Don Juan de Marana ou la chute d'un ange* (1836); Richard Strauss, *Don Juan* (1889); and George Bernard Shaw, *Man and Superman* (1903).

In Spain, the Don Juan legend also appears repeatedly in literature, and one treatment of the legendary hero dates before Tirso de Molina's famous *El burlador de Sevilla*; Antonio de Torquemada's *Jardín de flores curiosas* (1570) is about a student named Lisardo who witnesses his own funeral and, after being led on a mysterious journey, repents and converts before his actual death. The story of Miguel de Mañara was recorded in 1680 by Juan de Cárdenas in his *Breve relación de la muerte, vida y virtudes de Miguel de Mañara*, in which the protagonist also views his own funeral procession and repents before his death. Moreto's play, *San Franco de Sena* (1654) includes the motif of the cross and the statue of Christ and ends with Franco's conversion and repentance. José de Espronceda's *El estudiante de Salamanca* (1840) treats a Don Juan figure as the protagonist, Félix de Montemar who, like Miguel de Mañara and Lisardo, also witnesses his own funeral, but instead of redemption, Félix dies a horrible death never having discovered the answer to his existential ponderings.

TECHNIQUE

While Dicenta certainly borrows from a rich tradition, he adds an entirely new perspective in Don Miguel de Mañara's redemption through parental love. The concept of having Don Miguel compete against his own son, Don Juan, is Dicenta's idea. In *La conversión de Mañara*, Dicenta successfully adheres to the Romantic tradition surrounding the Don Juan legend. It is full of action, from the beginning until the end, and its main theme revolves around unrequited love and honor. The mysterious night scenes performed with very little light at the stroke of midnight, the constant presence of masked figures, the time dedicated to elaborate sword-play, the motif of vengeance on the part of Don Juan and Don Miguel, the unbridled emotion, the violence and murder on stage, and the positive influence of Christianity are all attributes of Romantic drama. There is a scene that is hauntingly similar to a scene in *Honra y vida* (1891) in which Inés, desperate after having been threatened by Don Miguel, cries out to the Virgin Mary:

> ¡Señora, amparadme vos!
> ¡Virgen del cielo, valedme!
> ¡Contra ese hombre defendedme,
> bendita madre de Dios! (57)

In *Honra y vida*, Inés (same name) also begs the Virgin for help after the king threatens to take her by force. Both women's prayers are answered, for as soon as they throw themselves on their knees in front of the statue of the Virgin, help arrives in the form of their true love. For Inés of *Honra y vida*, however, the solution to their situation results in her death; Don Juan's Inés, on the other hand, trusts that her lover will be able to defend her, knowing that he had successfully done so earlier with Don Rodrigo, who had also threatened her.

IDEOLOGY

Although *La conversión de Mañara* was intended primarily for entertainment, there is a hint of a thesis in Dicenta's positive end to the *comedia*. This is not the first time that Dicenta focuses on what he considers to be the right attitude of a father towards his child. Fernando (*El suicidio de Werther*, 1888) and his mother were abandoned by his father, and since he was considered illegitimate, the resultant prejudice suffered by Fernando plagued him throughout his life and ruined his career as an artist. In *La conversión de Mañara*, Don Miguel's powerful words, "Juan, toma mi nombre / y dáselo á esta mujer," represent his recognition of his duty as a father, and for Dicenta, this is a father's most sacred obligation (79)[2]. Earlier in the *comedia*, Don Juan describes to Inés his painful past and his deepest desire, also reflecting Dicenta's ideology:

> Un infame seductor,
> justicia es que así le llame,
> aunque es mi padre, un infame
> robó á mi madre el honor....

---

[2] For further evidence of Dicenta's opinion of a father's duty, see *El crimen de ayer* (1908) on page 206.

> Mi anhelo está en que aquel hombre
> devuelva á mi madre nombre,
> fama y honra. (17)

CONCLUSIONS

There is no information available concerning the premiere of *La conversión de Mañara*, Dicenta's first full-length *comedia*. It is one of the few genuinely Romantic plays Dicenta has written, and together with *Honra y vida* (1891), *El Duque de Gandía* (1894), and *Raimundo Lulio* (1902), *La conversión de Mañara* represents a distinctly different side to Dicenta's talent, as he seeks to entertain his audiences with Romantic themes by resuscitating a legendary figure of Spain's past. As he did in the earlier dramas, Dicenta faithfully adheres to the ideas that are borrowed while skillfully adding his own twist to the story. The lyrical verse, the air of mystery and suspense, and the abundance of action on stage all appeal to the audience's senses, and Dicenta's proficient handling of an age-old story is a new and original contribution to the Don Juan cycle.

EL VALS DE LAS SOMBRAS (1906)

Dicenta's next play, *El vals de las sombras*, premiered in the Teatro Eslava on March 8, 1906. *El vals de las sombras* is a *juguete cómico lírico* that Dicenta reworked from his original, *De tren a tren* (1902), and although completely identical to the original in plot, the inclusion of music and verse in the newer version invests it with an even lighter tone than that of the humorous *De tren a tren*.[3] The music, provided by Quinito Valverde, is not present throughout the drama, instead, only certain scenes are sung, and the remainder of the drama remains true to the original.

TECHNIQUE

The opening scene is musical, as Tadeo, Aurelia, and Escolástica argue back and forth about preparing Tadeo's hot water for his shave. As in the original, Escolástica is slow to bring her master the water, and her sarcastic nature is still blatantly evident in her response to Tadeo's reprimands:

> ¿Cree usté que es culpa mía,
> señor, que el agua al salir
> de la fuente salga fría
> y no eche al momento á hervir? (6)

Tadeo burns himself with the boiling water, and the scene ends as he screams in

---

[3] For a complete plot summary of *El vals de las sombras* see page 157.

pain, Escolástica laughs heartily at his misfortune, and Aurelia tries unsuccesfully to quiet Escolástica's laughter:

ESCOLÁSTICA:	¡Ja, ja, ja, ja!
AURELIA:	¡Cállate, cállate ya!
TADEO:	¡Ah, ah, ah, ah!
ESCOLÁSTICA:	¡Ja, ja, ja, ja!
AURELIA:	¡Cállate, cállate ya! (7)

The next musical scene is as Aurelia describes the "vals de las sombras" from across the street. Aurelia alternates between singing her lines and reciting them, and there is very little difference from the same scene in *De tren a tren*. The following scene, in which Carlos appears, is musical, but rather than rewriting the scene into verse form, Dicenta changes nothing from the original, as the actors sing the lines that were spoken in *De tren a tren*. The most lyrical scene is the exchange between the mayor and Marcos, the man from across the street, as they demand to search the entire home for the adulterer:

MARCOS:	Yo soy un hombre atroz,
	feroz;
	usted no sabe
	lo que soy yo;
	busquemos al adúltero,
	aquí tiene que estar;
	recorramos esta casa
	desde el patio hasta el desv'an.
	por arriba, por abajo,
	por delante y por detrás.
CORO:	Por arriba, por abajo,
	por delante y por detrás.
MARCOS:	Y si al infame logro encontrar,
	yo lo cojo, yo lo rajo
	por arriba, por abajo,
	por delante y por atrás. (22-23)

CONCLUSIONS

The newer version of *De tren a tren* remains true to the original while adding lighthearted music to enhance the comic nature of the play. *El vals de las sombras* is a whimsical piece intended for entertainment purposes only, and it represents Dicenta's versatile talent on stage as he manipulates what was once prose into verse.

AMOR DE ARTISTAS (1906)

Dicenta's next play, *Amor de artistas*, premiered in Seville on May 14, 1906 in the Teatro de San Fernando de Sevilla. Written entirely in prose, *Amor de artistas* is a four-act *comedia* that focuses on the bohemian world Dicenta knew so well, as he explores the lives and loves of a company of actors and one budding playwright.

Plot

The play opens in the home of Amelia, a prominent actress, as the acting company is waiting for the arrival of Emilio Rojas, a successful playwright who plans to read his most recent play to the group. Emilio's newest *comedia* has been written especially for Amelia, and also present at the reading are a number of individuals of the theatrical world and its patrons. As they wait for Emilio to arrive, the group's conversations revolve around the love affair between Emilio and Teresa, his devoted companion and mistress. Emilio arrives, and the curtain falls as he begins to read his latest drama aloud to his friends.

The *comedia* is a big success, and the actors and the dramatist are given a standing ovation at its premiere. After the final curtain call, Amelia and Emilio find themselves alone, and their heightened emotional state makes them both imagine that they have fallen in love with each other. Emilio abandons his lover, Teresa, and he and Amelia begin living together; however, it is soon obvious that the two do not get along well at all, as others describe the constant fights that they have. After a long argument in which nothing is resolved between Amelia and Emilio, the Duke of Martoria arrives to invite Amelia on a lunch excursion to France by automobile. Not caring that Emilio will be greatly angered if she goes, Amelia agrees to accompany Martoria and his friends. When Emilio finds out, he forbids Amelia to go and challenges Martoria to a duel. While the men are gone, Amelia realizes the mistake she has made and admits that Teresa is Emilio's one true love. Emilio returns from the duel wounded, but not fatally. And he returns to Teresa, while Amelia joins Martoria.

Technique

Although the plot is weak in *Amor de artistas*, the subject matter has certain realistic aspects which constitute the play's main interest. None of the characters, not even Emilio and Amelia, is individualized; instead Dicenta presents a generalized concept of artistic people, especially playwrights and actors, as he knew all of this information as a firsthand witness. The extreme emotions felt by the artists, jealousy of each other, nervousness during the performance, the relief afterwards, the overheated passion, and bitter hatred, all represent a realistic picture of the artists' world. While talking with Martoria, who claims he does not understand, Amelia describes the effect the success of

Emilio's premiere has on the dramatist and the actors:

> Es natural. Usted no es artista. Para Emilio esta noche no existe, no puede, no debe existir en el mundo más que una cosa, su comedia.... Con ella juega su reputación, su talento, su aureola de autor insigne. En ella están la victoria sobre sus rivales, los aplausos del público. Los aplausos del público son para nosotros lo primero.... porque en ellos, en esos aplausos conquistados, arrancados por fuerza, conseguidos á costa de nuestra sangre, de nuestra salud, de nuestra dicha muchas veces, está nuestra superioridad sobre las otras criaturas. (33)

The backstage perspective of the nervous players and the excited dramatist is very realistic, and for Dicenta's contemporary audiences, it allowed them a revealing glimpse behind the scenes. Emilio and the actors pace around Amelia's dressing room in an obvious state of anxiety, as Emilio claims: "¡Ay! Si el público supiera lo que sufre un autor la noche del estreno, no se silbaba una obra" (29). Emilio believes his suffering is much greater than that of the actors: "Nosotros tenemos que aguardar cruzados de brazos, con pasividad desesperante. Ustedes no; ustedes salen al escenario, pelean con el público cuerpo á cuerpo" (30). Amelia agrees:

> Yo temo al público antes de salir á escena. Después no. Cuando estamos frente á frente le desafío; aunque se irrite no me asusta. Solo pienso, solo quiero una cosa: domarle, esclavizarle, hacerle aplaudir. (30)

After the play is over, the public receives the playwright and the actors with great enthusiasm, much to the relief of the company and Emilio. Dicenta describes the scene in detail in the stage directions:

> Procúrese que esta escena dé idea del aspecto que ofrecen los saloncillos de teatros después de un éxito. Los personajes secundarios pueden entrar, salir, renovarse, en una palabra; unos abrazarán á Emilio, otros estrecharán su mano ó la de Amelia; cuáles hablarán aparte. En fin, ya está dicho. El saloncillo de un teatro después de un éxito. (42)

The realism in this scene is commendable, especially in Dicenta's tongue-in-cheek criticism of the way people form their opinions:

LA DE PEÑAGRÍS:	¡Qué obra! Qué obra, ¿eh? *(Dirigiéndose al Personaje primero, un sietemesino muy peripuesto.) (Aparte.)* ¿A tí, qué te parece?
PERSONAJE 1º	Hombre, yo he aplaudido; pero hasta ver qué

dicen
mañana los periódicos, no tengo opinión. (42)

Other realistic elements are placed throughout the play to remind the spectator of the contemporary reality of the situation. The setting is particularly realistic, as Dicenta describes the nature of the coastal resort in San Sebastián. The occasional reference to automobiles, a rarity in 1906 Spain, is significant in the portrayal of the wealthy theatergoers that attend Emilio's premiere. This is the first time Dicenta utilizes such a symbol of mechanized prosperity, and it is interesting to note that the automobile is used to leave Spain by driving over the French border to Biarritz, a French resort popular among the wealthy.

IDEOLOGY

Although there is no apparent thesis, nor is there any reference to class struggle or other social problems that were presented in Dicenta's earlier realistic dramas, *Amor de artistas* allows Dicenta the opportunity to present a detailed theory of what constitutes an artist. In Act I, the dialogue is dominated by Antonio, one of Amelia's fellow actors, who lectures on psychological truths about artists. He feels that, although they may inspire love, artists are incapable of feeling it deeply: "los artistas... son incapaces de ser felices en amor, y de hacer feliz á quien les ame" (18-19). After Amelia confronts Antonio, he questions her:

> ¿Sacrificaría usted por nadie su orgullo de actriz? ¿su vandiad de comedianta? ¿sus extravagancias é independencias de criatura excepcional que á nadie necesita y por consiguiente, no se sujeta á nadie? ¿Dejaría usted de vivir en exhibición permanente por evitar á su amante disgustos? ¿Inmolaría usted en obsequio suyo un éxito en el mundo, un aplauso en la escena?... No, y cien veces no.... Porque es artista; y á los artistas nos tocó nacer de este modo; porque así, para vivir del público y con el público y en público, nos ha hecho interior y exteriormente la santa madre Naturaleza. (20)

Amelia responds with the typical Romantic expression: "Lo que nos ocurre es que no encontramos quien nos comprenda" (21). Antonio replies sarcastically: "¿Quién nos va á comprender si empezamos por no comprendernos nosotros?" (21). Throughout the play there are constant references to the incompatibility the artist experiences, as Amelia relates to Antonio: "Usted es artista y, según propia declaración, los artistas somos inaguantables" (64).

The final scenes, in which Teresa confronts Amelia and the latter recognizes her excessive pride and arrogance, are significant in Dicenta's attempt to draw a realistic picture of the difference between the artist, Amelia, and the average woman, Teresa. Teresa, who earlier in the play had recognized her own limitations in her competition for Emilio's attention, now realizes her power:

> Digo que en horas de placer y de exhibición y de triunfo usted puede hacerle más feliz que yo porque es más hermosa, y más inteligente y más atractiva para halagar las pasiones de un hombre como él. Yo soy una pobre mujer, una criatura insignificante; no tengo grandes éxitos que ofrecerle. Apenas si me queda hermosura que darle; pero en mi humildad y en mi insignificancia sé lo que no sabe usted. Perdonar y sufrir. (82)

Amelia, overcome with admiration for Teresa, responds sincerely:

> Cierto. No somos nosotras, criaturas turbulentas que sentimos con la imaginación y no con el alma, hechas para endulzar dolores. Hechas estamos para provocarlos.... Nervios, sangre, sentidos, todo lo gastamos en la lucha por el éxito, por la gloria, y cuando bajamos á la realidad, bajamos destrozadas, rotas, sin alma, nuestra alma quedó allá en el mundo de la ficción y del aplauso. (83)

Amelia graciously allows Teresa to take her proper place as Emilio's lover, knowing that she would never be able to satisfy Emilio the way that Teresa can.

Conclusions

Amor de artistas provides an excellent perspective of the world of theater at the turn of the century in Spain, and its elements of realism enhance Dicenta's attempt to draw a picture of typical theatrical life. However, the weakness of the plot and the underdeveloped characters make this *comedia* unfit for the stage. In the overall perspective of Dicenta's work, *Amor de artistas* represents Dicenta's continued desire to use realism on the stage, and despite its defects it redeems itself in content by painting a realistic picture of the behind-the-scenes activity of a turn of the century stage production.

Marinera (1907)

On February 11, 1907, Dicenta's next play, a dramatic monologue, was performed in the Teatro de la Princesa. Written for Mimí Aguglia Farrau, *Marinera* is a tragic story told by a young fisherwoman as she looks out at the sea.

Plot

As the curtain rises, Ana, who is sitting on a rock that juts out into the sea, talks aloud to herself as she waits impatiently for the return of her fiancé, Pedro, by boat. It is the night before their wedding, and as she waits, she reminisces about their relationship. When they were children, they used to build sandcastles on the beach, and even then they pretended to be married as they argued about the location of the bedroom in relation to the kitchen. That particular day, they got so angry at each other that Pedro slapped her, knocking her off her feet and on top of the sandcastle, destroying it completely. Ana, refusing to be victimized, threw a heavy rock at Pedro, who still has the scar on his forehead.

Ana describes the many seashells they used to find and how Pedro used to make jewelry for her with the different shapes and sizes. One day, Pedro was so overcome by Ana's beauty, that he grabbed her and kissed her; she was twelve-years-old, and he was fifteen. From that moment forward, they were forced to steal kisses and hugs out of the sight of their disapproving mothers. While she is talking, the sky gets darker, and she realizes that a northwest wind is approaching. The waves get higher as she describes the horrible struggle of the fishing boats off in the distance trying to make their way to shore. She sees Pedro and witnesses his death. The curtain falls slowly as she faints on the beach.

TECHNIQUE / IDEOLOGY

Marinera is loosely based on one of Dicenta's short stories from his collection titled *De la batalla* (1903). In "Los dulces de la boda" Dicenta relates a similar story of two young lovers who suffer unbearable tragedy in the death of the fisherman at sea. Dicenta's fascination with the sea and the people who make their living in the many seaside fishing villages is evident not only in both *Marinera* and "Los dulces de la boda," but also in *Juan Francisco* (1904) and later dramas, *Lorenza* (1907) and *Entre rocas* (1908).

This is not the first time Dicenta has used a woman to tell a story; in *Aurora*, *De tren a tren*, and *El vals de las sombras*, the protagonists are women, allowing the audience to view the female perspective. As in these three dramas, in *Marinera* there are references to the mistreatment of women. In *Aurora*, the protagonist describes the rape and abuse she suffered as a pretty young girl, and in both *De tren a tren* and *El vals de las sombras*, Aurelia laments her situation, having been forced into marriage with an older man. In *Marinera*, Ana explains the importance of being in control and not allowing any man to dominate her. As children, she and Pedro had argued over the location of the bedroom in their sandcastle, and when Pedro became violent with her, she fought back. Now that they are adults, she proudly declares that just as it was in their sandcastle, the bedroom is where she wants it to be in their new house,

> la alcoba estuvo donde yo quería, donde está la alcoba de la casita que vamos á vivir. ¡Claro que estuvo! ¡Hubiera faltado otra cosa! Tonta es quien se deja mandar por los hombres. ¡Lo que es yo! ni de niña. De mujer, excuso decirles á ustedes. (7)

Conclusions

Marinera is an excellent example of Dicenta's skill, not only as a playwright, but also as a storyteller. Ana's monologue is interesting and witty, and in it, Dicenta succesfully captures the essence of a young fisherwoman the night before she is to marry, fully expressing her fears, excitement, and nervousness. *Marinera* is similar to *Juan Francisco*, another drama that is set in a small fishing village, as another young woman looks longingly out to sea, waiting for her beloved to return. It is no coincidence that her name is Anita, the diminutive of Ana, for their characters are very similar. *Marinera* marks Dicenta's third attempt at dramatic monologue, yet it is his first piece written entirely for one specific actress. In this poignant drama, Dicenta continues to demonstrate his sensitivity for those who are victimized, in this case, a young woman who refuses to be dominated by her future husband, even as a child.

Overall Conclusions to Chapter Five

In the years following Dicenta's highly acclaimed *Juan José* and his subsequent failure, *El señor feudal*, Dicenta wrote many Romantic musical pieces, with the presentation of one lyrical drama every two years from 1898 to 1906: *Curro Vargas* (1898), *La cortijera* (1900), *Raimundo Lulio* (1902), *Juan Francisco* (1904), and *El vals de las sombras* (1906). Interspersed among these *zarzuelas* are short dramatic pieces written for the *teatro por horas* (*El tío Gervasio* and *El león de bronce*, both in 1900, and *¡Pa mí que nieva!*, 1904), *comedias* (*De tren a tren*, 1902; *La conversión de Mañara*, 1905; and *Amor de artistas*, 1906), and one "social" drama (*Aurora*, 1902). All of the dramas that fall into this intermediary period of Dicenta's career maintain many of the same characteristics evident in his early plays, yet there is an obvious development in Dicenta's versatility and skill as he incorporates humor, religious elements, realism, innovative social commentary, and legendary figures of Spain's past into a variety of theatrical genres.

Before the success of *Juan José* in 1895, Dicenta was highly praised for the *zarzuela* that premiered a year earlier, *El duque de Gandía* (1894). Perhaps it is the memory of that great success that inspired him to return to the lyrical drama. In 1898, *Curro Vargas* premiered after two years of silence following the failure of *El señor feudal* (1896), and despite the controversery concerning its similarity to Pedro de Alarcón's novel, *El niño de la bola* (1880), Dicenta, along with his co-writer Manuel Paso, again enjoyed a period of adulation. *Curro Vargas* and Dicenta's next two full-length dramas, *La cortijera* and *Raimundo Lulio*, are thoroughly Romantic in theme and technique, as Dicenta returns to his neo-Romantic roots first developed in *El suicidio de Werther* (1888). *Raimundo Lulio*, unlike *Curro Vargas* and *La cortijera* however, shares more characteristics with Dicenta's first *zarzuela* (*El duque de Gandía*), as Dicenta returns to a medieval setting by reworking a legendary theme. This also occurs in *La conversión de Mañara* (1905), which, although not a *zarzuela*, is purely Romantic. Dicenta skillfully recreates the legends surrounding the figures of Raimundo Lulio and Don Juan, while remaining faithful to the original themes. One other Romantic drama that falls into Dicenta's intermediary period is *Juan Francisco* (1904), which, although Romantic in theme and technique, contains a thesis, an unusual combination for a lyrical drama. *Juan Francisco* indicates Dicenta's continued interest in portraying contemporary problems on the stage; unfortunately for Dicenta, a lyrical Romantic drama does not provide the proper format for social criticism.

Dicenta's critics focus on his "social" dramas, ignoring, with the exception of *Aurora* (1902), all of the plays that premiered between *El señor feudal* (1896) and *Daniel* (1907), yet these eleven overlooked plays are essential in the study of Dicenta's development and versatile talent. In his many *zarzuelas*, Dicenta shows great skill in playwrighting, especially in the lyrical verses and humorous sketches. Throughout many of these plays, Dicenta often inserts amusing touches, and in one play in particular, *De tren a tren* (1902), Dicenta uses humor to his fullest advantage, later rewriting it into a lighthearted lyrical drama, *El vals de las sombras* (1906), further emphasizing its comical nature. Amusing characters such as Varillas (*La cortijera*, 1900) and Pascual (*Juan Francisco*, 1904) provide comic relief in situations that would otherwise be serious.

Religion also plays an important role in many of Dicenta's dramas, both positive and negative. In *Curro Vargas* (1898), Dicenta characterizes Padre Antonio as a sympathetic, real, and understanding priest, a man who feels both the divine and human side of every issue. On the other hand, in *Aurora* (1906), Dicenta criticizes religious people like Homobono who use their fanatical beliefs to manipulate others for their own benefit and to oppose social progression. In the majority of Dicenta's dramas from this period, however, religion is used as a positive force on the lives of the characters; in both *Raimundo Lulio* (1902) and *La conversión de Mañara* (1905), the Romantic hero recognizes and atones his sins at the end of the play, and in *Raimundo Lulio*, as in the earlier *El duque de Gandía* (1894), the protagonist converts to Christianity and dedicates his life to priestly matters.

In the years between *El señor feudal* and *Daniel*, Dicenta does not avoid using realistic techniques on the stage, contrary to the opinion of his many critics. In fact, after a careful study of Dicenta's wide variety of dramas between 1896 and 1907, it is immediately evident that Dicenta constantly returned to incorporating realism into his work. The two monologues, *El tío Gervasio* (1900) and *El león de bronce* (1900), both show realistic touches, despite their limited length. Both protagonists comment on the reality of the society surrounding them, lamenting their unfortunate fate of having been born poor. In other dramas, such as *Curro Vargas*, *¡Pa mí que nieva!*, *Aurora*, and *Juan Francisco*, Dicenta uses dialect to realistically reflect the social status of the speaker, and in *¡Pa mí que nieva!*, Dicenta has the characters call attention to the change in their manner of speaking after becoming rich. *Amor de artistas* also indicates Dicenta's repeated use of realism on stage, as it represents Dicenta's attempt to recreate the world of the artist, providing the spectator a glimpse of what goes on behind the scenes of the premiere of a succesful play.

One of Dicenta's most striking innovations in the years between *El señor feudal* and *Daniel* is his portrayal of the suffering of the female working class, as he describes the violation and rape of young girls and the rampant child abuse in *Aurora*, a "social" drama that most critics agree is significant in Dicenta's development as a social dramatist. Heavily cloaked with symbolism, *Aurora* provides a daring and biting commentary of the decadence and hypocrisy of the ruling class while pushing for social progress through education obtained abroad and the amalgamation of the upper and lower classes. In other dramas, such as *De tren a tren* (and its remake *El vals de las sombras*) and *Marinera*, Dicenta also brings the female perspective to the stage; in these dramas, the female protagonists, all with names that begin with an "A", like Aurora, stare into the distance and describe what they see, while making a social commentary based upon their experience. Anita (*De tren a tren*) suffers because she has been forced into a loveless marriage with an older man, and Ana (*Marinera*) expresses her defiance against the traditional role of the woman, one who is dominated and physically abused by her husband.

Overall, the intermediary period of Dicenta's career is rich with often ignored plays that deserve attention, especially the whimsical lyrical *zarzuelas*, the dramatic monologues, and the entertaining *comedias*. Unfortunately for Dicenta, however, because of his great success with *Juan José*, critics expected Dicenta's drama to continue in that same mode of "social" theater, and when Dicenta showed his great versatility and skill in other theatrical genres, he was criticized for not using the stage for the sole purpose of social commentary.

6
Dicenta's Final Contributions: 1907-1916

DANIEL (1907)
IN THE SPRING OF 1907, DICENTA triumphed with the production of one of his most significant social dramas, *Daniel*, presented by the company of Fernández Díaz de Mendoza in the Teatro Español on March 7. After more than a decade of lyrical Romantic dramas, interspersed with an occasional realistic piece, Dicenta returned to the treatment of the exploited worker in *Daniel*, which, according to the critic Pedro de Répide, both a friend and a collaborator of Dicenta, was Dicenta's favorite contribution to the stage: "la obra teatral que más gustaba a su autor, entre todas las que había escrito, era *Daniel*" (qtd. in González-Blanco 293). Mas Ferrer describes *Daniel* as Dicenta's "creación más perfecta dentro del drama social" (*Vida* 163). The primary theme in *Daniel*, a four-act drama in prose, is the plight of lead miners who suffer greatly because of the conditions in which they work and the poverty induced by those who exploit them.

PLOT
    The play begins in Daniel's home as he and his family and friends awaken at four o'clock in the morning to share each other's company and some coffee before going to the mines to work the long day. Daniel is an older miner who has two sons and a daughter. One son, Pedro, is a sergeant whose company often controls the riots and strikes of the rebellious miners, while his other son, Pablo, is a miner and a revolutionary. Daniel's daughter, Anita, who also works in the mines, has been seduced by Luis, the son of the *amo* (Lucas), who pretends to love Anita in order to fulfil his own selfish desires.
    Pablo is in love with Cesárea, another revolutionary, yet the love theme is overshadowed by her aspiration to organize a strike among the workers because of an impending wage-cut. Throughout the play these two revolutionaries are referred to jokingly as "the apostles." The workers are hesitant to join Pablo and Cesárea in their plans for a strike, as the memory of the most recent strike is too painful. The results were damaging; Daniel lost both his wife and his youngest

child because they starved to death, and Cesárea, who is only twenty-five years old, lost her husband in the violent rebellion led by the striking miners. The miners complain about the extended hours, the low wages, the dangerous working conditions, the excessive rent paid for the houses rented by the workers, and the high prices of goods sold in the stores run by the company.

Once the wage-cut is officially announced, Cesárea and Pablo are successful in encouraging the workers to a strike. Daniel refuses to join them, even though he is unhappy about earning less money. For him, earning less money is better than earning no money and suffering even more. Ignorant of the discontent among the workers, the *amo* invites a group of wealthy friends to visit the mine and all of the machines. The group discusses the workings of the mine, and it is evident that none of them cares or understands what goes on there. They witness the miners at work, ignoring the slave-like conditions and the hazards that face them, and while wandering through the mineshafts, Luis invites them to an elaborate dinner to be held in one of the biggest areas of the mine sometime in the future.

Once the strike begins and the workers have been replaced by imported laborers, the miners devise a way to keep the latter from going to work. The striking miners hide in a long-forgotten former entrance tunnel to the mine and instigate a riot once the imported laborers arrive. As the soldiers, including Daniel's son Pedro, arrive, the miners destroy the furnaces and machinery in a fit of violent rebellion. Daniel, who up to this point has refused to help the workers, tries to save his precious "horno," which represents his entire life's work. Luis, who accompanies the soldiers and the imported laborers, orders the soldiers to fire upon the striking miners to regain control of his father's mine. Daniel is injured, and many soldiers and miners are killed, including Daniel's two sons, Pablo and Pedro. As he mourns their deaths, Cesárea informs Daniel of his daughter's seduction by Luis.

Time passes, and Daniel begins his new job as the elevator operator in the mineshaft, since his injuries have left him incapable of the more demanding work in the mine. As the time approaches for the banquet hosted by Luis, Daniel transports all of the supplies for the dinner party in his elevator. Once the day arrives, Daniel is responsible for lowering the visitors to the bottom of the mine. After the guests have finished their meal and are ready to return to the surface, Daniel begins to hoist the elevator full of guests to the top. Just as they are about to arrive to the surface, he slices the elevator cables, and the car plunges to the bottom of the mineshaft, killing all on board. He screams, "¡A la mina! ¡Al infierno!" (89).

SOURCES

Daniel is the result of Dicenta's fascination and horror of the mining community in Linares, which he visited four years earlier and wrote about in

1903 in the autobiographical *Espumas y plomo*, fully describing the effect the misery of the miners had on him:

> Todo se mezclaba y confundía dentro de mi cráneo; los rayos del sol, recostados en el cielo, con el resplandor de los hornos encendidos para la fundición; el rodar estrepitoso de los carruajes, cuyos tiros campanilleaban gallardamente por los andenes del paseo, con el resoplar áspero de los motores en faena; el verde vivo de la campiña adornado con besos de luz y cantos de pájaros, con la negrura sepulcral de los fondos mineros, donde los candiles brillan como en el cementerio los fuegos fatuos, y la voz de los hombres suena á gemido engrosado por una bocina mostruosa. (*Espumas* 63)

Just as the group of wealthy individuals had the opportunity to visit the mineshaft, Dicenta too witnessed the suffering of the miners firsthand; however, unlike the ignorant and insensitive visitors in *Daniel*, Dicenta was profoundly moved and saddened by the extreme conditions in the mine, the physical state of the miners, and the indifference of the foreman and the *amo*. Before boarding the elevator, the foreman of the mine assured Dicenta that the elevator was safe enough for him to visit the mineshafts, despite the fact that it had failed in the past: "Cierto que algunas veces se rompe un cable, y ¡cataplum!; pero hoy puede usted bajar sin temor; los cables son nuevos; los han renovado hace pocos días; no hay peligro" (77). Dicenta recreates this event in *Daniel*, as the mine foreman and the mine owner assure the wealthy visitors that the elevator in which they will be lowered is not one of the less reliable ones that the miners use, and therefore, it is inspected daily to insure safety. The total disregard for the safety of the miners is evident in their cold observations:

> FERNANDO: Hay orden de que los cables se reconozcan á diario. En diez años solo una vez.
> LUCAS: Y fué en un ascensor de los que utilizan los obreros. En este no ocurre nunca nada. (*Daniel* 32)

When Dicenta arrived at the bottom of the mine, fifteen hundred meters below the earth's surface (*Espumas* 79), he found himself face to face with a group of miners who were severely handicapped by the conditions they had suffered while working in the mine: "Aquellos hombres producían espanto á los ojos y dolor en el alma" (115). Concerned about the wellbeing of the miners, Dicenta questioned the foreman, who heartlessly responded:

> El obrero se queja sin razón. El trabajo de hornos y cámaras no es tan malo como ellos dicen. Aquí los hombres, con pocas precauciones, no tienen que

temer nada por su salud. Esto no es tan malo, no es tan malo; de veras. (119)

As the "ricacho" spoke, Dicenta noticied a malnourished dog that was "flaco, tísico, casi moribundo" and pointed it out to the foreman (119). Without realizing the descrepency in his claim that the workers are safe in the mine, the foreman stated that the dog would not live long in those conditions: "Vivirá poco. Perro que anda por estos sitios, no dura un año" (119).

In *Espumas y plomo*, Dicenta describes the misery he witnessed in the mine in poignant detail, as he emphasizes his own preoccupation with the exploitation of the miners. Dicenta, so overcome by the experience, explains that it would be impossible to describe the entirety of the suffering he saw in a simple newspaper article or diary entry:

> Un libro sería necesario para escribir el poema de miserias y de torturas que los mineros graban con sus picos en las lucientes láminas del filón, en las paredes grises de la mina, en los artesones donde lavan el plomo para convertirlo en albayalde y envenar poco á poco á los hombres qu lo fabrican. (63-64)

Dicenta's "poema de miserias y de torturas" comes to life in *Daniel*, as he composes the play with the memory of his visit to the lead mines of Linares fresh on his mind:

> Veía á los obreros de la mina levantarse un día protestando de sus sufrimentos, negándose á continuar el trabajo servil, pidiendo mejora en sus jornales para comer como personas, y en sus derechos para vivir como hombres; veíalos declararse en huelga, ponerse en frente de sus explotadores, procurar por todos los medios que sus compañeros, sin faltar uno, les ayudaran en la empresa; veía á los patrones acudir demandando auxilio á los poderes públicos, y veía á los soldados, á los oficiales, á los hermanos del obrero empuñar el fusil, meter en los cañones de éste el plomo que aquél, después de arrancarlo del filón, de purificarlo en los lavadores, de cocerlo en los hornos y de vaciarlo en los moldes, había convertido en balas; los veía empuñar los fusiles con manos que la disciplina hace inflexibles y el instinto de fraternidad temblorosas, ponerse dar cara á los obreros sublevados, y á la voz terrible de ¡fuego!, devolverles en forma de golpe mortal el plomo que ellos fabrican á costa de su sangre, de su sudor y de su vida. (110)

Dicenta's skillful portrayal of the exploitation and suffering of the miners in *Daniel* is also greatly influenced by the French novelist Émile Zola and his

Germinal (1885), a novel that explores in graphic detail the situation of coalminers in northern France. As Peak notes, the proof of the influence Zola had on Dicenta is immediately evident in "Dicenta's editorship of the Madrid weekly *Germinal*" (Peak 117). Peak describes Dicenta's mission in *Germinal*: "According to its program, 'Germinal' would devote itself chiefly to economics and social problems, 'cuyos pavorosos conflictos describe el gran poeta francés en su inmortal obra *Germinal*'" (Peak 117). In the sixteenth volume of *Germinal*, August 20, 1897, in an article titled "La gente nueva" written by Mérida, the influence of Zola is emphasized:

> Dicenta, Benavente, Bark, Fuente, Delorme, Jurado de la Parra y Palomero; que forman el núcleo director de la simpática revista en el arte son decididamente partidarios del naturalismo de Zola, socialista y positivista. (qtd. in Pérez de la Dehesa 56)

In the novel *Germinal*, as in *Daniel*, the primary theme is the exploitation of the miners and their struggle to survive, and as Dicenta, Zola describes in detail the daily lives of the miners, depicting them at home as well as at work. Morby describes the similarities:

> The elaborate luncheon that they enjoy while hunger forces a strike upon the miners has a parallel in the one that gives Daniel an opportunity for revenge. Several characters, old Bonnemort, la Brûlé, Mouquette, and Pierron, who closes his eyes while his wife finds means to improve their circumstances, have more or less accurate counterparts in Daniel himself, la Greñuda, Irene, and Nemesio and his wife Bastiana. The little soldier who would fire upon the workers if commanded to do so, and the subsequent intervention of the army, may have inspired Dicenta's ironical use of brother against brother. (Morby 389)

Despite their many similarities, the cause of conflict in *Germinal* is the survival of the coalminers in the advent of technology as the introduction of machinery leaves them without employment. Zola's *Germinal* ends on a note of optimism as Etienne, the leader of the strike that had just been broken, looking back upon the mining community he has chosen to abandon, thinks of the miners working far below him as seeds, ready to burst through the soil; "Germinal," or seedtime, was a month in the calendar of the French Revolution. Cesárea, the female protagonist of *Daniel*, also uses the seed imagery. Her belief is that the only way to improve the miners' plight is to die for their cause: "Con nuestra sangre regarán gérmenes de amor y justicia" (*Daniel* 62).

Technique
Realism

In *Daniel*, Dicenta portrays the daily activities of the miners, filling the play with accurate realistic details of their lives not only at work deep in the mines, but also at home, in the few hours that they are not working. Dicenta's use of realism is most evident in the convincing setting for the industrial workers. The miners live in company houses, purchase their food at company stores, and are completely controlled by the owners in every aspect of their lives. Cesárea complains bitterly about their sad lot in life: "Nos obligaban á vivir en casas construidas por ellos, y nos obligaban á comprar en tiendas que eran suyas también. Para aprovechar el terreno, nos regateaban el aire; para aumentar sus ganancias nos envenenaban la comida" (14).

The stage directions are extremely detailed as Dicenta provides an accurate picture of the lives of the miners. In Act II, which takes place in the mine, Dicenta writes two full pages of stage directions describing exactly how to depict realistically the workings of a lead mine. Dicenta explains the importance of following his instructions: "Procúrese dar al público la impresión exacta de una fundición en tarea; el espectáculo de uno de esos infiernos mineros donde los trabajadores se asfixian y se tuestan durante largas horas" (*Daniel* 29). There are heavy carts filled with molten lead running back and forth across the stage; there are bright hot furnaces where molten lead flows; and there are men, women, and children working together in the dangerous conditions of the mine, each completing his or her particular task. Hall describes the difficulty the players must have faced in their effort to follow Dicenta's detailed stage directions:

> The management of large groups on the stage, especially at the moment of the smashing of the foundry plant and of the shooting, no doubt presented serious problems, but these must have been slight in comparison with those raised by the play's unwonted reliance on elaborate scenic effect. The spectacular use of the pit headgear at the end of the play is only the last of a series of examples of this. (64)

Dicenta continues to emphasize the need to portray these difficult scenes as realistically as possible:

> Procúrese dar á esta escena, como a todas las anteriores, grandes caracteres de vida y de realidad. Es el medio, el vivir de los trabajadores lo que hay que meter plásticamente en el alma del público, para que éste se impresione, se compenetre con ese vivir y lo esté viviendo á la par de los personajes. (*Daniel* 40-41)

The realistic setting is further emphasized by the details of the lives the miners are forced to lead. The play opens at four o'clock in the morning, as the miners are preparing to begin another day's work. Rising before dawn in complete darkness and descending into the dark mineshafts soon afterwards, the miners rarely see sunshine, and the never ending dismal and grey atmosphere of the set serves to reflect the extreme social oppression of the miners. As the workers slowly prepare to begin the long day in darkness, they provide glimpses into their daily lives in their morning conversation. Daniel describes to Pablo, who hopes to encourage a strike among the workers, how he lost both his wife and his infant son to starvation as a result of an earlier strike: "Tu madre reventó; tu hermanillo, como el pecho de la madre por mor de la necesidá no escurría leche, también reventó" (21). Daniel's sad story is reminiscent of Tío Gervasio's description of how his wife and baby died of malnutrition after he found himself without employment (*El tío Gervasio* 1900).

As in many of his previous plays, Dicenta continues to use dialect to reflect the social status of the individual. Throughout the play, the miners consistently speak with the same dialect, expressing their great emotions with speech that is full of human feeling, while the ruling class speaks coldly and frivolously, using perfect grammar and never resorting to the use of colloquialisms. In this way, Dicenta humanizes the workers, pushing the spectator to identify with the injustice of their situation. The difference in the dialect between the workers and the owners is most evident when the miners are interrupted at their work by a visit from the curious friends of the *amo*. As the wealthy visitors complain about the unbearable heat deep below the surface of the earth where the miners work the furnaces to melt the lead, Lucas, the mine owner, states nonchalantly that it is only a matter of becoming accustomed to the temperature. Lucas turns to Daniel and asks coldly: "¿No es cierto, Daniel?" (35). Daniel answers his *amo* with respect while maintaining the dialect common to the miners: "Sí, señor, tóo es acostumbrarse. Ya ve usté nosotros… Claro que no tóos tién mi resistencia" (35).

NEO-ROMANTIC CHARACTERISTICS

Despite the overwhelming realism of *Daniel*, Dicenta continues to manifest elements of neo-Romanticism. Daniel is not the typical Romantic hero, but his violent reaction against his oppressors is the result of his daughter's dishonor and his deep desire for revenge for the suffering of his family and his fellow-worker. The themes of honor and vengeance, however, are minor in the development of the drama, as the dishonoring of Daniel's daughter is only one of many evils he has faced. Unlike Jaime (*El señor feudal*, 1896), who is pushed to violent action solely because of his sister's dishonor, Daniel's motivation for revenge is not limited to Anita's seduction by his employer's son; instead, it is the combination of the deaths of his wife and three sons, his own crippling injuries, the unjust treatment he and his fellow-workers have received, and finally, the seduction of his daughter that lead him to murder the wealthy visitors to the mine. Dicenta's use of sensationalism, not only in the final scene of death but also in the furious rebellion of the miners and the deadly confrontation with the soldiers, is further evidence of his inability to escape his neo-Romantic roots.

The unrequited love theme is also present, but again, in a minor way. The love between Pablo and Cesárea is subordinate to their common cause of revolution, and their love for each other is insignificant in the development of the drama. In *Daniel*, for the first time in his entire body of full-length plays, Dicenta presents a drama in which the cause of the action is not the result of a sexual relationship. Other social dramas, like *Juan José* and *El señor feudal*, rely heavily on the relationship between a man and a woman for the source of the conflict, and despite Dicenta's attempt to portray the severe exploitation of the working class in both dramas, the love theme dominates the action. In *Daniel*, on the other hand, the seduction of Anita is minor to the plot, and the love shared between Pablo and Cesárea only serves to provide Cesárea a platform to express her extreme revolutionary views.

CHARACTERS
CESÁREA

Dicenta's most innovative character creation is Cesárea, a woman who has no counterpart in any of Dicenta's previous dramas. Having lost her husband in an earlier strike, Cesárea is bitter and driven by her husband's dying words, "otros hombres vendrán: hay que seguir, seguir siempre, siempre," to bring about change in the life of her fellow worker (13). The spectator's first impression of Dicenta's strongest leading lady is provided in the conversation between Anita and Pablo as the play opens. Pablo, who is in love with Cesárea, listens intently as Anita expresses her opinion about the woman everyone calls "la Apóstola":

Ella es guapa y trabajaora. Lo malo pa tí y pa tós los que la requiebran, es que sólo echa cuenta de sus hijos. Amás, está un poco... (*Dando vueltas sobre la sien con uno de sus dedos.*) ¡Tiene unos dichos! En el taller la llamamos la *Apóstola*. ¡Y cómo nos reímos de ella! (7)

Anita is perceptive in her analysis of Cesárea's personality, as Cesárea soon confirms her devotion to her children and the "dichos" that Anita fails to understand: "Fuera de mis hijos, no existo más que para la venganza y el odio" (13). Despite her love for Pablo and his extensive effort to coax her into marrying him, Cesárea rejects him, saying:

¡Ser de otro! ¡Tener á otro hombre estos brazos que han tenido á Manuel

> ensangrentado, muerto, muerto por defender la felicidad de nuestros hermanos! ¡Dar otro padre á los hijos del mártir! No, Pablo; déjame; sigamos siendo lo que somos. (16)

Throughout the play, Cesárea urges her fellow workers to join her and Pablo in a strike against the mine owners in protest of the wage cut, and her speeches, each time more passionate than the last, inspire the miners to action. The miners, who are at first suspicious about a woman with such enthusiasm and liberal ideas, go from outright ridicule of Cesárea to a genuine appreciation for her strength and courage. Irene, a simple-minded laborer, responds to one of Cesárea's great speeches with sincere admiration: "¡Qué bien dices las cosas! Yo no las entiendo del to, pero vaya que se me clavan en el corazón" (59). Other miners agree:

> Y en el nuestro se meten. Anoche cuando nos reunimos pa ver lo que hoy se hacía, ya viste que la gente andaba duosa. Pero cuando te levantaste en mitá del bosque, iluminá por la luna y hablaste, tos fuimos unos. (59)

The same miners who at first mocked Cesárea by calling her "la Apóstola" are so enlivened by her revolutionary speeches that they equate her to the Virgin Mary: "Paecías mesmamente una virgen del cielo que bajaba á la tierra á decirnos: 'Esto y esto es lo que hay que hacer. ¡Confiar en mí!'" (59). Cesárea seems to have an almost mystical effect over her fellow workers; for the first time in their miserable lives, they have hope for a better future.

Cesárea, in contrast to Pablo who fears that many will lose their lives, feels they all must be prepared to die in order to provide a better life for future generations: "¿Es precisa la muerte suya, y la nuestra, las de miles y miles de hombres para el bien de los que nos sucedan? ¿Sí? Pues entonces la muerte es una obligación. Las obligaciones, se cumplen" (61). Pablo disagrees, stating strongly that he is not afraid to die but that he does not believe it is fair that the simple-minded miners should die without realizing the reason: "¿Es justo que hagamos morir á los otros, á los que no tienen cabal conciencia de por qué mueren y para qué mueren?" (61). Cesárea's passionate response proves that she is only focused on one goal, regardless of the consequences of achieving it:

> Arrancarles para la muerte, de la miseria, de la esclavitud, y hacer con sus cadáveres una bandera que aliente á sus hijos, es, para ellos, misericordia; para sus hijos, porvenir; para nosotros un deber.... Con nuestra sangre se regarán gérmenes de amor y justicia. Por obra suya brotarán sobre la tierra generaciones en las que los hombres erán hermanos y el trabajo fiesta; en la que nadie se atreverá á verter la sangre de nadie, porque la sangre de todos será para todos común. (62)

As the play progresses, Cesárea becomes increasingly more coldhearted, especially upon the death of Daniel's two sons, Pablo and Pedro, as she mocks the miner for having defended his precious "horno" from the rioters: "¡Anda, defiende el horno! ¡Vé detrás del amo! ¡Suplícale! ¡Pídele perdón! ¡Anda! ¡Anda, imbécil!" (75). Cesárea's revelation that Daniel's daughter has been dishonored by the son of the *amo* is even more heartless: "Menos mal que tu hija está viva para que el matador de tus hijos la goce" (75). Her stinging words injure Daniel when he is at his lowest point emotionally.

Following the unsuccessful strike, Cesárea is fired, and the surviving miners, who have returned to work, blame her for their misfortune; instead of freedom from the many injustices they suffered, they received death, and their situation has deteriorated, as the *amo* notes: "Ya murmuran de ella, recordando que les ofreció la independencia y les llevó á la muerte. Pronto la odiarán" (80). When Daniel confronts her, expecting to elicit an apology, Cesárea arrogantly claims: "No he procedido mal en nada ni con nadie" (84). Her failure to improve the miners' situation has not changed her strong revolutionary views. She coldly tells Daniel that if time were reversed, she would still tell Pablo that he must die: "Pues si Pablo resucitara y si por la redención de todos tuviese que morir otra vez, no vacilaría en decirle: muere" (85).

Cesárea is present in the final scene in which Daniel releases the elevator sending his oppressors to their deaths, yet, unlike the rest of the drama, Cesárea finds herself speechless as she realizes Daniel's plan. Daniel's statement, "No hablo. Hago," emphasizes the difference between the two of them (88). While Cesárea has spent all of her time lecturing others about her beliefs, nothing is accomplished. Daniel, on the other hand, says nothing, and with one simple act, takes revenge on those responsible for his pain. Cesárea's lack of protest and ensuing silence is uncharacteristic of her, and as the curtain closes, she slowly backs away from the horrific scene.

DANIEL

Just as Juan in *El señor feudal* (1896), Daniel represents the conscientious worker who does not question his position and remains loyal to the *amo*, following the custom of generations before him:

> Pa trabajar nacimos. Trabajó mi padre y el padre de mi padre, y trabajo yo y trabajais vosotros, y trabajarán vuestros hijos; y los amos seguirán siendo amos, que esa es la ley. En la mina nací y en la mina quiero morirme. (23)

Unlike Juan, however, Daniel is not a member of the "obrero masa" described by García Pavón: "Hombre indeciso, que conoce perfectamente la crueldad del amo, pero incapaz de rebelión alguna sin cabecilla que le anime" (57). Instead, Daniel is the stereotypical "viejo obrero honrado":

> Conformista, amante del orden y de su trabajo. Hombre de otros tiempos, que rechaza las nuevas ideas revolucionarias y los procedimientos violentos.... Pero que al final, por haberle matado al hijo—proletario consciente—o haber sido seducida su hija por el burgués, se suma a los revolucionarios e incluso toma la venganza más espectacular. (García Pavón 57)

Upon learning that his employers are contemplating a wage cut, Daniel reacts with the typical fatalistic attitude of one who accepts injustices without question:

> ¿Que vais á componer el mundo? Siempre hubo pobres y hubo ricos. Siempre los habrá. Los más trabajamos pa los menos. Así está hecho el mundo, y no lo desharéis la apóstola y tú con discursos. (23)

Daniel is of an older generation and tends to have more respect for authority than his own children. He feels that the situation is fixed; there will always be a large gap between those who are wealthy and those who suffer at the hands of the wealthy. Therefore, in his mind, a strike is useless because the established order is not going to change.

As Pablo and Cesárea encourage the laborers to strike, Daniel stubbornly refuses to join them. Having lost his wife and infant son to starvation because of a previous strike, Daniel fears that the only possible results from another strike would be more death, misery, and starvation for the miners. Daniel's objection to the strike, however, is the result of something much deeper: his honorable yet foolish pride in his work. As García Pavón describes the typical "viejo obrero honrado," Daniel is "amante del orden y de su trabajo" to a fault (57). Daniel describes the extreme pride in his furnace and the work he has done over the past forty years:

> Cuando estoy frente del horno, con la barra en la mano, revolviendo la pasta y echando por cá pelo una gota de suor como el puño, no me cambiaría por naide.... Si me cambiasen de horno ó de mina, me parecería que yo ya no era yo. Hace cuarenta años ¡cuarenta que tengo el mismo amo y el mismo horno! (*Daniel* 23)

This is the only life Daniel has ever known, as he has been working the same furnace since he was fifteen years old. A strike would not only mean a total loss of income, but it would also force Daniel to leave his precious furnace behind, to be worked by someone else. This is a thought that Daniel cannot bear, and in an effort to stop the strike, Daniel begs his fellow workers to reconsider: "Podemos esperar. Todo menos la huelga. Quizás hablando con don Lucas. No es mala persona. Pué que nos atienda.... Hay que hacer el último esfuerzo" (50).

The miners push Daniel forward to confront Lucas, the *amo*, who explains to the group that the wage cut is only temporary: "Cuestión de unos días" (52). Daniel, completely satisfied with Lucas's explanation, returns to his furnace and encourages his fellow workers to do the same. They ignore him, and he is left alone as the rest of the miners refuse to receive less money for their labor.

As the strike forces the owners to arrange for imported laborers to take the place of the striking miners, Daniel is incapable of staying away from his beloved furnace. Despite the fact that the mine has not been operating for several days, he continues to go to work, guarding his furnace from others. Pablo, who is discouraged by his father's seemingly irrational love for the furnace, tells Cesárea that Daniel is not alone:

> ¿No le ves, cuando suena la hora del trabajo, alzarse de la cama como un autómata y venir aquí á contemplar, á adorar su horno, ese horno en queestá dejando la vida hace cuarenta años?... ¡Hay tantos obreros como mi padre! (62-63)

Daniel compares his love for his furnace with his love for Pablo as he tries to dissuade his son from rebelling against the *amo*:

> ¿Sabes si yo te viese muerto lo que sentiría cuando tocase el cuerpo tuyo? Pues talmente me pasa cuando llego á mi horno y lo tiento y lo hallo muerto, acarambanao, sin que por su boca abierta salga el vaho del plomo. Me da verlo así mucha pena, mucha, pero no pueo dejar de verlo. (64-65)

Daniel is horrified when he learns that the striking miners plan to destroy all of the furnaces in an effort to keep the imported laborers from working the mine. His reaction, as his fellow workers approach his furnace, is a desperate and pitiful plea:

> No lo romperéis. No quiero que me lo hagais pedazos. Cá ladrillo arrancao, sería un cacho de carne que me arrancaríais á mí. Oidme. Nunca pedí por Dios á hombre alguno. ¡Por Dios os lo pido ahora! ¡No destrocéis mi horno!... Romperlo es matarle. ¡No quiero que me lo mateis! ¡No mateis á mi horno! ¡Os lo suplico con brazos en cruz! (71)

As they destroy his precious oven, Daniel collapses and breaks into sobs, screaming "¡Mi horno! ¡Mi horno hecho pedazos!" (73).

Following the deadly confrontation between soldiers and miners, Daniel at first appears unchanged by the tragedy of losing his two sons and learning that his daughter has been seduced by the son of the *amo*; he is as humble and submissive as before. Crippled in the skirmish, Daniel is incapable of returning to the furnaces that defined his existence; thus, as he becomes the elevator operator, he is stripped of his pride, the only thing remaining him. However, his attitude towards his superiors is characterized by the same respect he had for them prior to the strike, and although he mourns the loss of his job at the furnace, he vows to set his mind to his new obligation: "De más han hecho con no ponerme de patas en la calle. Por lo que hace al cambio de trabajo, ya me acostumbraré. Mierándolo á derechas, el hombre debe saber estar ande le coloca su suerte" (78). Daniel's subservience, however, is feigned, and only after Cesárea arrives to bid farewell to him does he express his bitterness and desire for revenge. Cesárea, as well as the spectator, is surprised by Daniel's newfound rebellion:

> ¿Imaginas que estoy sirviendo á los que mataron á mis dos hijos, al que disfrutó y barrió á mi Anita, por ganarme un mendrugo de pan? Vaya, mujer, entonces eres tonta. No has mirao hondo pa aquí dentro. No conoces á este hombre.... Este hombre cuando le hacen un mal, no lo olvía; este hombre, cuando le hieren, hiere. (85-86)

Daniel explains to Cesárea the reason for his change of heart:

> He cambiao tal que si me hubiesen puesto un hombre nuevo. ¡Y decir que este cambio fué en un día, sólo en un día! Bien es verdá que en un día perdí tó lo que tenía que perder.... Primero mi horno destrozao; despu'es el señorito Luis gritando ¡fuego! Y los soldaos tirando y los obreros tirando á la par y Pablo de un lao y Pedro de otro, en tierra,... mientras tú me gritabas que mi hija era quería de don Luis. To en una hora. (86)

After having lost everything that mattered to him, Daniel, like Juan José, is fueled by a violent rage that leads to the culminating tragedy of exacting revenge upon those who have been the source of his personal pain. When Dicenta's contemporaries charged that Daniel suffered an unbelievable amount of tragedy in his life, Jacinto Benavente defended his fellow artist:

> Sí, son muchas desdichas para un solo hombre si fuera un hombre solo. Pero Daniel es algo m'as: no es un hombre, son muchos, son muchas generaciones.... La visión amplia, abarcadora de Dicenta concentra lo esparcido ¿No es un derecho del artista? (*Sobremesa* 21)

MINOR CHARACTERS

Daniel is a drama rich with minor characters, who, although not well developed, accomplish Dicenta's goal of creating a realistic environment. Besides the character types represented by the major characters (Cesárea and

Pablo, revolutionaries; Daniel, respected and conscientious worker; and Luis and Lucas, indifferent and abusive employers), the remaining characters all fall into the category of "obrero masa." They recognize the injustice of their situation, but it takes a leader like Cesárea to encourage them to action. Individually, they are powerless, as is evident in the scene in which they attempt to confront the *amo*:

> LUIS: *(A los obreros.)* ¿No oís que llaman al trabajo? *(Con imperio.)* ¿Qué hacéis ahí quietos? *(Los obreros bajan la cabeza, cobardemente sin atreverse á contestar. Cesa la campana.)*
> OBRERO 1°: *(Tartamudeando.)* Ya ve usté... estamos... Pues estamos... Ya hemos oído la campana... Estamos...
> LUIS: ¿Por qué estais? Decidlo de una vez.
> OBRERO 1°: *(A los otros.)* No sé qué decirle.
> PACORRO: *(Al Obrero 1°)* ¡Qué blando eres! Fíjate. *(Se estira la chaqueta y se dirige á Luis; fuerte.)* ¡Estamos...! *(Se detiene como atragantado, balbuceando.)* Estamos... estam... ¡Anda, se me traba la lengua!

Although ready to strike, the stuttering miners cannot bring themselves to say so to the *amo*; they are totally dependent on Pablo and Cesárea who, without the fear and habitual respect for the *amo* that is so deeply ingrained in the majority of the miners, are able to express their plans to strike to protest the extreme injustice of the salary cut.

Pacorro is an interesting minor character in that he provides the same comic relief in the daily lives of his companions as does Andrés in *Juan José*. He teases Pablo and Cesárea about their relationship; he jokes with Anita about having to get up so early; he makes fun of Pablo and Cesárea for their revolutionary ideas; he pretends to be in love with one of the wealthy visitors to the mine; he mocks the singing of the ladies while they work; he repeatedly shouts "¡Ole! ¡Ole!" once he joins the strike, as if it were just a game; he flirts shamelessly with Irene and other miners; and he spends the majority of his time drunk. Pacorro's attitude towards marriage is humorous, as he explains his reasoning for not getting married: "[Women] Beben mucho.... No me gusta partir el vino. El pan, bueno. Es mi idea: el pan como hermanos; el vino como tigres. Cuando me case, sólo habrá en mi domicilio un borracho: yo" (18).

IDEOLOGY

In *Daniel*, Dicenta explores in depth the problems of the worker in a modern, industrialized society. The entire play is a treatise on the ills and injustices suffered by the miners, as they constantly express their dissatisfaction with their inability to overcome extreme oppression and improve their situation. García Pavón describes the thesis of *Daniel* as a "verdadera consigna del movimiento marxista, repetida hasta la saciedad" (60), yet the ideology of the play, as expressed in the words of Cesárea, is anarchist rather than Marxist. Dicenta's argument is multifaceted: he mocks the frivolity and ignorance of the wealthy; he condemns the callousness of the mine owners towards the workers; he criticizes the dangerous and harsh conditions under which the miners, including elderly and children, are required to work; he emphasizes the injustice in the exploitation of working women by their superiors; he argues against the government's involvement in breaking up the strike; and finally, he illustrates the difficulty faced by the miners in their effort to improve their situation.

In his argument, Dicenta draws a clear distinction between the two classes, in their speech, personality, and appearance, especially on the two occasions that the mine owner's wealthy friends visit the mine. The miners, hardened by years of physical labor, are bitter and unhappy; whereas the superficial wealthy guests, completely oblivious to the dangers of the mine and the suffering of the miners, are foolish in their contentment.

Upon the first visit of the friends of the *amo*, the young miners are impressed by the beauty and grace exhibited by the visitors, but La Greñuda, an elderly laborer, quickly dispells their praise: "Ropa, chica, ropa. En cuanto se la quitan son igual que los nuestros" (31). The wealthy young ladies are oblivious to the suffering of the miners as they delight in the excitement of the workings of the mine: "¡Estoy contentísima! He pasado un gran rato. Creía soñar mientras bajaba por aquel boquete sin fin.... ¿Verdad que es un espectáculo muy bello?" (32-33). One lady laughs at the gentlemen, saying: "¡Y ustedes con las vestimentas de mineros! ¡Parecían bandidos!" (32). Another suggests that someone should film the wonderful scene for others to enjoy: "Debían sacar cintas para los cinematógrafos de Madrid. ¡Cómo se divertiría la gente! (33). Their description of what they have witnessed indicates their ignorance and complete lack of concern for the miners: "Los obreros cantan mientras trabajan. Son muy bonitos sus cantares. Oyéndolos imaginé que estaba en una función de teatro" (33). Dicenta's audience distances itself from the callous visitors, forgetting that they too are watching a performance by talented actors, for the suffering of the miners is too real to ignore. Fernando, one of the engineers of the mine, explains to the ladies that all is not as they see it: "Función penosa, llena de peligros para los actores, señorita. Ganan su vida muy rudamente los mineros" (33). Isabel's "¿Sí?" is interrupted by Lucas, the *amo*, as he expresses his opinion about the working condition of the miners; for him, they are good for nothing else: "Hay que contar con que los mineros son también gente ruda y no sirven para otra cosa" (33). Later, as Fernando describes the dangers of arsenic poisoning to the group, Isabel ignorantly responds: "¿Y esto mata? ¡Quién iba á pensarlo! ¡Con unos colores tan bonitos!" (35).

In the final act, there is an enormous contrast between the significance of the mine for the wealthy, who view it as a prime location to host a grand banquet, and the miners, who have spent their entire lives working in dangerous conditions under the oppression of the *amo*. It is difficult to forget the years of suffering experienced by the miners as the foreman describes the changes that have been made deep below to accommodate the guests:

> Abajo han improvisao un comedor que me río yo de la fonda. Lo han puesto en la plazoleta, ande están los ventilaores, pa que el aire circule bien y no sientan la pesaez y el ahogo que trae respirar en los pozos. A más, luminarias por toas partes. La mina, á cuenta de una mina, paece un palacio. (78)

The audience cannot help but be disgusted that the visitors plan to flaunt their prosperity in the midst of those who are starving. Following the banquet, as the guests are being hoisted to the earth's surface, the ladies' foolishness is again emphasized, as they describe the effect the light has on the elevator shaft:

> JOSEFINA: *(Abajo riendo.)* ¡Qué bonito efecto el de la luz tras la obscuridad!
> LUISA: *(Abajo.)* Parece que vamos á la gloria. (89)

The irony of their words is disturbing, as Daniel completes his vengeance, screaming: "¡Al infierno!" (89).

The suffering of the average miner is extreme, but Dicenta intends to show that those who struggle to survive under such harsh conditions are not limited to strong young men and women; both children and the elderly are forced to work in the mine alongside their more physically capable companions. Dicenta's argument against the abuse of the elderly is especially vehement in his characterization of La Greñuda, a widow who, after working the mine for fifty-five years, finds herself alone. Her situation is similar to that of Tío Gervasio who, in his sixties, has lost everything that ever mattered to him, and just as La Greñuda, he continues to perform hard labor to survive (*El tío Gervasio*, 1900).

La Greñuda is older and wiser than her fellow workers, and it is she who makes the first move towards any action against her oppressors, as she pushes a loaded cart in the path of the elegantly dressed visitors. No one is harmed, and although she denies having pushed the cart on purpose, she later admits to her companions her intention to injure the pretty ladies: "Lástima de mandao. A las piernas tiraba.... Por verlas á toas uncías á la vagoneta, daba lo que me quea de vivir" (38). Later, as she complains about her meager lunch, La Greñuda describes her bitter hatred towards the wealthy:

> Un cacho de pan más duro que el plmo, y un tomate. Luego queréis que no aborrezca á tóos esos hartos de jamón. Como los cogiese entre mis uñas ande no hubiera Guardia civil, les sacaba el pellejo á túrdigas. (41)

When chastized by her younger companions for her attitude, La Greñuda angrily reminds them that she is no longer young, and that not only is she poor, she is also alone:

> Vosotras tenéis un padre ó un hermano ó un hombre, ó un chiquillo. ¡algo que os llama y que os alegra! ¡Yo! Mi juventú, ¡anda con Dios! Mi marío cerró el ojo ya. Los hijos… me los mató un desprendimiento. Cuando se han cumplío los sesenta y se está pobre y fea y hay que agarrarse á una vagoneta pa vivir y á un cacho de pan duro pa afilar las encías, no se pué ser güena, muchachas. (42)

Cesárea sees a reflection of herself in La Greñuda and fears that without action, she too may end up poor and lonely. Dicenta argues for a more humane treatment of Spain's elderly laborers who have no choice but to continue working until their death without any special treatment or compensation for their life of service.

As in *Aurora* (1902), Dicenta attacks the exploitation of the female worker, who feels forced to submit to superiors to please their whims. Anita, Daniel's daughter, is young and naïve; she is quick to believe that Luis, the son of the *amo*, is sincere in his attention to her, and she freely gives herself to him, believing in the possibility of marriage. She ignores Cesárea's wise advice: "ese hombre, el hijo del amo de la mina, sólo á la desgracia te puede llevar con sus requebrares…. Vale más ser compañera de un obrero pobre, que querida de un amo rico" (25-26). Anita realizes the truth when Luis openly rejects her in the presence of the wealthy young women:

> ANITA: *(Bajo.)* ¿Por qué te acercas tanto á esa señorita? *(Celosa.)*
> LUIS: ¿Por qué? *(Sorprendido.)* ¿Vas á venirme ahora con historias? *(Desdeñoso y altivo.)* ¡Pues tendría gracia! Anda. (44)

Anita is not the only woman who has sold herself to her employer. Bastiana, another young miner, is the wife of the mine foreman. Dicenta describes her in the stage directions as a beautiful twenty-five-year-old woman who, besides being very well dressed for a laborer, gives off "aires de importancia" (40). As the workers break for lunch, Bastiana separates herself from the rest, "teniendo cuidado de escoger el sitio más limpio" (40). The other women despise her, and Irene feels especially bitter towards Bastiana, claiming that the reason her husband has been named foreman is because Bastiana exchanged sexual favors with the *amo*. Irene compares herself to her rival:

> Sé que cuando he puesto mis ojos en un hombre, minero ha sío él y querer por querer le he dao; y si él ha pagao unas copas con los dineros de su

jornal, con los del jornal mío he pagao otras yo.... En cambio otras, se compinchan con sus maríos pa hacer cucamonas á un amo viejo y pa que el viejo haga capataz al marío y capataza á la mujer. De mó que yo, con lo que hago, me doy y otras, con lo que hacen, se venden. (45)

Although both Anita and Bastiana are exploited by their superiors, Bastiana chooses to be victimized, hoping to improve her situation. After Bastiana gives in to the desires of the *amo*, her husband is promoted to foreman, allowing Bastiana the opportunity to move one step up the social ladder. Dicenta not only condemns the ruling class for taking advantage of working women to meet their own needs, but he also rebukes women like Bastiana who encourage that type of exploitation.

The dominating theme in *Daniel* is the discontentment among the miners, as they complain constantly about the dangerous working conditions in the mine, the long hours they are forced to work, the insufficient income, the low standard of housing provided by the owners, the high prices charged at the company store, the cruel and indifferent attitude of their employers, and their inability to improve their situation without resorting to a strike. Although at first hesitant, the miners, with the exception of Daniel, agree to join Cesárea and Pablo in a strike because they realize that they have no other option to improve their situation. Their hesitancy is the result of two factors, first, the memory of the suffering caused by the previous strike, and second, the ingrained fear and respect they feel towards their employers. The situation has become so unbearable, however, that they recognize the strike as the only possible solution to their pain.

As the miners take action by violently attacking the furnaces and throwing rocks at the soldiers that were brought in to break the strike, they openly unite to oppose the tyranny of their opressors. Not only is this the first time that this has occurred in Dicenta's plays, but it also marks a breakthrough in the development of social drama on the Spanish stage, as Hall notes: "*Daniel* is of interest primarily because it was the nearest approach to proletarian mass drama which had been seen on the Madrid stage" (63). Their revolt, however, is a total failure because the miners are defenseless against the armed soldiers. Lives are lost, and the mine is reopened, as the surviving miners return to work accepting the wage cut they had opposed. The tragedy is more the result of the loss of faith of the strikers in their leaders; the miners' inability to comprehend fully the vision of the future as seen by Cesárea and Pablo limits their strength in uniting against their oppressors.

There is evidence of anti-governmental criticism in the practice of using soldiers to quell the disturbances among the working class. By creating the brother against brother situation, Dicenta humanizes both sides. Pedro struggles with his conscience as he explains to his fellow soldiers the difficulty in having to oppose his family and friends:

> ¿No sabes que mi padre y mi hermano y todos mis amigos de cuando era mozo trabajan en la mina? ¿Crees que me sonaría el cuerpo á gloria si tuviese que encarar contra ellos el fusil? Vosotros no conocéis en la mina á nadie, y, claro, ¿qué os importa nadie? Tirar del gatillo entretiene. Si fuéseis de este pueblo, estaríais como estoy yo. (56)

The soldiers are quick to agree with Pedro, but not because he defends his family and friends, but rather, they emphasize the barbarity of having to shoot innocent victims who are just in their desire to improve their conditions: "¡Pero de eso á tirar al montón, no sabiendo á quién vas á darle!" (56). The lieutenant best expresses the soldiers' unrest as they prepare to do what they have been ordered:

> Sería una atrocidad que llegase á haber tiros. ¡Maldita huelga! ¿Por qué nos traerén á esto á los soldados? ¡Nosotros llevamos las armas para cosas más grandes; para pelear contra los enemigos de la patria, no para disparar contra los hambrientos! ¡Ojalá no sea preciso hacer fuego! (57-58)

Dicenta does not find fault in the soldiers personally; instead, he screams out against a society that, instead of providing a force that works for the benefit of the miners' cause, sends soldiers to attack the defenseless workers. Dicenta criticizes the absence in Spanish society of an organization whose sole concern is to help better the lives of the exploited industrial workers. Any improvement in the miners' situation must be obtained through means of self-regeneration; there is no available help from without.

Conclusions

González-Blanco believes that "*Daniel* representa el sindicalismo, el revolucionarismo fuerte y crudo, sin atenuantes" (221). What makes *Daniel* stand out from Dicenta's previous social dramas is the fact that the social question itself is the source of all the dramatic action; it is not concealed behind other themes such as love and honor. Pedro de Répide praises *Daniel*:

> Este drama, más bien tragedia por su grandeza de concepción, es de un gran atrevimiento y de una magnífica belleza artística.... esta obra será siempre considerada como una de las más importantes del moderno teatro europeo. (qtd. in González-Blanco 293)

The revolutionary message in *Daniel* is strong. Although the workers are unsuccessful in their attempt to oppose their employers by striking, there is hope for the future in Daniel's singular violent act. In his sacrificial act of revenge,

Daniel clears the way for future organizational action. The owners are gone, and since Daniel will be shackled with the guilt of mass murder, no one will stand in the way of the miners. The solution to their suffering is found in their ability to seek out a common good in organization; Daniel's sacrifice represents the death of old ideas. It is no wonder that *Daniel* is Dicenta's favorite play, for in it he successfully returns to the social question that catapulted him into the spolight some twelve years earlier with *Juan José*.

LORENZA (1907)

On December 12, 1907, Dicenta's next play, *Lorenza*, premiered in the Teatro Español. A three-act *comedia* written entirely in prose, *Lorenza*, like *Juan Francisco* (1904) and *Marinera* (1907), is set on the Spanish coast, as Dicenta explores the lives of the people in a small fishing village. Although not well-received, *Lorenza* is a significant drama in Dicenta's continued attempt to criticize a society unwilling to accept progress. Dicenta's friend and collaborator, Pedro de Répide, remembers *Lorenza* fondly:

> Estrenó Dicenta una obra que no fué un éxito; pero que también era de su trabajo predilecto, y a mí me parece de las más bellas comedias que se han escrito en estos últimos tiempos. La ví escribir en San Vicente de la Barquera hace diez años y se publicó luego con un prólogo mío. Me refiero a *Lorenza*. Un [sic] ansia de ideal y una noble rebeldía de mujer en un rincón de la costa cantábrica. (qtd. in González-Blanco 293)

PLOT

Lorenza and Mónica are sisters who live with their mother in a small seaside fishing village on the northern coast of Spain. Their father, who was an aspiring artist, died four years earlier and left the family in abject poverty. Before he died, however, he educated his daughters with the hopes that they would someday move up the social ladder and overcome the poverty that oppressed them. Life in the village is unexciting and dismal due to the long cold winters, but when summer arrives, the villagers welcome vacationers from Madrid, Rome, and other cities, who bring with them stories from afar.

Lorenza and Mónica do not fit in any social group because they are too educated to be fisherwomen like their friends and are too poor to be accepted by the wealthy. Because they are the most beautiful women in town, however, they receive much attention from the wealthy young bachelors who come to the beaches to vacation for the summer. Two men in particular, Alberto and Jerónimo, have fallen in love with Lorenza and Mónica, respectively. The wealthy women of the village, especially María, who is consumed with jealousy because of the sisters' love affairs with Alberto and Jerónimo, despise Lorenza and Mónica.

Alberto, who is an accomplished painter, is in love with Lorenza, and Jerónimo, a talented musician, is in love with Mónica. But all four know that as summertime nears its end, the men will have to return to the city, leaving the ladies heartbroken. Lorenza, who is the rebellious sister, struggles with their impending departure, but Mónica accepts the situation, having told herself from the beginning that their relationship was only temporary.

María hopes to embarrass the sisters by not inviting them to the traditional end-of-the-summer party to be held at her home. Alberto and Jerónimo, who are invited, refuse to go, and together with Lorenza and Mónica, they plan to host their own celebration on the beach, by the light of the moon. At their private party, while Mónica and Jerónimo say goodbye, Lorenza and Alberto express their undying love for each other. Alberto asks her to join him on his adventures, but she rejects him, knowing that duty requires her to stay in the village with her mother and her sister.

Later, as the ladies say their last goodbyes, Alberto asks Lorenza once more to consider his offer. Overcome with emotion, she agrees and tells him she will join him. Mónica tries but fails to convince Lorenza to stay, and without saying goodbye to her mother, Lorenza escapes with Alberto, as she pleads with Mónica to forgive her and to ask forgiveness of their mother for her sake. The curtain closes as Alberto and Lorenza embark on a new life together, far from the oppresive village.

SOURCE

During the summer of 1906, Dicenta recorded and published his impressions of his trip to San Vicente de la Barquera, a small fishing port on the Cantabrian coast, in *Desde los rosales*. In one of the essays included in this collection, "Para un drama," Dicenta describes one of the local village girls whose sad situation caught his attention. Her story inspired him to write the essay, "Para un drama," which later became *Lorenza*. Just as Lorenza and Mónica are isolated from the others in their small fishing village, "la niña de la Barquera" also finds herself alone:

> La niña de la Barquera habita un pueblo de sesenta vecinos y es pobre; por su educación, ni gusta el trato de las aldeanas humildes, ni éstas gustan de ella para el trato suyo; por su pobreza, no puede alternar con las señoritas del pueblo; tampoco éstas la conceden alternativa. Se halla entre las unas y las otras, aislada, a distancias iguales, sin poder unirse á ellas, viviendo entre las dos solitariamente. (*Desde* 94).

Even the young men are inaccessible to the young lady for the same reasons, and the summer vacationers are only interested in a brief courtship before they return to the big city. Dicenta describes the tragedy of such a life:

Este es el drama; no el de la niña de la Barquera, el de todas las mujeres destinadas por la suerte á vivir dentro de las aldeas, con hermosura, con educación y sin capital.... ¿Qué porvenir es el de esa niña? En él se halla el asunto, no de un drama, de dos. El un drama es el drama terrible, el trágico, de la mujer que quiere amar á un ser digno, siquiera sea exteriormente, de los amores suyos; el de la que se rebela contra su destino, y ansiosa de volar, de tender las alas que Naturaleza le dió, emprende el viaje con el primero que entona á su oído el soñado cantar, para caer después con las alas rotas. El otro drama es el drama silencioso, manso, más trágico quizás que el primero; el drama de la juventud agostada en la dolorosa faena de esperar lo que jamás ha de venir; es el drama de los días, de las horas, de los minutos, que van dejando huellas en el espíritu y en la carne, y acaban por hacer de la joven soñadora, hermosa y alegre, una solterona agria, fea y ridícula. (*Desde* 95-97).

These two "dramas" described by Dicenta are the inspiration for the two sisters in *Lorenza*, in which he develops the lives of two young ladies who choose opposite paths. Dicenta returns to the same subject in *Rebeldía*, a novel published in 1910, in which he explores the plight of the two sisters, whose names he has changed, at a greater depth.

TECHNIQUE

Lorenza, although Romantic in theme, is a realistic drama full of everyday details of the villagers' lives. The first scene is an entertaining *cuadro de costumbres* in which several townspeople are playing the lottery. They are disappointed when they find they have the losing numbers, except for Pepe, who discovers that he has won a small prize. His hopes are dashed, however, when he receives a baby's rattle. This scene represents the limited options the villagers have for excitement; even the winning prize for the lottery is a joke. *Lorenza* is written entirely in prose, and although many of the characters speak in rural dialect, Lorenza and Mónica do not. As in his previous dramas, Dicenta uses dialect to accurately represent the social status of the individuals on stage. The villagers use colloquialisms, but because Lorenza and Mónica have been educated by their father, their speech is unaffected by the vernacular used by their peers. Instead, they speak with the knowledge learned from the many books in their father's library. As Alberto begins to explain the nature of one of the elaborate celebrations of the wealthy to Lorenza, she quickly interrupts him:

No hace falta. En la biblioteca de mi padre hojeé libros que hablan de esas fiestas. A ser como los poetas griegos las pintan, eran encantadoras. Y eso que hice en traducciones la lectura. Mi sabiduría no llega al griego. (41)

In the same way that the young sisters use a language appropriate to their education, the speech of Alberto and Jerónimo reflects their artistic nature, as one is a painter and the other, a musician. Their language is poetic:

> ALBERTO: ¡Qué deliciosa playa! Mar, cielo y montaña se reunen en ella para que todos los verdes y todos los azules compitan.... No hay forma de recoger en un cacho de lienzo tan diversas tonalidades.
> JERÓNIMO: Ni, de recoger en un pentágrama todos los poemas que aire y mar cantan por aquella atmósfera azul. (14)

Lorenza is essentially Romantic, as it is a story of typical young lovers faced with many obstacles as they try to realize their love. Besides the two sisters and their lovers, there is another pair, La Gibiona and Trasmallo, who provides a different perspective of love between two villagers. Instead of pursuing the "novios de verano," (25) La Gibiona has fallen in love with another fisherman, Trasmallo; however, because her father is so against their relationship, the two are forced to see each other privately. Lorenza envies La Gibiona, saying: "¡Qué feliz eres tú, Gibiona! Sin salir de la aldea hallas tu ventura. Con él puedes realizarla" (60). La Gibiona, however, is forced to suffer physical abuse from her father when he realizes that she has been seeing Trasmallo against his will. Not only is their relationship against her father's wishes, but also Trasmallo's mother discourages it:

> LA GIBIONA: Padre jura que no he de hablar ocntigo y que ha de romperme las costillas si te hablo.
> TRASMALLO: Madre dice que muerto me prefiere á hablando contigo. (35)

The two decide to follow their hearts and rebel against their parents, which futher emphasizes Dicenta's theme of rebellion witnessed in Lorenza's choice to escape the village.

IDEOLOGY
The ideological aspect of *Lorenza* is minor because Dicenta favors the development of the protagonists to a detailed exploration of the problems faced in small towns by growing depopulation and the flight to large cities. However, in his portrayal of the two sisters, Dicenta stresses the boredom and lack of opportunities available to those who live in small Spanish villages, and the inability to improve their situation. Throughout the play, in the mouths of the villagers, Dicenta condemns society for not recognizing the need for progress, and as he did in "Para un drama," Dicenta claims that there is no future for young ladies such as Lorenza and Mónica:

GUNDEMARO: Educadas como señoritas y pobres de solemnidad. ¡Figúrense que provenir el suyo!
PEPE: El de todas las señoritas aldeanas, pobres como ellas ó como ellas con inteligencia y corazón. Desesperarse mientras envejecen y jugar á matrimonios irrealizables con novios de verano. (16)

The two sisters, however, are not the only ones who suffer; all of the villagers complain about the long harsh winters and the short summers. As the summer nears its end, Pérez explains what awaits the fishermen: "Para los pescadores sólo quedan diez ó doce días de buen comer. Luego se entra el invierno y con el invierno las hambres" (32).

The difference between the two sisters is clear from the beginning; while Mónica is timid and unadventurous, Lorenza longs for a faster paced life in the city. Mónica defends their mother, Petra, when Lorenza complains that she does not understand how much they are suffering. Lorenza claims that life would have been more tolerable if their parents had educated the two girls in the business of fishing: "Mal hizo nuestro padre en no educarnos como á las pescadoras. Seríamos dos bestias más" (24). Instead, they were educated in the manner of the wealthy young women of the village. Unfortunately, their extreme poverty, when combined with the education provided them by their father, makes the two sisters incapable of fitting into any social group. Lorenza laments their limitations to the mayor of the village who has the luxury of attending two separate parties:

Usté puede estar en los dos sitios, nosotras en ninguno. Para el baile del casino nuestro vestir es poco, para el baile de la plaza, mucho. En el uno no nos sacarían por descote de menos. En el otro nos quedaríamos sentadas por volante de más. (38-39)

Mónica, on the other hand, seems content with her life, willing to accept what fate has given her. Unlike her sister who is fascinated by the stories of the big cities told by Jerónimo and Alberto, Mónica is frightened: "Me asusta esa vida y ese mundo de que usted me habla.... No podría vivir en ellos" (45). When Jerónimo encourages her to follow him on his adventures, Mónica explains to him that she is not the type: "Algunas suben mucho, porque tienen las alas grandes; las que tienen pequeñas las alas, vuelan á ras de tierra. Yo debo ser de estas, Jerónimo" (46). Lorenza, however, has always dreamed of leaving the village for the city, as she describes to Alberto: "Mi imaginación, educada para otros horizontes, sufría en esta cárcel imbécil de la aldea. ¡Soñar soñar con el amor que tú realizas, era mi exclusiva ventura" (64). While Mónica claims that the thought of living in the big city makes her sick, "respiro mal y me ahogo"

(45), Lorenza declares that living in the village suffocates her: "me ahogo aquí. Esta atmósfera concluirá por matarme" (65). Both women are well developed, and their decisions at the end of the drama are in keeping with their personalities. Dicenta does not mean to express to his audience that one has made a better choice than the other, but rather that they each have chosen the correct path. Perhaps the title of the play is the only indication of Dicenta's preference for Lorenza's choice.

CONCLUSIONS

Although *Lorenza* could have been a powerful social drama treating the widespread discontent among those living in small Spanish villages and the problems associated with the depopulation of these towns because of the increase in the number of people migrating to large cities, Dicenta chose to develop the tragedy of a pair of sisters and their personal struggles. Although the theme is Romantic, the characters and the setting are convincing and realistic. There is no doubt that *Lorenza* would have achieved more fame had Dicenta developed the play in a more realistic manner with less sentimentality.

EL CRIMEN DE AYER (1908)

In the same way that one of Dicenta's earliest plays, *Los irresponsables* (1890), questions the traditional view of marriage, *El crimen de ayer*, which was first performed in the Teatro Español on February 18, 1908, examines the traditional view of the family, as Dicenta argues for the rights of the illegitimate child. As in *Lorenza*, *Marinera*, and *Aurora*, the protagonist of *El crimen de ayer* is a woman; however, unlike the leading women in Dicenta's previous plays, Carmen has more in common with Dicenta's most well known male protagonists, Juan José and Daniel. Rather than seeking social justice through legal means, Carmen takes justice into her own hands by punishing her oppressor. In comparing Carmen to Juan José and Daniel, Manuel Bueno finds: "Todos ellos son seres humillados y ofendidos que, en vez de pedir á la justicia social un amparo que no había de darles, aplican por su propia mano el castigo adecuado á sus opresores" (121).

PLOT

Much like *Amor de artistas* (1906), *El crimen de ayer* focuses on the more glamorous lifestyle of the artist rather than the poor oppressed working class. The play begins in an artist's studio as Mariano is celebrating his success as a painter. All of the guests, with the exception of Julián, share the same interests as they are all part of the artist community. Julián, a law student who is about to complete his studies, is accepted into their social group because of his love for art and his generous gifts of money and alcohol. Julián and his lover, Carmen, have a newborn son, and although Julián seems unenthusiastic about his child, their friends praise the infant.

The majority of the play takes place at Mariano's studio or an art exhibit where Mariano has the opportunity to show his work. There is much dialogue between the characters concerning art, as they each describe their current projects and their personal views about art in general. One of Mariano's most recent paintings is a poignant portrayal of a mother and her child who have been abandoned by the father. It is such an excellent piece that everyone is mesmerized by it, especially Carmen, who sees her own image in the realistic representation of the mother's tragedy. Mariano's friends mingle with the wealthy guests at the exhibit in order to eavesdrop on their conversations about Mariano's paintings. Carmen overhears two young men discuss Julián's impending marriage to a wealthy young lady who lives in the countryside near his parents. Carmen is overwhelmed with shock and despair as she realizes that Julián's plan to leave the following morning for his yearly summer trip to visit his parents is more than likely a one-way trip. Now that his academic responsibilites are finished, the only reason he would have to return to the city is Carmen and their son.

The final act takes place in Carmen and Julián's home. When Julián arrives, Carmen demands that he tell her the truth about his future plans. While admitting that he is planning to get married, Julián denies having had anything to do with the arranged marriage his parents have orchestrated, and he insists that he never planned to leave Carmen and the baby. Realizing that Julián is marrying another, Carmen no longer mourns for her own loss, but rather the loss her son will suffer the rest of his life. Carmen angrily rejects Julián, claiming that the relationship between a man and a woman may be broken, but the one between a father and child should never be torn apart. For the child's welfare, she demands that Julián provide the infant with his name, to ensure that Julianito will not suffer undue prejudice from a society that condemns the illegitimate child. Julián weakly promises to do so when Julianito is older and the name is needed. Carmen fears that she is the reason that Julián hesitates; thus she pleads with him to take the child to raise in a traditional manner and give him his name. Carmen is futher overcome with hatred when Julián denies the child, as he explains that all he is able to provide for now is love and support. She recognizes the truth behind his empty promises; if their baby has his name, the existence of this child would be scandalous for him in his new career. As he begins to walk out the door, she takes her sewing scissors and stabs him to death.

TECHNIQUE / IDEOLOGY

El crimen de ayer returns Dicenta to the treatment of the artist and the bohemian lifestyle reminiscent of *Amor de artistas* (1906) and *El suicidio de Werther* (1888). In *El crimen de ayer*, Dicenta combines the skillful character development of *El suicidio de Werther* with the realistic and convincing setting of *Amor de artistas*, but rather than place the artist as the protagonist, Dicenta gives the primary role to a young woman who is part of the social circle of a group of artists.

The Romantic characteristics of his first drama, *El suicidio de Werther*, are no longer evident in *El crimen de ayer*; instead, Dicenta treats the same thesis more effectively in a less adorned, more realistic manner. Much like the characters in *Amor de artistas*, Carmen and her friends are realistic in their conversations, interests, and actions. Dicenta's stage directions are extremely detailed, demanding that the setting and the execution of the scenes be as realistic as possible. The details of the domestic preparation at Mariano's home during dinner and the planning and management of the art exhibit further enhance the overall realism of the drama. Much like the well-written descriptions in *Amor de artistas* of the behind-the-scenes activity of a a successful drama as it is being performed, the nervousness of Mariano and the excitement of his friends as he presents his art to the public in an exhibition are convincing representations of life at the turn of the century. Even the background characters are more individual and realistic than in Dicenta's earlier dramas, and although violent and full of passion, the tragic murder that closes the play is credible because of the situation leading up to the event, not because of any Romantic formula. The use of the painting as a mirror of the protagonist's tragedy is not new, for Dicenta had already used this device in *El suicidio de Werther* (1888). Carmen's words, "Este cuadro me parece un espejo. Creo que no es ella, sino yo, la que está dentro de él," are reminiscent of Fernando as he contemplates the tragic suicide of Werther in his painting (44). As it was in Dicenta's first drama, the painting is effective as a symbol of fate in *El crimen de ayer*, casting a dark shadow of impending doom throughout the drama.

The structure of *El crimen de ayer* is different from any of Dicenta's previous plays; the first two acts, while setting the stage for the tragedy of the final act, are full of satire, allowing Dicenta, through his characters (fellow artists), to express his opinions about art and life in general; whereas in Act III, all semblance of satire is abandoned as the play is brought to its dramatic end. Dicenta's message, as usual, is multi-faceted: he argues for the rights of the illegitimate child, attacking society for victimizing innocent children and condemning fathers who do not provide a name for their offspring outside of marriage; he praises free love, forcing his audiences to reevaluate the significance of marriage; and finally, he criticizes the French theory of "art for art's sake."

Dicenta's strongest argument is that in defense of the illegitimate child. Juan José grew up without a father or mother, and the lack of love and affection coupled with the condemnation of an unforgiving society pushed him over the edge towards a life of crime. Fernando (*El suicidio de Werther*) was also abandonded first by his father and later his mother as an infant, and he too struggled throughout his life to make a name for himself through his talent as an artist. Again, society would not allow an illegitimate child to succeed. In *El crimen de ayer*, however, Dicenta approaches the issue from a different angle; rather than portraying an adult who fights for justice for his own well-being after having been victimized his whole life for not having a legitimate name, Dicenta starts at the source of the problem: the moment the father abandons the child. While contemplating the painting, one of Mariano's friends, Pedro, is overcome with hatred for such a man who could abandon his child: "a él, a ese tío que la abandona, le estrangularía..." (43). In a conversation with Irene, Carmen complains that Julián refuses to provide their baby with his name until he is older:

> Un hijo sin nombre a nada obliga. Cuando se convierte en obstáculo se le da con el pie y a otra cosa. ¿Quién va a salir por él? ¿La madre? ¿La que se entregó como amante?... para el mundo la mujer que se entrega así es una perdida. Así me entregué yo. (46)

Upon the realization that Julián is planning to marry another, Carmen claims that their son suffers more than those who live in the streets and starve: "Más pobre que los que aguardan con su madre, en la calle, en el quicio de una puerta cualquiera, el regreso del padre. A veces viene éste sin pan, pero viene siempre con amor" (59). Confronting Julián, Carmen begs him to provide a name for his son, and when he replies that the boy will always have his financial support, Carmen becomes enraged, shouting:

> ¡Qué pido!... Tu nombre para él... La protección, el apoyo moral que el oro no compra ni regala ¡Es el hijo tuyo, Julián! ¿No será horrible que el hijo tuyo tenga que bajar los ojos mañana y no se atreva a responder cuando le pregunten: ¿Quién eres tú? ¿Quién era tu padre? ¿No será espantoso que le digan: "¡Vete! No eres a nosotros igual. De los dos seres que dignifican con sus nombres del hijo te falta uno, por desconocido o por negado..." Ve que son heridas incurables las que tales frases producen. (69-70)

Carmen's act of revenge at the close of the drama is not done on her own behalf, but rather, it is an act of punishment against Julián for invoking those prejudices against their son by denying him a name. Following the murder of Julián, the future for mother and child is not improved, despite Carmen's explanation to the infant: "Vale más que no tengas padre que tengas ése" (71). Carmen will be imprisoned for her crime, and Julianito will be left with neither a father or a mother. The only hope that Dicenta provides is in Carmen's dear friends, Irene and Mariano, who upon several occasions have made it clear that they will support Carmen in any way possible, perhaps by adopting the child.

The relationship between Irene and Mariano is important in the development of Dicenta's thesis, because through them he intends to prove that free love is an acceptable and even preferable choice, and that those who do not marry can still live fulfilled lives, perhaps even more so than their married counterparts. Dicenta has long been an advocate of free love, for based upon his own experience, he found it to be far more satisfying than marriage. After his short-lived marriage, Dicenta spent the rest of his life with his beloved Amparito, a gypsy with whom he had children. Manuel Bueno believes *El crimen de ayer* represents "un ambiente que él [Dicenta] conoce mejor que nadie" (124). Manuel Bueno continues:

> Un mundo de bojemios que funciona á espaldas de la ley, sin que eso prive de alegría á sus moradores...las gentes viven más á gusto fuera de la legalidad que dentro, y una mujer y un hombre son más dichosos cuando "se juntan" que cuando "se casan." (124)

This world that Dicenta creates in *El crimen de ayer* consists of a group of friends, none of whom are married. Each pair at Mariano's dinner is joined by common consent and affection. Their relationships are stable without any hint of promiscuity, they maintain established homes, they appear to be permanently attached, and they observe the same domestic obligations any married couple might.

The dysfunctional relationship between Carmen and Julián, however, contrasts greatly with the seemingly perfect relationships of their friends, and throughout the play Dicenta draws a clear distinction between them. While the other couples live together as if they were married, Julián maintains a separate house from that of Carmen, as Mariano describes: "Julián me presta su criado. El que le sirve en el cuarto de soltero, donde vive Julián para su familia y para las personas graves. Julián es inmenso. ¡Un hombre con dos casas!" (13). Irene's response, "Y con dos caras: una para cada domicilio," is acrimonious as she reveals a truth about Julián that foreshadows the tragedy to follow. Later, as Carmen complains that Julián rarely laughs or pays any attention to her, Pepa responds: "Pedro y yo por qualquier cosa nos reímos. Siempre estamos alegres" (14). Carmen, however, is so lonely for company in the house she shares with their newborn son, that she often finds herself talking to flowers, "hasta creo que me responden" (16). She claims that Julián calls her "romanticona y cursi," while Irene describes the fun and loving relationship she and Mariano enjoy:

> Las horas muertas hemos ido Mariano y yo de campo en campo como dos criaturas. El deshojando flores y arrojándomelas a la cara, yo arrojando una a una las hojas de las margaritas y preguntándoles: ¿Me quiere?

Sí... No... Sí...No... Cuando la margarita acababa en no, sentía ganas de arañar a Mariano. Necesitaba él repetir: ¡Te quiero!...¡Te quiero!...cien y cien veces, para quitarme el mal humor. (16-17)

Carmen's friends know that she suffers, and they pity her, saying: "Si nosotras hubiésemos encontrado antes lo que hemos encontrado después, quizás no tendríamos después" (22). They love Carmen deeply, but their affection for Julián is shallow: "Si él gasta su oro con nosotros, nosotros gastamos nuestro ingenio con él" (28). Perhaps the most obvious difference between Julián and the other men of the group is his lack of affection for his child. When he complains that Carmen brought the infant to the celebration, Mariano exclaims loudly with pride: "El día que tenga un chico, lo llevaré en brazos hasta a las sesiones académicas, dado caso que me rematen de académico" (30). Julián recognizes the difference: "Ustedes, los artistas, son muy distintos a nosotros. Nosotros necesitamos ser formales" (31).

Besides Dicenta's generous support of free love and his argument against child abandonment, a third issue exists in *El crimen de ayer*. As he recreates the world of the artist, Dicenta seizes the opportunity to express his opinion on a particular literary movement that was becoming increasingly more popular, that of "Art for Art's Sake." Originally propounded by Théophile Gautier in 1835 in the preface to *Mademoiselle de Maupin*, "Art for Art's Sake" experienced a new popularity towards the end of the nineteenth century, as it became fashionable in symbolist circles. In the character of Ruderico, who is extremely exaggerated, Dicenta builds a witty satire against this new theory, yet without resorting to any bitterness. In one of Dicenta's most amusing scenes, Ruderico, a dramatist, when provided an opportunity to describe his latest play, proudly tells of his hard work: "Há tres meses laboro en él. Ya llevo burilados tres versos...." (32). Dicenta mocks the frivolity of having spent three entire months writing only three verses. Ruderico also insists that the most important thing in his drama is color and tone. Rather than putting any importance on the meaning of the play, he contends that "cada oración debe ser un lirio" (33). Ruderico elaborates:

> Mi propósito es dar idea de la tristeza del asunto por medio del color.... El morado es el color esencialmente triste.... La escena se desarrollará en las gradaciones de un crepúsculo vespertino. Resplandores morados descienden de un cielo morado: morados estarán árboles y plantas; morado será el pergeño de los personajes ; morado... (32)

Angel teases Ruderico as he interrupts his friend: "Morado va a ponerte el público si representan tu berengena literaria" (33). Ruderico begs his friends to listen to the three verses it has taken him three months to write, and despite Angel's sarcastic "Déjalo para cuando esté completa la estrofa, el siglo venitiuno," Ruderico recites the verses emphatically:

¡Din! ¡Don¡ ¡Din! ¡Don¡ La campana toca, doncella.
¡Din! ¡Don¡ ¡Din! ¡Don¡ Su son es la fragancia de los lirios que oprimes; lirial tú, pálida hija de la tarde muriente. (33)

Ruderico's friends make fun of him in a loving way as they joke about the ridiculousness of his ideas.

CONCLUSIONS

Dicenta's critics have failed to recognize the quality of *El crimen de ayer* in their discussions of his work, perhaps because it is not defined as a social drama due to the lack of a class struggle. Dicenta's artistic development, however, shows great improvement in *El crimen de ayer* as he reworks an earlier thesis, that of the abandoned and illegitimate child from *El suicidio de Werther* (1888). Dicenta's thesis is clear and his characters are well developed. Gone are the Romantic characteristics that defined his first play as they are replaced by realistic elements that make *El crimen de ayer* a superior drama.

LOS MAJOS DE PLANTE (1908)

Dicenta's next drama, a *sainete*, was performed two months following *El crimen de ayer* on April 11, 1908 in the Teatro Español and was written in collaboration with Pedro de Répide, a fellow dramatist and dear friend of Dicenta. The second of four dramas by Dicenta that were performed in 1908, *Los majos de plante* is a lighthearted one-act play set in Madrid in 1800. Keeping in form with the one-act *sainete* made popular by Ramón de la Cruz in the second half of the eighteenth century, *Los majos de plante* is written in the *costumbrista* manner as it pokes fun at the low social classes.

PLOT

As is customary in a *sainete*, there is little plot development as the characters playfully interact with each other; however, because of a thirty-year-old secret, *Los majos de plante* follows a short story line that culminates in the secret being revealed. The play takes place in Madrid in the *barrios bajos* as the characters make their way to a party to celebrate the victory of Joselito and "El Rondeño," two bullfighters who barely escaped death the day before. Among the characters who plan to attend the dance are a priest whose main interest is good food, an abbé who constantly complains about his duties, Alonso el Bueno, a newcomer to Madrid who is known for his charity and his saintly nature, and several *petimetres, petimetras, majos*, and *majas*, including "La Resalada" and her mother, Mochuela. Mochuela is surprised to find out that Alonso el Bueno has heard about a tragic event in her past that she has not been able to forget.

Thirty years earlier two young men fought over her; one was killed, and the other, "El Castizo," fled, never to be heard from again. At the party, "El Remellao," a mean bully who enjoys intimidating everyone in his presence, pulls a knife and demands that the dancing cease and that everyone leave. His wishes are granted as the *majas* run inside, shrieking in fear, and the *majos* follow to protect them from such a wild man. "La Resalada," who is in love with "El Remellao," remains with him, as she flirts shamelessly with the mean spirited *majo*. Alonso el Bueno arrives late, and after he pulls off his mask, "El Remellao" draws back in shock as he recognizes Alonso el Bueno as "El Castizo." Alonso demands that "El Remellao" ask forgiveness of the partygoers and that he humbly leave. His secret being revealed, Alonso ("El Castizo") begs mercy of Mochuela and the rest for his life of crime. "La Resalada" embraces him, and the dancing and partying begin anew.

TECHNIQUE

Following in the tradition of Ramón de la Cruz, and more recently Dicenta's childhood friend, Carlos Arniches, Dicenta and Répide model their *sainete* after the established form, including many of the devices characteristic of the *sainetes* of the eighteenth century. Intended to be a comedy, *Los majos de plante* is quite humorous as the characters make fun of each other, argue, flirt, and go about their lives. Two of the most amusing characters are religious figures, Fray Serapio and Abate Jalea. Fray Serapio's main concern is food, and whenever given the chance, he discusses his irrational love for it. His comments are funny and mostly inappropriate. For example, upon learning that Alonso el Bueno has forced "El Remellao" to allow the party to proceed, Fray Serapio approaches "El Remellao" and shouts angrily at him: "¡Y para esto perturbaste la digestión de un cristiano!" (37). While most everyone humors the priest by providing him his favorite dishes, the common feeling towards Abate Jalea is disdain. His constant complaining and insistence that he deserves better have embittered the people towards him. "La Resalada" expresses her opinion with contempt: "Si en lugar de ser abate fuérais hombre, quizá habláramos" (18). The Abate is a character type common in Ramón de la Cruz's *sainetes*, and as John A. Moore describes, he is "usually a socially ambitious member of the poor class" (26). This definition explains Abate Jalea's constant grumbling about his position. Another character type is the *majo* or the *maja*. Moore's description of the *majos* typical of Ramón de la Cruz's one-act plays also applies to both "El Remellao" and "La Resalada" of *Los majos de plante*: "A boastful man with a chip on his shoulder, the *majo* is ready to fight on the slightest provocation. The *maja* is also quite quarrelsome and prone to violence if she is provoked or threatened by another *maja*" (26). The *petimetres* and the *petimetras* are also typical of Ramón de la Cruz's *sainetes*, and although their presence on the stage in *Los majos de plante* is minimal, they serve to accurately reflect the French influence in Spain that was popular in the eighteenth century. In one particular scene, one of the most humorous of the play, several *petimetres* find themselves in the company of a "poetastro famélico" who seizes the opportunity to express his opinion about the decline of the Spanish stage:

> ¿Dónde hay algun ingenio en quien se junten
> el pensar grave y el decir honesto?
> ¿Decís que Jovellanos? *¡Retro vade!*
> ¿Decís que Moratín? *Párvula* gente.
> ¿Es Ramón de la Cruz? ¿Qué oído pulcro,
> su lenguaje al oir rubor no siente?
> Los modernos, ¿qué son? *Pulvis vermícula.* (27-28)

Dicenta and Répide poke fun at the criticism that Jovellanos, Moratín and Ramón de la Cruz endured in their attempt to bring life to the Spanish theater at a time when the Spanish stage suffered from a lack of quality drama.

CONCLUSIONS

Dicenta's only *sainete*, the one-act, three-cuadro *Los majos de plante*, was a feeble attempt to capture the fame and success achieved by his friend Carlos Arniches, who together with the Quintero brothers, Martínez Sierra, Linares Rivas, and Jacinto Benavente, dominated the Spanish stage in the first quarter of the twentieth century. Dicenta and Répide adhere to the definition of *sainete* as *Los majos de plante*, which is written in verse, depicts a *costumbrista* dialogue, parodies the low social classes, and makes fun of the *afrancesados*. The play, however, is weak as a whole. The comic element, although present, does not predominate, and the underlying plot of Alonso el Bueno's true identity seems to be a forced addition to the *cuadro de costumbres*. More accustomed to portraying society's ills, Dicenta is awkward in the genre of the *sainete*. Although successful in his earlier *zarzuelas*, Dicenta's attempt to recreate one of Spain's most popular forms of theater was a failure. Perhaps that is the reason he never again returned to the *sainete* in his work

ENTRE ROCAS (1908)

A month following the premiere of *Los majos de plante*, Dicenta's next play, *Entre rocas*, made its debut in the Gran Teatro de Madrid on May 21, 1908. *Entre rocas* is a revised shortened version (one-act) of the lengthier lyrical drama *Juan Francisco*[1] (three acts), first performed on December 22, 1904. The plot is nearly identical to the original, with the exception of several minor

---

[1] For a plot summary of *Juan Francisco*, see page 169.

changes to make the drama more appropriate for the *teatro por horas* and to correct the awkward combination of a thesis with an exaggerated Romantic plot, present in *Juan Francisco*. Besides changing the title of the drama, Dicenta changes only one name, that of Juan Francisco, who becomes Pedro Antonio in *Entre rocas*; all of the remaining characters have the same name, with the exception of Sargento, the humorous bachelor who provides comic relief in his constant flirting with Curra, who is no longer present in the new one-act version of the play. Neither is the melodramatic yet amusing relationship between Pascual and María as detailed as it was in the original. The biggest changes in *Entre rocas* are in Dicenta's decision to remove the heavy thesis and to minimize the Romantic nature of the drama, making it a much more simple play without the strong message and emotional excessiveness that made *Juan Francisco* one of Dicenta's weakest dramas. In fact, *Entre rocas* is lighthearted and funny, and the murder scene that closes *Juan Francisco* is completely removed in *Entre rocas* to avoid spilling blood on the stage. In the original, Juan Francisco defends Anita's honor by killing Gaspar, thus winning the approval of her father once again. In *Entre rocas*, however, Pedro Antonio (who is Juan Francisco) allows Gaspar to escape uninjured, having proven himself enough to his future father-in-law. Although totally ignored by critics, *Entre rocas* is a well-written drama that successfully avoids the errors made in the original, and its superiority over *Juan Francisco* proves Dicenta's skillfullness at adapting prior works into more successful pieces.

CONFESIÓN (1908)

Dicenta's last of four plays performed in 1908, *La confesión*, made its debut on September 5, 1908 in the Teatro Salón Regio. A one-act *comedia* in prose, *La confesión* is a moving representation of the suffering of one man and his family as he nears death.

PLOT

Many years ago Santiago went to Africa in search of adventure and gold. After discovering a seemingly bottomless gold mine, he and his family have lived a life of luxury ever since. Now in his sixties, Santiago is suffering from heart disease and is near death. His wife, Feliciana, and dauther, Antonia, are concerned about his spiritual state, but not necessarily because of religious reasons. They fear that Santiago's refusal to repent and receive his last rites will disgrace them among their wealthy peers. With the help of one of their affluent friends, Adela, they arrange for a priest to meet with them to discuss methods of convincing Santiago to listen to their wishes. The priest, Father Enrique, explains to the two women that they are better equipped to influence Santiago than he is since they are his family. Father Enrique encourages them to enter into Santiago's room to talk to him, and if they should need his help, he will be available in the front room.

At first Santiago is annoyed at his wife and daughter's insistence that he speak with the priest, but when they continue to discuss the hereafter, he becomes increasingly more frightened. Santiago asks his daughter if she believes that the good are rewarded and the bad are punished in the afterlife, and upon her emphatic "lo creo," he begins to sob. Santiago demands that they both listen carefully because he plans to confess a horrible crime of his youth. When he was in Africa many years ago, he and a fellow miner had promised each other that if they discovered gold, they would share it with each other and split the fortune. The other young man accidentally came across a mineshaft that led to another area further away where there was gold. Overcome by his selfishness, as his partner pointed the way, Santiago stabbed him in the back, killing him. He hastily threw the body in some rocks and claimed the fortune for himself. After his heartfelt confession, Santiago orders his wife and daughter to search for the family that rightfully deserves half of their fortune, and then he begs them to bring the priest in to him to administer his last rites. The two women ignore Santiago's plea, and they leave the room, shutting the door behind them. Santiago falls dead on a chair, and the women tell the priest that it is too late.

TECHNIQUE / IDEOLOGY

Set in the "época actual," the first decade of the twentieth century, *La confesión* is a harsh attack on the selfish and shallow nature of the wealthy and the negative power of money. The stage is divided in half, with the result that the audience witnesses the events of two separate rooms simultaneously; the one on the left is the sitting room, and the one on the right is Santiago's bedroom. At first it seems that Feliciana and Antonia are sincere in their grief and in their fear that Santiago will die a heretic since he has consistently rejected all articles of faith his entire life. We soon realize, however, that money has poisoned them; the two women are only concerned about keeping up appearances. When Adela and her daughter stop in to visit with them briefly, they talk about all of the high society functions that Feliciana and Antonia are missing because of Santiago's illness. After a long description of all that they have done, Adela exclaims: "¡Cómo os echarán de menos en todos esos sitios!" (9). Their conversation turns quickly to Santiago's refusal to accept the beliefs of the church. Adela says aloud what Feliciana and Antonia are most worried about:

> Por todos los medios hay que evitar semejante desgracia. ¡Un hombre de la posición de Santiago morir como un hereje!... ¡Y verle camino del cementerio civil con cuatro coches á la zaga... porque no llevaría más de cuatro coches!... ¡Ir así, á un cementerio donde no entierran más que golfos, un personaje que puede recibir telegráficamente la bendición papal y tener sufragios en las principales iglesias y llevar cruz alzada junto al carro

fúnebre, y detrás del carro fúnebre todos los carruajes propios de Madrid! ¡No, hija, de ninguna manera! Aunque sólo sea por "el qué dirán" debe presentarse á ello Santiago. (11)

The two women are more concerned about the disgrace they will suffer if Santiago refuses to repent than they are about his eternal damnation. This is especially obvious in the final moments of Santiago's life as Feliciana and Antonia are horrified at his confesion of murder, as Feliciana exclaims selfishly: "¡La miseria para nosotros!" (25). Santiago, who at once feels released from the heavy burden that he has suffered for most of his life, tells his wife and daughter to immediately begin searching for the family of the young man he killed so long ago: "Hay que dárselo todo, ¡todo! ¡Es suyo! Nuestro no es nada. ¡nada! Pronto, hija mía, ¡pronto!" (25). He then remembers that they had asked a priest to come to talk to him, and excited about the possibility of repentance before his death, Santiago asks: "¿Dices que un hombre de bien quiere hablarme? ¡Que entre! ¡Porque yo muero!… ¿Qué os detiene? ¡Llamadle! ¡Habré de ir yo en su busca!" (25). Dicenta's stage directions clearly indicate the mutual decision made by the two women:

> Feliciana y Antonia se miran un momento fijo, muy fijo y abriendo la puerta que comunica con el gabinete, salen á el, cerrándola tras sí, mientras Santiago se desploma en el sillón donde queda inmóvil, agonizante, con los ojos clavados en la puerta. (25)

Rather than taking the risk that their peers find out the horrible truth about their great wealth, they sacrifice Santiago's soul, because, for them, it is far worse to lose their fortune than to suffer the disgrace that Santiago died a "hereje."

Dicenta also uses this short powerful drama to ridicule the role religion plays in the lives of many, especially the role it plays in the lives of the wealthy. For Feliciana and Antonia, being religious was one of the many obligations they had as members of the upper class. Adela explains her shallow opinion: "Vaya que mientras una vive descuide á Dios algunas veces, pero a la hora de la muerte hay que quedar bien" (12). It is clear that Feliciana and Antonia were never truly concerned about Santiago's soul; their only concern was maintaining their high social position. Although Dicenta condemns the use of religion to manipulate people, *La confesión* is not anticlerical. Padre Enrique is characterized as a warm, intelligent, and caring individual, one who is not willing to force a belief on anyone who is not ready to listen. As he waits in the sitting room to hear from the two women, Padre Enrique quotes a passage from the Bible: "En verdad os digo que más fácil le es á un camello entrar por el ojo de una aguja que 'a un rico en el reino de Dios" (20).

CONCLUSIONS

A very powerful drama, *La confesión* is an excellent example of Dicenta's ability to take a simple theme, that of a father on his death bed, and use it to his own advantage to attack the selfish and shallow upper class. As in previous dramas, Dicenta exhibits little mercy for the wealthy, especially those who have obtained their wealth by criminal means (Roque in *El señor feudal*).

LOS TRES MARIDOS BURLADOS (1909)

On February 5, 1909, Dicenta's next play, *Los tres maridos burlados*, premiered in the Teatro Eslava. Written in collaboration with Pedro de Répide, *Los tres maridos burlados* is a *comedia de enredos* inspired by the novel of the same name by Tirso de Molina (1584-1648). The drama treats the dissatisfaction of three married women with their husbands and their separate acts of revenge.

PLOT

Brígida, Hipólita, and Mari-Pérez are three married women who each complain about their husbands. Brígida's husband, Diego, is an alcoholic, and his excessive drinking is more than she can bear. Hipólita's husband, Lucas, is a miser who does not share any money with her, forcing her to borrow from friends, and Mari-Pérez's husband, Gonzalo, is an extremely jealous man, always keeping a watchful eye on his young wife. One particular afternoon, the three ladies discover a large diamond in the bushes, and they begin to fight over the beautiful jewel. Fray Bernardo breaks up the fight, and tells them that he has an excellent solution. He challenges the three women to teach each of their husbands a lesson by playing a practical joke on them. She who does so with the most success wins the diamond.

With the help of her neighbors and friends, Hipólita convinces her husband, Lucas, that he looks very ill. She calls the doctor, a friend of hers, who examines Lucas carefully. The fake doctor tells Lucas that he is near death, and that he must do all of the necessary preparations before he dies. Horrified, Lucas mentions the money box he has buried behind the church, and he immediately leaves to retrieve it. Upon his return, he finds his wife dressed all in black, weeping. He overhears his neighbors talking about his own death. He enters his house, and all who are inside recoil in shock, pretending that Lucas is a ghost. He claims that he is still alive, and they demand that he leave, assuring him that Lucas already died. Convinced that he is dead, Lucas leaves. After his departure, Hipólita and her friends are overcome with laughter.

Brígida also takes advantage of her neighbors and friends to help her in her attempt to trick her husband. When he arrives home, she is lying on the sofa complaining of horrible aches and pains. She convinces him that he must go to the other side of town, even in the pouring rain, to get the only doctor whom she will allow to see her. After much convincing, Diego finally leaves. As soon as he is gone, everyone begins to rearrange the furniture, remove wall hangings, replace doors, and redecorate the house, even changing the sign outside from "Taller de Morales" to "Casa de posadas." Upon his return, Diego is surprised to hear music and dancing coming from inside his house. He knocks on the door, and the music stops. He demands to know what is going on, and he is told that there are no rooms available for him. Brígida claims that she owns the inn, and she asks him to leave. He becomes angry at his wife, as he reaches for his sword. Brígida's friends come to her aid, as they accuse Diego of being drunk. They carry him ouside, and tell him never to return. As he leaves, everyone laughs heartily at their success.

By slipping a sleeping potion into Gonzalo's soup, Mari-Pérez and her friends are able to transport Gonzalo to the convent, where they undress him, shave his beard, moustache, and head. They place him in bed, and Mari-Pérez escapes outside to a window from which she has an excellent view of the scene about to occur. Cleto, one of the brothers, passes smelling salts under Gonzalo's nose to awaken him. Once awake, Gonzalo calls for his wife, for his maid, and no one answers. Soon he hears a knock on his door, and Cleto enters, calling him Father Rebolledo. Gonzalo is confused and insists that he is Gonzalo Santillana. When Cleto holds up a mirror for Gonzalo to see for himself who he is, Gonzalo becomes violent as he tries to choke Cleto. Fray Bernardo and the other *frailes* enter the room and listen to Gonzalo's story. They conclude that he must be possessed by the devil. They begin the process of exorcising the demons from Gonzalo, who, in order to make them stop, finally admits that he is Father Rebolledo. Mari-Pérez comes to his aid, running into his room as she claims that she has been searching for him all evening.

Father Bernardo explains to Gonzalo that he was punished for being so jealous and mistreating his wife. Gonzalo begs forgiveness of the priest and his wife. Hipólita arrives with Lucas, whom she chastises for hiding money away from her. She tells Father Bernardo that Lucas never came home all night, and the priest reprimands the miser. Finally, Brígida drags Diego in by the ear, complaining that his drinking has gone too far. Not being able to defend himself, Diego accepts the rebuke of Father Bernardo. At once the three men realize what has happened to them. Father Bernardo explains to them that they had to be punished for their bad behavoir. They all three agree to treat their wives with respect and to cease all activity that gives into their vices. The women each receive a diamond, and the one that they found in the bushes is donated to the church.

Technique

In *Los tres maridos burlados* Dicenta and Répide follow the Golden Age formula for drama, giving the action the most important role. Rather than providing a detailed character development, Dicenta and Répide create a drama that is essentially a drama of action. Because plot is paramount, character analysis is unneccessary, and audience involvement is essential. A play full of incident, with three separate actions, *Los tres maridos burlados* is divided into a prologue followed by three *cuadros*, each *cuadro* focusing on a specific couple. As is typical in Golden Age plays, the main theme in *Los tres maridos burlados* is poetic justice, as each of the three husbands is punished for his wrongdoings and the wives are justly rewarded, leaving the audience with a feeling of satisfaction. Another more minor theme, that of baroque disillusionment, also plays a role as the wayward husbands find themselves questioning reality, much like Segismundo in Calderón de la Barca's *La vida es sueño*. Just as Segismundo recognizes that he must be responsible for his actions, the three husbands are forced to reevaluate their treatment of their wives. One cannot ignore the similarity between the *engaño* of Gonzalo, who, like Segismundo, was drugged and taken someplace else where he was awakened to what he thought to be a dream.

Unlike the Golden Age dramas that *Los tres maridos burlados* was modeled after, Dicenta and Répide's play is not so heavy with a moral lesson as to turn away twentieth century audiences. Whereas Calderón de la Barca's main intent in *La vida es sueño* is to push the public to question reality and to recognize the consequences of bad behavior, Dicenta and Répide's purpose for writing *Los tres maridos burlados* is entertainment, a way to breathe life back into the genre that represents Spain's most glorious moment on stage. Greatly contrasting with the selection of dramas available to the public in Madrid in 1909, Dicenta and Répide's newest play was written with the intention to excite and entertain. Although the plot was provided by Tirso de Molina in his novel, Dicenta and Répide developed the story into a successful play fit for twentieth century audiences, as González-Blanco notes:

> *Los tres maridos burlados* viene a ser una anticipación feliz del género difícil, apretado y denso de la novela corta, hoy tan en boga. El mercedario les dió la esencia, el argumento, el nudo; pero ellos dramatizaron y la aderezaron para que no repugnase a nuestro moderno gusto. (261)

CONCLUSIONS

Los tres maridos burlados marks Dicenta's last play before a four-year silence, and although it was written in collaboration with Pedro de Répide, it does share characteristics with some of Dicenta's previous plays, in the humor, the skilled verse, and the management of the set. It is yet another example of the scope of Dicenta's talent, as he is successful in recreating a typical Golden Age drama that could be appreciated by his contemporaries.

SOBREVIVIRSE (1913)

One of Dicenta's last plays is *Sobrevivirse*, which premiered on January 21, 1913 in the Teatro Español. In it Dicenta explores a moving theme that no doubt touched him deeply. In this tragic drama, the main character is a dramatist who suffers a stroke, and as a result of his paralysis, he loses all that he had once enjoyed.

PLOT

César, a prominent and successful playwright, has just been informed that he will be receiving academic honors from the state. As he is preparing himself for this great honor, he suddenly collapses from a stroke. Months later, César continues to struggle to accept his strange new life. He has lost his mistress, the starring actress in all of his plays, who left him as soon as she realized he could no longer serve her needs, and one by one all but two of his friends have abandoned him. With his name no longer on the boards, César is overcome with depression. It is as if he has been forgotten. Secretly, he begins to write a drama that he plans to send to his producers, yet instead of putting his name on it, he signs it with a pseudonym. With no money coming in as before, the family soon feels the effects of poverty. They no longer live in the city, and a family doctor friend, Soto, looks after the invalid for free. The only money coming into the family is that made by Emilia, César's wife, who sews and Ámparo, his sister, who teaches. The family prays for César's improvement, and they make a strong effort not to allow him to find out the extent of their poverty.

The financial burden is more than the two women can handle , but fortunately they begin to receive a small amount in royalties that has been accumulating from César's publications. César consistently becomes more and more difficult to live with as both his mind and body deteriorate. As his brain loses its capacity, César accuses everyone of betraying him. First he claims that Alberto, a dear friend who studied under César's instruction, is trying to steal his plays and sell them as his own, when in reality Alberto simply plans to finish them so that they can bring in more money for the family. César then suggests that Alberto and Emilia are lovers, yet this is not true. Actually, what César does not know is that Alberto is generously allowing his own royalties to come to the household under César's name, a deal which he had arranged with his publisher. No one knows this until a friend of the family, Don Mariano, accidentally lets the information slip. The two women are stunned by this news. They feel that they cannot accept such a donation; thus they continue to try to support the family with their sewing and teaching.

In the meantime, César sends his play to his former producers. They reject it because the most important stage actress of the period, Felisa, César's former mistress, refuses even to read it. Rather than blaming her selfishness, however, César accuses Alberto of having something to do with the play's rejection. When his own wife defends Alberto, César is even more inclined to believe they are having an affair.

Emilia confronts Alberto about his motives in having his royalties transferred into César's name so that the family can receive the money. He tries to explain that he feels a lot of affection for his old teacher and that his generosity is innocent. Once she pushes him, however, Alberto confesses that he has always been in love with her. She too admits that she loves him, yet they both decide to ignore their feelings for César's sake. As they are saying goodbye for the last time, Alberto kisses Emilia's hand. Unfortunately, César witnesses this act, convinced that his wife and *protegé* have dishonored him.

From this point on César is decidedly different. He takes a trip to Madrid without letting anyone know, and upon his return he claims to have cleared his mind. He contemplates his past and his future, as well as all who surround him. He realizes how horrible he has been, recognizing Emilia's sacrifice for him and giving Alberto credit for his great nobility. He calls for them to come to him so that he can beg for their forgiveness. After a long lamentation in which he expresses his incompetence in the game of life, César swallows poison and slumps to the floor. He tells Emilia and Alberto to go on living as he sacrifices his own life for their happinness.

TECHNIQUE / IDEOLOGY

Sobrevivirse has very little in common with *Amor de artistas* (1906), another drama that focuses on the theatrical world, for rather than exploring the bohemian atmosphere associated with dramatists and actors, Dicenta treats a family situation that is far more profound, more tragic, than the lighthearted *Amor de artistas*. *Sobrevivirse* is one of Dicenta's most serious plays, as well as realistic. The characters are convincing, and the scenes, conversations, and behavior of César and his family and friends are natural. All Romantic characteristics have been cast aside as Dicenta traces the decline of a fellow dramatist. It is certain that Dicenta draws from his own experiences, observations, and associations in his characterizations of the main characters; however, nothing suggests that César is a representation of Dicenta. Unlike César, Dicenta never suffered any mental illness, but as a child, Dicenta experienced life with a father, who because of a war injury, lost his mental capacity. It is Dicenta's development of César's mental condition that most enhances the play and attests to Dicenta's great skill in portraying realistic situations. The fact that César's decline is gradually brought about reflects truthfully the nature of mental illness.

Emilia's extreme self-sacrifice is also very realistic, as most women in early nineteenth-century Spain felt they had no other choice but to stay with a husband who treats them badly. Because of their two young children, Emilia believes her most important role is that of mother, with the result that she maintains her duties as wife. It is impossible not to pity her, for she has suffered more than anyone else. During César's success, she was disregarded, as he lavished all he had on an undeserving mistress. Once he steps out of the spotlight and is ignored by the crowds, Emilia cares for him in every detail.

In *Sobrevivirse*, Dicenta departs from his usual portrayal of the need for social justice, as he concentrates solely on moral justice. César, who has lived a selfish life by neglecting his wife and children, is brought to understand the sacrifice made for him by his wife and his dear friend Alberto. After he becomes ill, César becomes increasingly more ill-tempered. Even though everyone around him showers him with affection and love, he shows no appreciation for all that has been given to him. César behaves like a child, and his constant insults are stinging. He complains about everything, and his exasperation is expressed with great sarcasm. He only thinks of himself, and he treats those who have helped him with disdain. His contemptible behavior is greatly contrasted with that of his devoted wife, Emilia. Although she has been mistreated for so many years, she does not hesitate to take care of César now that he needs her most. Her rejection of Alberto and their mutual decision to part ways is yet another example of her sacrifice for an undeserving man. César's final realization of the truth brings about a complete change in his perspective: "¡Qué asco me produjo mi acción al mostrarse la verdad enfrente de mis ojos!" (64). Through his final act of self-sacrifice, César atones for the wrongs he has done his loved ones and opens up a way for them to discover happiness in each other, as his dying words express: "¡Siga su camino la vida! (70).

As he does in *El crimen de ayer* (1908), another drama that focuses on the artists' world, Dicenta seizes the opportunity to express his opinions about art. In *Sobrevivirse*, Dicenta's voice is clearly heard in the character of Seco del Árbol, a devoted friend of César and his family who, because he is a theater critic, has developed strong opinions about quality drama versus poor drama. Seco describes the difficulty of his position:

> He visto hacerse y deshacerse tantas reputaciones. Lo peor es que ayudé a hacerlas y ayudé también a deshacerlas. ¡Qué remedio! La moda se impone en arte como en todo, y las modas cambian deprisa; de ahí que los grandes hombres sean remudados, para los efectos de actualidad, casi casi con igual rapidez que los figurines.... Acaso entre los figurines artísticos haya un genio de los llamados a perdurar. ¿Y qué? De momento, como si no. Cuando su moda pase, cuando llegue la hora de substituir el figurín, quedará el genio arrinconado. Lo reemplazaremos con lo que haya, y lo más último, aunque lo que haya y lo más último valga poquita cosa. (6-7)

This is the case for César, who, although once applauded by critics, because of his decision to please the public and increase his fame, now receives bad reviews for the majority of his plays. The opinion of the critics, however, is of little significance, as César is awarded prize after prize for his talent. The fact that César is about to receive academic honors from the state is an example of Dicenta's sharp satire of the quality of literature that is chosen for such awards.

Long before César's poor physical and mental condition leads to his loss of fame and success, his mistress, Felisa, initiates the slow decline in the quality of César's work. Taking full advantage of her effect over César, Felisa becomes Madrid's most applauded actress. César is completely smitten by her, without realizing that she is only using him. It is obvious that he ignores his responsibilities as both a father and a husband in order to submit to her desires, and as a playwright, his integrity is sacrificed as he chooses to write plays that will promote her as an actress. Dicenta intends to show that many women are attracted to the fame of a dramatist, and many times it is a woman who is responsible for the downfall of the artist. Mariano, an older playwright who retired long ago, describes a memory he has from when he used to work as a secretary for another famous dramatist. His master was so accustomed to receiving invitations from strange women, that one day he decided to teach one particular young lady a lesson. Mariano describes:

> A pocos días recibió mi maestro una carta. Era de la desdeñosa señora. La dama le invitaba a almorzar con ella. "Almorzaremos solos," decía el postscriptum.... No acudió. Envió a la dama un ejemplar de su obra y otra carta donde decía: "Como con quien usted desea almorzar sola es con mi libro, se lo remito dedicado envidiando su buena suerte." (16)

If anything autobiographical can be found in *Sobrevivirse*, it is in the character of Mariano, who appears to have experienced the same highs and lows as Dicenta in his reign as a leading dramatist. Unlike César, Mariano never submits to the temptations to increase his fame by prostituting his talent, but also unlike César before his illness, Mariano's fame decreases with every passing year. His words could very well be those of Dicenta: "Mis comedias estrenadas no producen un céntimo. El estreno de mi comedia nueva va para largo, suponiendo que vaya alguna vez.... No es la pena por mí; recordando las miserias del principio sufriría las del final" (16). Although Dicenta never really suffered any financial hardship after his early success with *Juan José*, he never equaled that success. Dicenta's advice for the next generation of dramatists is clearly heard in Seco's speech to Alberto as he advises the young dramatist not to sacrifice his artistic integrity:

> Sobre todo no se venda usted nunca, Alberto. ¡Nunca!
> Ni al oro, ni al placer, ni a la ostentación, ni al aplauso.
> El artista y la mujer se rebajan y se prostituyen cuando se

venden.... Quien se vende, sea por lo que sea, sólo asco produce. (29)

CONCLUSIONS

It is no coincidence that Dicenta's first play after a four-year silence treats the difficulties that face a dramatist who has once achieved fame but who now is mostly ignored. Eighteen years after the landmark success of *Juan José*, Dicenta has yet to equal its achievement, despite his constant return to treating the social question in his plays. Daniel, although a major success, did not generate the same amount of praise as *Juan José*, mostly due to the fact that social issues were no longer novel themes for playwrights. In *Sobrevivirse* Dicenta explores the world he knows best, and by doing so he brings to light issues that are most significant to him.

EL LOBO (1914)

Dicenta's final play, *El Lobo*, premiered in 1914 in the Teatro Price. In his last theatrical effort, Dicenta makes another successful attempt to explore the cry of "los miserables." Together with *Juan José*, *El Lobo* represents one of Dicenta's finest works, however simple it may be. Just as the title character of *Juan José* is forced into crime because of the tragedy of his circumstances, the same holds true for the title character of *El Lobo*. What Dicenta explores in the latter, however, is the aftermath; el Lobo is already sixty-five years old, having served most of his life in prison for his crimes.

PLOT

El Lobo is the most respected inmate in the prison, and although he is sixty-five years old, he remains strong, tough, and fearsome. His fellow inmates respect him more out of fear, based upon El Lobo's personal history, than for any other reason. After being orphaned, he was raised by shepherds who used him to tend to their flocks. They treated him with cruelty, pushing him to bond more with animals than with humans at an early age. Bitter, el Lobo learned to be strong and ferocious in order to defend himself. His power was proven when one day a wolf approached the sheep he was guarding. He immediately attacked and killed the wolf, but it is the manner in which he did so that is exceptional; he tore at the wolf's throat with his own teeth, severing the jugular. This is the reason he is called "El Lobo." It was not long after this event that he committed his first crime: murder. After having been mocked and ridiculed his entire life by the shepherds, one day he decided he could no longer take their abuse. Without hesitation or premeditation, he killed one of the shepherds who was guilty of making fun of him. After that he lived in the "sierra" where he was lord over man and beast. Although he was hunted by the Civil Guard and hated by the local farmers, he was able to maintain his freedom by frightening those who might betray him. His ferocity was legendary, and all who knew him avoided him at all costs. El Lobo was finally captured by the Civil Guard while he was sleeping in a cave, and he has been in prison ever since.

As el Lobo wastes away his life in prison, he dedicates the majority of his time to knitting socks. In the prison yard, one of the inmates approaches el Lobo to ask him if he would be interested in joining a group of prisoners in their planned escape because their goal is to live in the "sierra" where el Lobo used to reign many years ago. El Lobo declines, claiming that he is too old and that the "sierra" is for youth. He goes back to his knitting. The prisoners are interrupted by the warden, Don José, who has come to find out which ones were planning to escape, for he has learned of their scheme from a spy. After he punishes them all by declaring a general suspension of privilege, a little girl wanders into the prison yard. She is the prison warden's only child, and she refuses to stray very far from him since her mother's death. The prisoners are shocked by her voice and are unable to ignore her presence. El Lobo, however, continues to knit, unaffected by what is happening around him. As the other prisoners discuss her beauty and innocence, Aurora slowly approaches el Lobo without him realizing it. She is curious about his work, and she questions him about his knitting. El Lobo is shocked, unable to respond to the little girl. Aurora grabs the sock and dances around with it, praising its color and quality. She tells him that he must make some socks exactly the same color for her doll, and in return she promises to give him kisses. In response to his incredulous, "¿Besos, a mí?... ¿Besos?," Aurora demonstrates a kiss on his cheek (25). His pipe falls from his mouth as his body trembles at her touch, and he grabs the child and lifts her high into the air, looking at her with a tenderness he has never before experienced. When her father realizes what is happening, he becomes frightened and demands that el Lobo let her go.

El Lobo dedicates all of his free time to knitting for the child, unable to even think about taking his allotted time to exercise in the prison yard. He has made friends with Metrio, one of the guards, who delivers the tiny clothing that el Lobo knits for Aurora's doll. He brings news of her delight and satisfaction to el Lobo, encouraging him to make more. The other prisoners are slowly losing the respect they once held for el Lobo; now they make fun of his silly knitting. None of this matters to el Lobo, who begs Metrio to tell him everything about Aurora. Meanwhile, the prisoners begin to plan a new outbreak, yet this time they decide not to include the old man. El Lobo, however, pretends to be sleeping as he listens intently to their plans to kill the prison warden and escape. Pajarito, one of the prisoners who is watching el Lobo sleep, insults him, claiming that he is no longer the ferocious "lobo" after which he was named. El Lobo ignores their taunts as he feigns sleep. When the time arrives for them to kill the warden, el Lobo makes his move. He jumps out at them and shouts "¡Cuidiao [sic], Don José, que asesinan!" (40). All at once mayhem breaks loose, and in the struggle el Lobo is stabbed by Pajarito. In retaliation, he grabs Pajarito with full force and severs his throat with his own teeth, killing him.

El Lobo is taken to the prison infirmary, suffering from a mortal wound. In saving the warden's life, el Lobo gives his own. There is a feeling of sadness among the prison guards and the doctors. All treat him with the utmost respect, and when Don José thanks el Lobo for saving his life, el Lobo explains to him that he should not thank him because he too hated the warden just as much as the other prisoners did. However, due to the presence of one tiny child, el Lobo's perspective changed, and she is the one who deserves the thanks. Once Don José realizes why el Lobo defended him, he falls to his knees to thank the prisoner, asking him if there is anything more he can do to make his last moments less painful. El Lobo's dying wish is to see Aurora once more. Don José complies, and when Aurora arrives, she asks the old man if she can hug him in gratitude for saving her father's life. El Lobo stops her, explaining that his hands are covered in blood. The warden pushes her towards him and commands her to hug him anyway. She promises el Lobo that whenever she plays with the doll, she will always think of him. He asks her to give him one final kiss as he dies.

SOURCE

In 1904 Dicenta published *De piedra a piedra*, a collection of his impressions of his trip from the Monasterio de Piedra to Monserrat, which includes a description of his reaction to a performance of *Resurrección*, a translation of a drama by Leo Tolstoy (1899). Dicenta describes the main idea of the play:

> De un lado está Dimitri representando la humanidad triunfante, egoista, explotadora de almas y cuerpos, que al fin reconoce sus culpas y quiere lavarla. De otro, la Maslowa, representando la humanidad envilecida, desamparada y explotada, que, aun rehuyendo aparentemente su salvación, exige salvarse. Estas dos humanidades, unidas primero por un impulso de la Naturaleza, separadas luego por un estúpido decreto social, se funden al cabo empujadas por la justicia que impulsa á la una, por el ansia de redimirse que germina en la otra, ¡y forman una humanidad única, un solo cuerpo todo fraternidad y amor! (*Piedra* 234)

Following the performance, many spectators questioned the thesis that one who has been a criminal for so long is capable of redemption: "¡Salvar á quien cayó! ¡Hacer sano lo que está podrido!... ¡Eso es imposible! ¡Bueno está para una comedia! En la vida real, imposible. ¡imposible de todo punto!" (*Piedra* 234). Dicenta rejects their argument by describing an event that was told to him by the prison warden of the Cárcel Modelo. One of the prisoners on death row who had been convicted of murder entertained himself with two birds that he had tamed, "con quienes guarda todo género de afectuosas consideraciones y emplea las más dulces palabras" (*Piedra* 236). This violent and hateful man shared not only his food with the birds, but also his deepest feelings, as he talked to them incessantly. One day, the prison warden entered the cell and noticed that one of the birds was missing. After much questioning, the inmate finally admitted what had happened to his pet. In the cell next to him was a young man who was overcome with depression, crying all day long, never receiving visits from anyone. That particular day was more than the bird tamer could tolerate; he was so full of pity for his cellmate that he loaned him one of his birds: "Hoy ha llorado más que nunca. ¡Daba lástima oirle! Y yo, pues le he prestado uno de los pájaros pa que se distrajese una miajas" (*Piedra* 237).

TECHNIQUE

El Lobo is one of Dicenta's most realistic dramas. The character delineation, their behavior, attitudes, emotions, and speech all reflect an accurate representation of the dynamics inside a prison. There are different types of prisoners depicted in the play, those who are vicious, those who are weak, those who are sad and despairing, and those who are dominated by hatred and constant thoughts of rebellion. The lives that the prisoners lead are boring, and as there is in every prison, in this particular prison there is a system of secret rank and organization, a code of standards for behavior, and penalties for violation of the code, all devised by the prisoners themselves. The heavy feeling of hatred and the fatalistic attitude that permeate the drama add to the harsh realism of the setting.

More than any of Dicenta's previous dramas, *El Lobo* evokes an overwhelming feeling of pity that reflects the sentimental nature of the play, and although the spectator certainly pities society's other victims, such as Juan José, Daniel, and Aurora, the emotion expressed on stage by el Lobo is unequaled. His reaction to the child is poignant, especially after the detailed description of his animalistic nature. Never before in his entire sixty-five years has el Lobo experienced tenderness such as this. The profound effect that one little girl has on such a hardened criminal is touching. When Aurora first approaches him in the prison yard, el Lobo is hardly able to speak, as he repeats over and over again, "¿Qué?" (24-25). In the stage directions, Dicenta describes the manner in which the actor playing the title role should interpret this key scene: "El Lobo, al oir la voz de la niña, levanta la cabeza. En sus ojos se pintará un asombro imbécil.... Aurora arranca la media de las manos del Lobo. Este la deja hacer, sin hablar, mirándola como atontado" (24-25). When the child promises to give kisses to El Lobo, he looks at her incredulously. Aurora responds by wrapping her tiny arms around his neck and kissing him on the cheek. Dicenta describes el Lobo's reaction:

Un grito inarticulado, entre rugido y sollozo, brota de los labios del Lobo;

la pipa se escapa de sus dientes; su cuerpo retiembla; su mano restriega el carrillo donde besó la niña. Luego coge a ésta con sus brazos, la alza en alto y la deja suspendida en el aire, mirándola con tierno y angustioso mirar. (25)

In this particular scene, Dicenta uses the sun to symbolize hope. Upon entering the prison yard, Aurora is told that she will be taken to the garden soon where it is much prettier. Her response, "También esto es bonito. (Señalando hacia el sillar.) Allí hay sol," provides hope to an otherwise hopeless situation (24). After el Lobo places her back on her feet, he falls backwards into his chair, "bañado por el sol," another example of the hope that Aurora has brought into his life (25).

El Lobo is not the only one affected by Aurora's innocence, as is seen in the change of attitude in the other prisoners upon her entrance into the yard: "En sus rostros debe reflejarse una emoción, mezcla de curiosidad y ternura" (24). One of the most bitter prisoners, el Remellao, mentions that he too has a daughter about the same age as Aurora. The thought of his little girl and the idea that he will not see her grow up overwhelms the tough inmate, causing him to cry.

The effect Aurora has on el Lobo, however, is immeasurable. Following their chance encounter in the prison yard, el Lobo is so affected by her that he dedicates all of his time to making clothes for her dolls and questioning the guards about her constantly. His fellow inmates laugh at him, and although he hates to be ridiculed, his only concern is Aurora. One day, as he gives Metrio some doll clothes to deliver to Aurora, he hears the other prisoners approaching. He whispers to the guard:

Guárdala, que sube la gente. Si la vieran, podía rirse [sic] alguno, y a ese alguno podría cortarle yo la risa con la hoja del cuchillo. Por mí no es el cuidao. Un muerto más a mi cuenta, ¿qué importa? ; pero me daría reparo de que el osequio llegase a la chiquilla salpicao con sangre. (34)

The audience is immediately reminded of his ferocity. El Lobo does not want to have to kill one of his fellow inmates for laughing at him, not because it is morally wrong, but because he might get blood on the doll clothes he made for Aurora.

Rather than scheming to murder the prison warden with his cellmates, el Lobo only thinks about Aurora. Knowing that without her father Aurora would be devastated, el Lobo goes against the other inmates, who are planning to assassinate the warden, by warning Aurora's father just in time in order to save his life. The final scene is especially heartrending, as Aurora joins him in his final moments. As she kisses him, he dies with her angelic image in his mind.

IDEOLOGY

In his final play, Dicenta takes up the same argument he started in *Juan José* almost twenty years earlier. Returning to the prison scene, Dicenta portrays a man who, because of society's neglect, has passed a life full of crime and hatred. Just as Juan José is justified in blaming a negligent society for the fact that he has become a criminal, el Lobo too was never given any other option. Convicted criminals suffer even more prejudice, even if their crime is as innocent as stealing bread, as did Juan José. As el Cano says to Juan José: "La noche que robaste á un hombre, tomaste en tu mundo, en el mundo de las personas honrás, billete pa otro mundo distinto: el nuestro. En estos viajes no hay billete de vuelta" (*Juan* 63). El Cano's words are powerful, especially since Juan José is full of hope that he can return to society and regain his honor. Instead, he escapes, murders, and ends up just like el Lobo, wasting his entire life behind bars.

Juan José and el Lobo have a lot in common, not only in their troubled past, but also in their violent animalistic nature. Both were orphaned, left to survive on their own, Juan José in the city, and el Lobo in the "sierra." Both infants were taken in by cruel people whose only plan was to exploit the child. Juan José was forced to grow up begging for a family that was not even his, and el Lobo was treated like an animal as he tended the sheep for some shepherds in the hills. Neither man experienced any sort of affection or love. Juan José's temper is so violent that the thought of his lover leaving him for another pushes him to become almost animalistic, much like el Lobo. Juan José's words as he expresses his anger are hauntingly familiar: "¡Pues el animal, cuando se mira acorralao, muerde!... ¡Yo también morderé! Si la bestia tiene ese derecho, mejor debe tenerlo el hombre, porque vale más" (*Juan* 56). What Juan José fails to complete, el Lobo is unable to avoid; he murders his oppressor by tearing apart his jugular with his teeth. Both Juan José and el Lobo experience a sort of epiphany after receiving the slightest amount of affection. Unfortunately for Juan José, Rosa is undeserving of his admiration for her; Aurora, on the other hand, is truly an angel that provides hope to a dying man.

Dicenta argues that men such as Juan José and el Lobo are doomed because they are orphaned, mistreated, deprived of human love and affection, and ignored and victimized by an uncaring and unforgiving society. El Lobo is truly shocked by the gracious attitude of the prison guards and the warden after his brave, selfless act of sacrifice: "Paice que a la hora de morir tó se hace cariño. Hasta las manos de usté, señor director, andan suaves por cima de mis hombros" (45). For sixty-five years, el Lobo has never experienced any "cariño," and now that he is on his deathbed, he finally receives human affection. In his essay titled "Resurrección," in which Dicenta describes his reactions to Tolstoy's play, Dicenta plants the seed for the argument presented in *El Lobo*:

> Si esta sociedad, que luego de precipitar á sus indivíduos en la infamia, nada hace para redimirlos y no intenta nada tampoco por convertir en atmósfera honrada y pura, la atmósfera viciosa y criminal donde aquellos seres se agitan; si esta sociedad aplicase á la redención; á la regeneración, á la dignificación moral de esos indivíduos las fuerzas que acumula para perderlos; si el egoismo y la indiferencia de unos contra otros sustituyesen el amor de todos para todos y el cuidado de todos para todos, no imposible, fácil sería convertir en realidad augusta la fábula tolstoiana. (*Piedra* 234-235)

Dicenta argues that society must take action to educate and nurture not only children who are orphaned or abandoned, but also hardened criminals who have nothing left to live for. After being told the story about the prisoner in the Cárcel Modelo, Dicenta becomes fascinated with the life that goes on inside those walls. In an essay titled "Regando flores," published in *Traperías* in 1905, Dicenta describes the urge to stop and appreciate the beautiful garden that the prisoners have planted:

> Gracias al esfuerzo de aquellos hombres, que, probablemente, no tuvieron amparo en su niñez, ejemplos sanos en su mocedad ni enseñanza en su juventud; que, abandonados por sus padres primero y por la sociedad después, crecieron en medio del arroyo, hasta que un viento de tormenta saturado con todos los miasmas del vicio, los barrió á la cárcel, el jardín está hermoso, lleno de frescura y salud. (36-37)

In *El Lobo*, Dicenta intends to show that even the most hardened of criminals is able to recognize his or her tender side when confronted with humanity and sympathy. The total change that occurs in el Lobo is the result of one innocent child who was not yet influenced by a discriminating society; she freely kisses el Lobo, without any prejudice. Metrio, the prison guard, notices the change in el Lobo, stating: "Ya es cosa rara ese querer en un corazón tan duro como el tuyo" (30). El Lobo responds:

> Más raro es que en sesenta y cinco años que llevo sobre el lomo, naide me haya dao un beso a la güena, de los que se dan sin interés, porque el alma tié la voluntá de darlos. La chica me lo dió. Aquí lo puso, encima de esta cicatriz, hecha por un puñal. (30)

Had either Juan José or el Lobo been given the opportunity to show their good side, they may have been able to overcome their criminal nature that society brought out in each of them.

Mas Ferrer believes that in tracing el Lobo's background to his orphan roots, Dicenta has created a naturalistic play: "No hay duda de que en esta obra Dicenta intenta llevar el naturalismo al teatro, esta obra es naturalista, ya que se centra en la problemática de la herencia patológica" (*Vida* 97). Although Dicenta's description of el Lobo's past tends towards the naturalistic, the play as a whole is too optimistic and too sentimental to be categorized into the group of naturalist works by Émile Zola, his contemporaries, and his followers. The scientific eye of the naturalists is not present because for Dicenta, the profound emotion is paramount.

CONCLUSIONS

The theme of *El Lobo* fascinated Dicenta so much that in 1917 he published a *novela* with the same name.[2] In the novel, Dicenta elaborates on the same plot, giving even more life to the principal characters. The drama, *El Lobo*, is one of Dicenta's best works, as Hall concedes: "this is perhaps his most satisfactorily conceived play. There is no divergence between plot and social message; the one is the other" (65). The social criticism is at once powerful and moving, as Dicenta pleads with society to take a more active role in the rehabilitation of criminals and the education and care of orphaned children. Dicenta's final play fittingly culminates a rich career as he strikes out against an unjust society.

OVERALL CONCLUSIONS TO CHAPTER SIX

Following the premiere of *Daniel* on March 7, 1907, Dicenta returns to writing realistic dramas that contain a thesis. With the exception of the two dramas written in collaboration with Pedro de Répide, *Los majos de plante* (1908) and *Los tres maridos burlados* (1909), and the remake of *Juan Francisco* (1904) titled *Entre rocas* (1908), Dicenta's final contributions to the Spanish stage are characterized by their lack of Romantic features, his continued attempt to criticize a backwards society, and a completely realistic approach. Not once in his final years did Dicenta turn to the legendary historical figures of the past, as he had earlier in his career with *Honra y vida* (1891), *El duque de Gandía* (1894), *Raimundo Lulio* (1902), and *La conversión de Mañara* (1905). Dicenta's two variations from the norm, *Los majos de plante* and *Los tres maridos burlados*, are, for the most part, uncharacteristic of Dicenta, which must be due to the talents of his co-author, Pedro de Répide. The former, a *sainete*, is a weak drama that attempts, albeit in a mediocre way, to revive the most popular form of theater from the second half of the eighteenth century. *Los tres maridos burlados* enjoyed more success than Dicenta and Répide's first collaborated effort, for in reworking Tirso de Molina's plot into a stage performance, the two dramatists successfully capture the essence of Golden Age drama without the

---

[2] The novel, *El Lobo* is published in a collection of *novelas* titled *Paraíso perdido*.

excessive moral tone.

What is most obvious in the development of Dicenta's talent in the final years of his life is his decision to adhere to his goal of portraying society's ills without resorting to the use of Romantic devices. Gone are the Romantic elements that define the majority of his work, as Dicenta is determined to express in the most realistic way possible his opinions about Spain's need for reform. With the exception of *Daniel* (1907), Dicenta's second most famous drama, the remainder of his plays until his death are for the most part completley ignored by critics. While it is true that Dicenta never equals his success in the genre of "social" drama represented by both *Juan José* and *Daniel*, the social question is present in the majority of his final plays; in fact, the issues Dicenta presents are well-developed and clearly stated without being overworked or burdened by excessive Romantic characteristics, as in *Juan José*, or sensationalism, as in *Daniel*.

In Dicenta's final dramas there are a number of strong women who stand out in their roles on the stage. Cesárea, the revolutionary leader from *Daniel*, is one of Dicenta's best character creations; she is completely dedicated to her goal, she has tremendous strength of character, she is able to inspire action on the part of her fellow workers, and she is totally willing to sacrifice her own life for the benefit of future generations. Lorenza of *Lorenza* (1907), is also strong-willed, for she decides to follow her dreams and leave the oppressive fishing village where she was raised, despite the negative social stigma she knows she will suffer for choosing to leave. Carmen, of *El crimen de ayer* (1908), is also one of Dicenta's more powerful leading ladies. She is motivated by her motherly instincts in her decision to murder the father of her child in order to save their son the disgrace of having a father who does not provide him his name. Emilia, César's wife in *Sobrevivirse* (1913), also demonstrates strength in character in her sacrifice to an undeserving man. Her primary responsibility is her family, and despite her love for Alberto, Emilia denies herself happiness in order to care for her ailing husband. Finally, the child in *El Lobo*, Aurora, is powerful in her childish innocence. Through her, Dicenta intends to show the importance of unprejudiced kindness; Dicenta condemns a society that deprives its most needy citizens of affection, support, and encouragement.

In several of his final dramas, Dicenta attacks the frivolity of the wealthy, especially in *Daniel* and *La confesión*. In the former, Dicenta portrays the upper class in a very negative light; the ignorant women who visit the workings of the mine deep below the surface act as if they are touring an amusement park. Their giddy responses and complete lack of understanding of the suffering in the mine is reflective of the indifferent attitude of the rich regarding the poor. In *La confesión* (1908), the wife and daughter of a dying man are so self-absorbed in their desire to maintain their social position, that they selfishly allow Santiago to die without receiving his last rites and redeeming his soul.

As he has many times in the past, Dicenta continues to attack the institution of marriage. In *El crimen de ayer* (1908), Julián, who is a member of the upper class, plans to marry, out of convenience, a young woman whose wealth will substantially benefit his future. His total disregard for the mother of his child, his long time lover, is difficult for the group of friends to understand, for although they are not married, they are completely committed to their partners. Dicenta has long argued that marriage is an oppressive institution created and adhered to by those who perpetuate long-standing traditions without question. In *El crimen de ayer*, Dicenta argues for free love, for in his own experience, he has been completley fulfilled. In *Los tres maridos burlados*, Dicenta, together with Répide, explores the lighter side of the suffering of young married women; each woman is forced to deal with her husband's vice. In *Sobrevivirse*, Dicenta indicates, through the self-sacrifice of César, that Emilia and Alberto should pursue their love without hesitation.

Overall, Dicenta's final dramas are superior in quality in comparison to his earlier plays due to his successful realistic approach. The themes are poignant and thought-provoking, as he pushes society to take a more humane approach to its treatment of the underdog. His final play, *El Lobo*, is perhaps his best-written drama, for the manner in which he combines the theme with the social message that is present throughout is not only powerful but also successful in Dicenta's attempt to force his audiences to reevaluate their perspective.

7
Conclusions

TECHNIQUE

THE THIRTY PLAYS BY Joaquín Dicenta y Benedicto, beginning with *El suicidio de Werther* in 1888 and ending with *El Lobo* in 1913, represent a broad spectrum of theatrical styles. Dicenta's early efforts adhere to the Echegarayan neo-Romantic school, after which Dicenta became a leader in his own right. These first dramas, *El suicidio de Werther* (1888), *La mejor ley* (1889), *Los irresponsables* (1890), *Honra y vida* (1891), and *El duque de Gandía* (1894), are characterized by Dicenta's use of the Romantics' themes, such as unrequited love, vengeance, inexorable fate, medieval themes, honor, Christian elements, exalted emotion, mysterious situations, the use of verse, and violence resulting in blood spilled on stage. One year prior to his landmark *Juan José* (1895), Dicenta attempted to break away from the neo-Romantic school in *Luciano* (1894), his first prose drama. In *Luciano*, Dicenta moves more towards a realistic portrayal of the necessity for divorce in a marriage turned sour, an autobiographical approach to a serious issue. Dicenta's attempt to preach to his audience weakens the overall artistic effect of his first drama with realistic tendencies.

Although he failed in *Luciano*, Dicenta achieved phenomenal success in *Juan José* one year later. By far Dicenta's best known play, *Juan José* pushed Dicenta into the spotlight as he became the first to give the proletariat the primary role on stage. Dicenta's art was slowly maturing away from the simple imitations of the master Echegaray, for whom he felt a deep admiration, towards his own style of reflecting his ideas and experiences in life. Even *Juan José*, however, was criticized by many for its neo-Romantic characteristics, as Dicenta seemed to struggle to shake free from the neo-Romantic movement. His subsequent play, *El señor feudal* (1896), was a total failure, more because Dicenta tried too hard to invest it with the social themes that brought him so much attention in *Juan José*.

Following the failure of *El señor feudal*, Dicenta experienced a period of fecundity that defies categorization. The group of plays written between *El señor feudal* (1896) and *Daniel* (1907) are so varied in theme and style, that it is easy to assume that Dicenta wished to try his talent in every possible genre. The majority of these plays are Romantic lyrical dramas, along with several one-act dramas written for the *teatro por horas*, and two *comedias*. The only play that stands out above the rest is *Aurora* (1902), which is also the only drama in the group to receive any critical attention, due to its social theme. Although Dicenta maintains many of the characteristics evident in his early plays, this group of dramas represents a significant development in the artist's continued maturation of technique and theme, especially in his use of humor, religion, realism, and social commentary.

Dicenta's final group of plays represents the artist's success at becoming comfortable with his own style. They are overwhelmingly realistic, skillfully written, and excellent examples of Dicenta's ability to accurately portray society's injustices in realistic settings without sacrificing the artistic nature of the play. The Romantic characteristics that define so much of his previous work are absent, and in fact, his best plays fall into this final period: *Daniel* and *El Lobo*. The former is a much more successful "social" drama than its more famous predecessor, *Juan José*, and *El Lobo* is Dicenta's most sentimental and best written play.

IDEOLOGY

Despite the wide variety of styles used by Dicenta, he never abandoned his goal to portray the political, social, and economic problems that plagued his country at the turn of the century. Although not every one of his dramas expresses some social criticism, in the majority of his plays, it is evident that Dicenta was concerned about the suffering caused by an indifferent society. Dicenta's most important contribution to the theater is those dramas that represent his constant preoccupation with social issues and his use of the victims of society as protagonists of serious drama. In fact, it is Dicenta's keen social awareness that catapulted Spanish theater into the twentieth century. In those plays that reflect a social message, Dicenta skillfully reveals his opinions about the following issues: art and the artist in his world; the church and its role in Spain's hesitancy to embrace progress; marriage and the need for divorce; the positive benefits of free love; the importance of a strong family structure; orphans and their need for affection and love; and the exploitation of the working classes by the ruling classes. Dicenta seeks to illustrate those practices he considers vicious and destructive to human happiness, but which are either ignored or openly approved by society.

ART AND THE ARTIST'S WORLD

In five plays, *El suicidio de Werther* (1888), *Luciano* (1894), *Amor de artistas* (1906), *El crimen de ayer* (1908), and *Sobrevivirse* (1913), Dicenta draws from his own environment, the world of art and letters. All but *Amor de artistas* end in tragedy, as Dicenta skillfully presents, in an interesting and detailed fashion, the lifestyle of the artist. Fernando, of *El suicidio de Werther*, hopes to prove to society his worth through his talent as a sculptor; unfortunately, he is incapable of single-handedly convincing an extremely prejudiced society that he should be judged by his own merits and moral character, not by the fact that he is an illegitimate child of a prostitute. In *Luciano*, Dicenta most accurately represents his own experience in a marriage that has gone bad. The sempiternal cry of the artist that he is misunderstood is best expressed in this drama. In *Amor de artistas* and *Sobrevivirse*, Dicenta explores the lives of two dramatists and their contemporaries. In this way, Dicenta skillfully injects his commentaries on art. In the former, Dicenta criticizes the way people form their opinions following the premiere of a play, as two spectators explain that they will have to wait until the morning to decide whether or not they liked the drama. In *Sobrevivirse*, Dicenta condemns those dramatists who succumb to the temptation to prostitute their art for money or fame. In *El crimen de ayer*, Dicenta uses light satire to poke fun at the popular new movement titled "Art for Art's sake."

CHURCH

Although Dicenta is far from anticlerical, he does not adhere to any particular creed, nor does he believe that the church's inflexibility in certain matters is justified, especially with respect to marriage and divorce. Dicenta criticizes religious people like Homobono (*Aurora* 1902) who use their fanatical beliefs to manipulate others for their own benefit and to oppose social progress. The majority of Dicenta's religious figures, however, are presented as kind individuals, priests who are respected by the people: Padre Andrés in *Los irresponsables* (1890), Fray Juan in *El duque de Gandía* (1894), Padre Antonio in *Curro Vargas* (1898), and Padre Enrique in *La confesión* (1908). In those plays where the clergy plays a part, Dicenta uses religion to represent the conservative attitude, yet the majority of the time Dicenta invests the order with dignity, sincerity, and intelligence. One exception is the humorous characterization of the priest in *Los majos de plante*, who is only concerned about good food.

MARRIAGE, DIVORCE, AND FREE LOVE

One of Dicenta's most recurring themes is the argument against marriage, and by doing so, the advocacy of divorce and the acceptance of free love. All of the following plays contain some commentary on Dicenta's view of marriage and/or free love: *El suicidio de Werther* (1888), *La mejor ley* (1889), *Los irresponsables* (1890), *Luciano* (1894), *Juan José* (1895), *Aurora* (1902), *De tren a tren* (1902), *Amor de artistas* (1906), *El crimen de ayer* (1908), *Los tres maridos burlados* (1909), and *Sobrevivirse* (1913). Dicenta never openly states that he is opposed to marriage, but he rarely exposes marriage in a positive light. The one exception is in *Honra y vida* (1891), in which Don Jaime and Doña Inés share a mutual love and appreciation for each other inside the bonds of matrimony, uncommon in Dicenta's dramas.

Dicenta condemns those marriages, which by their nature, protect more sin and blasphemy than any illegitimate union could harbor. The abuse suffered by Luciano at the hands of his wife's family (*Luciano*), the infidelity carried out by Gonzalo that is hidden by his marriage to Dolores (*La mejor ley*), and the manipulation of Matilde and her family to arrange the marriage between Matilde and Manuel in order to receive the large inheritance left them by an uncle (*Aurora*), are examples of this type of marriage. After they marry, Matilde plans to continue her affair with Enrique, using the marriage as a cloak for their sin, much like Gonzalo.

In *El suicidio de Werther*, Dicenta argues the injustice in Fernando's inability to seek marriage with his beloved because he is illegitimate. Without such prejudices, Fernando and María would be able to pursue their love freely, without restraint. In *La mejor ley*, *De tren a tren*, *El crimen de ayer*, *Sobrevivirse*, and in a lesser way *Los tres maridos burlados*, Dicenta argues against arranged marriages because both parties suffer in a marriage where love does not play a part. In *Los irresponsables*, Felipe is condemned by society because he has left his cheating wife and fallen in love with another. Felipe is the innocent victim, but because of society's strict adherence to tradition and blindness to the details of his situation, both Felipe and Margarita are forced to pursue their love outside the bonds of marriage. Margarita, knowing that she and Felipe will never be able to marry, decides that her love for him is worth the social condemnation she will experience if she chooses to become his lover. In *Los irresponsables*, Dicenta creates an understanding father, that of Margarita, who allows his daughter to have the right to choose her future mate. Ideally, Felipe should be allowed to divorce his wife so that he can be free to marry Margarita.

In *Luciano*, Dicenta continues his argument for divorce as the title character realizes that the woman he has married has no respect or understanding of his art. An interesting point about *Juan José* is the fact that none of the main characters is married, yet Juan José treats Rosa as if she were his wife, and there is no less importance given to her cheating on him because they are not married. In fact, they, together with Andrés and Toñuela, live together much like married couples do. Dicenta suggests no greater percentage of misfortune or infidelity in relationships of this kind than he depicts in unions sanctioned by the church and civil authority. Other dramas that focus on couples who are not married are *Amor de artistas* and *El crimen de ayer*, both plays in which the relationships are considered both permanent and sincere. In his argument for free love, Dicenta never intends to preach that the whole world would be happier if everyone followed a general practice of the doctrine of free love; instead, he contends that sincerity, fidelity and sanctity are found in many legally unsanctioned unions. Dicenta bases happiness on relationships that are built upon love, not ceremony. For Dicenta, love is the only thing that justifies relations between the sexes, and he makes no distinction between love in a marriage or unmarried love.

FAMILY

Related to Dicenta's views on marriage are his opinions about the family structure, especially the relationship between a parent and a child. Dicenta consistently condemns those parents who abandon their children, regardless of whether or not the parent is married. In his first play, Dicenta clearly draws a distinction between Fernando's blood mother and his foster father. Carlota, his mother, abandoned Fernando as an infant, and years later when she returns to his life and seeks the same love from him that she had earlier cast aside, Fernando only responds to her in so much as duty requires him. As he is dying, Fernando turns away from his natural parent and addresses his dying words of affection and loyalty towards the father who raised him with genuine care and affection. Dicenta portrays other commendable foster parents who take upon themselves the heavy burden of raising a child that has been cast aside in *Curro Vargas* (1898) and *La cortijera* (1900).

In *El crimen de ayer*, Carmen kills Julián when he plans to abandon their child and refuses to give their son his name. Carmen's violent act of murder is justified by Dicenta in that she does the only thing she possibly can to take vengeance for such a despicable act. Dicenta argues that every parent has the responsibility of more than just financial support; Julián owes his son moral support. On the opposite end of the spectrum is Emilia (*Sobrevivirse*), who is glorified by Dicenta because of her devotion to her children. She sacrifices her wishes in order to do what is best for the children. Even Alberto is seen as more fit to be the father to Emilia's children than their own father, and thus their union at the close of the drama is a positive one.

ORPHANED AND ILLEGITIMATE CHILDREN

One of Dicenta's strongest arguments is that in defense of the orphan or illegitimate child. He begins his exploration of the injustices suffered by the illegitimate child in his first play, *El suicidio de Werther*, in which Fernando, because he was abandoned by his parents as an infant, is incapable of rising above the prejudices of society. Juan José was also orphaned as an infant, but unlike Fernando, he was not adopted by a loving family. Instead, Juan José was forced to beg on the street for a family that was not even his own. Both he and el Lobo are able to trace their life of crime back to the fact that they were abandoned and ignored by society. Dicenta calls for support on the part of society in the rearing of young orphans, providing them with love and affection so that they can become a productive rather than counterproductive part of society. Dicenta's concern for the orphan manifests itself in other plays as well: *Curro Vargas*, *La cortijera*, and of course, *El crimen de ayer*.

EXPLOITATION OF THE WORKING CLASS BY THE RULING CLASS

There is no doubt that Dicenta's exploration of the abuse suffered by the working class at the hands of the ruling class is what brought him the most fame. Many times throughout his dramas, Dicenta seeks to portray the ruling or moneyed class as unscrupulous, intent on personal gain, and heedless of any hardship they inflict upon their employees. In *Juan José*, Paco abuses his power by discharging Juan José; in *Daniel*, the proprietors of the mine reduce the wages to an impossibly low figure and ignore the dangerous working conditions in the mine; also in *Daniel*, the mine owner's son, Luis, seduces Anita without any plans of marrying her; in *Juan Francisco*, Gaspar plans to ruin Tío Pedro's fishing business by unfair methods of competitions; Roque, in *El señor feudal*, intends to force the Marqués de Atienza to give his daughter in marriage to his son by threatening to foreclose a mortgage on the home in which the Marqués currently resides; and in *Aurora*, the factory owners abuse their power by requesting sexual favors of the innocent working girls.

An interesting device used by Dicenta in his attempt to condemn the ruling class for their exploitation of the working class is the use of the workers of their own tools to destroy their employers. In *Juan José*, the title character discusses his desire to use his trowel to stab Paco in the throat, and although he resists temptation, in the end he murders his employer. Cesárea (*Daniel*) urges her fellow miners to grab the tools they use in the mine to destroy the furnaces and machines in order to keep imported laborers from being able to take their places. The use of the vat in *El señor feudal* to murder the proprietor's son is especially symbolic as his blood is mixed with the blood of generations of workers.

Dicenta describes the working class as simple, hardworking, and loyal people. He argues that they are overworked and underpaid, and that the world fails to notice the physical and mental suffering inflicted upon them not only by their greedy employers, but also by society as a whole. Juan José is characterized as a good man, but due to circumstances beyond his control, he turns to a life of crime, much like el Lobo. Aurora, who although raped by her employers when she was a child, is viewed as a noble and generous person. In his social commentary, Dicenta condemns the rampant abuse of children (*Juan José*, *Aurora*, and *Daniel*), the mistreatment of the elderly after a life of service (*Daniel* and *El tío Gervasio*), and the negligence of society in providing help to the downtrodden (*Juan José* and *El lobo*). Dicenta believes that all men are born equally, and that it is up to society to ensure that all men are treated equally:

Cuando los hombres nacen, no nacen malvados ni justos, nacen hombres, materia dispuesta á producir el bien y el mal; todo consiste en el abono que reciben, en el ambiente que respiran, en la herencia fisiológica y moral que recogen. Con mayor ó menor esfuerzo, pero siempre según quién y cómo les empuja, pueden ir á la virtud ó al crímen, y pueden siempre, siempre, mientras quede en ellos un átomo de juicio y una partícula de conciencia, volver al bien, aunque el mal los tenga sujetos á su yugo. (*Piedra* 235)

Bibliography of Primary Works[1]

Dicenta y Benedicto, Joaquín. *Amor de artistas.* Madrid: R. Velasco, 1906.
———. *Aurora. Teatro.* Vol. 1. Madrid: R. Velasco, 1907. 5-81.
———. *Bajo los Mirtos.* Barcelona: Millá y Piñol, 1916.
———. *Confesión.* Madrid: R. Velasco, 1909.
———. *La conversión de Mañara.* Madrid: R. Velasco, 1905.
———. *Cosas mías.* Barcelona: A. López, 1900.
———. *El crimen de ayer.* Barcelona: Biblioteca Teatro Mundial, 1915.
———. *Crónicas.* Madrid: Fortanet, 1898.
———. *Cuentos.* Madrid: A. Marzo, 1900.
———. *Daniel.* Madrid: R. Velasco, 1907.
———. *De la batalla.* Madrid: Imprenta de M. Núñez Samper, 1903.
———. *De la vida que pasa.* Barcelona: Biblioteca Yris, 1926.
———. *Del tiempo mozo.* Madrid: Librería de los sucesores de Hernando, 1912.
———. *De piedra a piedra.* Cartagena: Artes Gráficas de Levante, 1904.
———. *Desde los rosales.* San Vicente de la Barquera, El Liberal, 1906.
———. "El desquite." *De la batalla.* Madrid: Imprenta de M. Núñez Samper, 1903.
———. *De tren a tren.* 2nd ed. Madrid: R. Velasco, 1903.
———. *El duque de Gandía.* Madrid: Imprenta de José Rodríguez, 1894.
———. *Encarnación.* Madrid: Librería de los sucesores de Hernando, 1913.
———. *Entre rocas* Madrid: R. Velasco, 1908.
———. *Espoliarium: Cuadros sociales.* Madrid: Librería de Fernando Fé, 1891.
———. *Espumas y plomo.* Madrid: Fortanet, 1903.
———. *Galerna.* Montevideo: Editora Elite, 1944.
———. *Garcés de Marsilla.* Madrid: E. Escolar Editor, 1981.
———. *El hampón.* Madrid: [no publisher given], 1913.
———. *El hijo del odio.* Madrid: E. Escolar Editor, 1980.
———. *Honra y vida.* Madrid: Imprenta de José Rodríguez, 1891.
———. *El idilio de Pedrín. Novelas,* Paris: Garnier Hermanos, 1922.
———. *Idos y muertos. Novelas.* Paris: Garnier Hermanos, 1922.
———. *Infanticida. Novelas.* Paris: Garnier Hermanos, 1922.
———. *Juan José.* 6th ed. Madrid: R. Velasco, 1897.

---

[1] As Dicenta published various collections of his newspaper articles and short stories, I have only listed them once. See <http://www.geocities.com/ Athens/ Forum/ 8915/ dicenta.html> for more information, yet remain cautious as to the accuracy of the bibliography attributed to Dicenta; there are serious errors.

———. *Juan José*. Madrid: Cátedra, 1992.
———. *Juan Francisco*. Madrid: R. Velasco, 1905.
———. *El león de bronce*. Madrid: R. Velasco, 1900.
———. "El león de bronce." *De la batalla*. Madrid: Imprenta de M. Núñez Samper, 1903.
———. *El lobo*. Barcelona, Biblioteca Teatro Mundial, 1914.
———. *Lorenza*. Madrid: R. Velasco, 1907.
———. *Los bárbaros*. Buenos Aires: [no publisher], 1930.
———. *Los de Abajo*. Madrid: Establecimiento tipografico de Antonio Marzo, 1913.
———. *Los irresponsables*. Barcelona: Biblioteca Teatro Mundial, 1915.
———. *Los majos de plante*. Madrid: R. Velasco, 1908.
———. *Luciano*. Madrid: Imprenta de José Rodríguez, 1894.
———. *Mares de España*. Madrid: Imprenta de Juan Pueyo, 1913.
———. *Marinera*. Madrid: R. Velasco, 1907.
———. *La mejor ley*. Madrid: Imprenta de José Rodríguez, 1889.
———. *Mi Venus*. Madrid: V. Rico, 1915.
———. *Novelas*. Paris: Garnier Hermanos, 1922.
———. *Página rota*. Madrid: [no publisher given], 1913.
———. *Pa mí que nieva*. Madrid: R. Velasco, 1904.
———. *Paraíso perdido*. Madrid: Sucesores de Hernando, 1917.
———. *Por Bretaña*. Madrid: A. Garrido, 1910.
———. *La promesa*. Madrid: Librería de los sucesores de Hernando, 1917.
———. *¡Quién fuera tú!*. Madrid: [no publisher given], 1917.
———. *Rebeldía*. Barcelona: E. Domenech, 1910.
———. *Raimundo Lulio*. 4th ed. Madrid: R. Velasco, 1902.
———. *Raymundo Lulio*. Madrid: Sociedad de Autores Españoles, [no date given].
———. *¡Redencion!*. Madrid: [no publisher given], 1912.
———. *El señor feudal*. Madrid: Sociedad de Autores Españoles, 1913.
———. *Sobrevivirse*. Barcelona: Biblioteca Teatro Mundial, 1914.
———. *Sol de invierno*. *Novelas*. Paris: Garnier Hermanos, 1922.
———. *El suicidio de Werther*. Barcelona: Biblioteca Teatro Mundial, 1916.
———. *Tinta negra*. Madrid: Librería de Fernando Fé, 1892.
———. *El tío Gervasio*. *Teatro*. Vol. 1. Madrid: R. Velasco, 1907. 82-94.
———. *Traperías*. Madrid: L. Arco, 1905.
———. *Una lección de amores*. Madrid: [no publisher given], 1927.
———. "Un divorcio." *De la batalla*. Madrid: Imprenta de M. Núñez Samper, 1903.
———. *El vals de las sombras*. Madrid: R. Velasco, 1908.Dicenta y Benedicto, Joaquín, and Manuel Paso. *Curro Vargas*. 2nd ed. Madrid: R. Velasco, 1899.
———. *La cortijera*. Madrid: R. Velasco, 1900.
Dicenta, Joaquín, and Pedro de Répide. *Los tres maridos burlados*. Madrid: R. Velasco, 1909.

Bibliography

Andrenio. "El homenaje a Dicenta." *La Gaceta Literaria*. March 1927.

Alarcón, Pedro Antonio de. *El niño de la bola*. Madrid: Impr. Central a cargo de V. Saiz, 1880.

Baroja, Pío. *Memorias. Obras Completas*. Vol. 7. Madrid: Biblioteca Nueva, 1949. 670-671, 735-784.

Benavente, Jacinto. *De sobremesa crónicas*. Madrid: F. Fé, 1910. 21.

Bieder, Maryellen. "The Modern Woman on the Spanish Stage: The Contributions of Gaspar and Dicenta." *Estreno* 7.2 (1981): 25-28.

Botrel, Jean François. "España, 1880-1890: el naturalismo en situación." Yvan Lissorgues, ed. *Realismo y naturalismo en España en la segunda mitad del siglo XIX*. Barcelona: Anthropos, 1988. 183-197.

Brady, Agnes M., and Margaret S. Husson, eds. *Five One-Act Spanish Plays*. New York: D. Appleton-Century Co., 1932.

Brockett, Oscar G. *History of the Theatre*. 5th ed. Boston: Allyn and Bacon, 1987.

Bueno, Manuel. *Teatro español contemporáneo*. Madrid: Biblioteca Renacimiento, 1909. 111-125.

Bustillo, José. "Los teatros." *La Ilustración Española y Americana* November 15 1895: 275-278.

Butler, Alban. *The Lives of the Saints*. Vol. 10. New York: P. J. Kenedy & Sons, 1936,

Calderón de la Barca, Pedro. *El gran Duque de Gandía*. Madrid: Guadarrama, 1969.

Campos, Jorge. *Teatro y sociedad en España (1780-1820)*. Madrid: Editorial Moneda y Crédito, 1969.

Carretero, José María [*El Caballero Audaz*]. *Lo que sé por mí: confesiones del siglo*. 2nd ed. Madrid: V.H. de Sanz Calleja, 1915. vol. 1 131-141.

———. "Joaquín Dicenta." *Galería: más de cien vidas extraordinarias contadas por sus protagonistas y comentadas*. Madrid: Ediciones Caballero Audaz, 1948. 631-637.

Campos, Jorge. *Teatro y sociedad en España (1780-1820)*. Madrid: Editorial Moneda y Crédito, 1969.

Cansinos Assens, Rafael. *La nueva literatura*. Madrid: Editorial Páez, 1927. 5-15.

Chapman, Charles E. *A History of Spain*. New York: The MacMillan Company, 1931.

Cook, John A. *Neo-classic Drama in Spain: Theory and Practice*. Dallas: Southern Methodist UP, 1959.

Cotarelo y Mori, Emilio. *Historia de la zarzuela*. Madrid: Tipografía de Archivos, 1934.

DeCoster, Cyrus. *Pedro Antonio de Alarcón*. Boston: Twayne, 1979.

Deleito y Piñuela, José. *Estampas del Madrid teatral fin de siglo*. Madrid: Saturnino Calleja, 1946. 55-60, 198-210.

Del Valle Ruiz, P. Restituto. "*Aurora* del señor Dicenta." *La Ciudad de Dios* 59 (1902): 560-569.

Dendle, Brian J. "Galdós, Zola y el naturalismo de *La desheredada*." Yvan Lissorgues, ed. *Realismo y naturalismo en España en la segunda mitad del siglo XIX*. Barcelona: Anthropos, 1988. 447-459

Díaz-Plaja, Fernando. *La vida española en el siglo XIX*. Madrid: Afrodisio Aguado, 1952.

Diez-Canedo, Enrique. *Conversaciones literarias*. Mexico: J. Mortiz, 1964. 46-49.
Dowling, John C. "The Madrid Theatre Public in the Eighteenth Century. Transition from the Popular Audience to the Bourgeois." In *Transactions of the Seventh International Congress: Studies on Voltaire and the Eighteenth Century*. Vol. 265. Oxford: The Voltaire Foundation, 1989. 1358-62.
Echegaray, José. *Teatro escogido*. 5th ed. Málaga: Aguilar, 1964.
Eguía Ruiz, Constancio. *Crítica patriótica*. Madrid: Tip.de la Revista de Archivos, Bibliotecas y Museos, 1921. 177-233.
Enciclopedia universal ilustrada. Vol. 49. Barcelona, Hijos de J. Espasa, 1924. 411-12.
Enciclopedia universal ilustrada. Vol. 24. Barcelona, Hijos de J. Espasa, 1924. 1039-45.
Escritores de Calatayud y su comarca: Joaquín Dicenta Benedicto. Centro de Estudios Bilbilitanos. 10 Jan. 2000 <http://www.geocities.com/Athens/Forum/8915/dicenta.html>[2]
Espina, Antonio. *Las mejores escenas del teatro español e hispanoamericano (desde sus orígenes hasta la época actual)*. Madrid: Aguilar, 1959.
Exum, Frances Bell. *The Treatment of Pedro I de Castilla in the Drama of Lope de Vega*. Diss. Florida State U, 1970. Ann Arbor: UMI, 1971. 7310210.
Farmer, David Hugh. *The Oxford Dictionary of Saints*. 2nd ed. Oxford: Oxford UP, 1987.
Feliú y Codina, José. *María del Carmen*. 5th ed. Madrid: R. Velasco, 1911.
Francos Rodríguez, Jose. *Contar vejeces, de las memorias de un gacetillero*. Madrid: Compañía Ibero-Americana de Publicaciones, 1927. 127-173.
García de la Huerta, Vicente. *Raquel*. Madrid: Editorial Castalia, 1987.
García Pavón, Francisco. *El teatro social en España (1895-1962)*. Madrid: Taurus, 1962.
Gies, David Thatcher. "Glorious Invalid: Spanish Theater In the Nineteenth Century." *Hispanic Review* 61 (1993): 213-246.
———. *The Theatre in Nineteenth-Century Spain*. Cambridge: Cambridge U P, 1994.
Gómez de Baquero, E. "Crónica literaria." *España Moderna*. 20.232 (1908): 155-162.
———. "Crónica literaria." *España Moderna* 84 (1895): 177-195.
González-Blanco, Andres. *Los dramaturgos espanoles contemporáneos*. Valencia: Editorial Cervantes, 1917. 204-294.
Gregersen, Halfdan. *Ibsen and Spain: A Study in Comparative Drama*. Cambridge: Harvard UP, 1936.
Guimerá, Angel. *Tierra baja*. Trans. José Echegaray. Madrid: Tipografía Yagües, 1924.
Hall, H.B. "Joaquín Dicenta and the Drama of Social Criticism." *Hispanic Review* 20 (1952): 44-66.
Klein, Richard Berry. *The Development of Realism in Late Nineteenth-Century Spanish Drama*. Diss. U of Illinois, 1970. Ann Arbor: UMI, 1975. 7020999.
Latimer, Elizabeth Wormeley. *Spain in the Nineteenth Century*. Chicago: A. C. McClurg and Co., 1907.
Literatura española. Universidad de Las Palmas de Gran Canaria. <http://orion.ulpgc.es/filologia/VSSWeb5c2LITESP3.htm>

---

[2] The information provided on this web site is questionable, as there are many works wrongly attributed to Dicenta. For example, *Los asistentes* 1895 was written by Pablo Parellada.

López de Ayala, Pedro. *Crónica de don Pedro Primero.* Madrid: Rivadeneyra, 1953.
Machado, Manuel. *Un año de teatro (Ensayos de crítica dramátcia).* Madrid: Biblioteca Nueva, 1918. 57-58, 151-154, 247-250.
Maeztu, Ramiro de. *Autobiografía.* Madrid: Editora Nacional, 1962. 53-60.
Mainer, Jose Carlos. *Literatura y pequeña burguesía en España.* Madrid: Edicusa, 1972. 29-57.
Martínez Cachero, José María. *Siglos XIX y XX.* León: Editorial Everest, 1995. Vol. 3 of *Historia de la literatura española.*
Martínez Ruíz, José. *Charivari. Obras completas.* Vol. 1. Madrid: Aguilar, 1947. 245-287.
Martínez Ruíz, José. *Ejercicios de castellano.* Madrid: Biblioteca Nueva, 1960. 105-108.
Mas, Jaime. "Introducción." *Juan José.* By Joaquín Dicenta. Madrid: Cátedra, 1992. 11-64
Mas Ferrer, Jaime. *Vida, teatro y mito de Joaquín Dicenta.* Alicante: Instituto de Estudios Alicantinos, 1978.
Mazas García, Alfonso de. Prefacio. *Garcés de Marsilla.* By Joaquín Dicenta. Madrid: Emiliano Escolar Editor, 1981. 11-50.
McCabe, Joseph. *Spain in Revolt 1814-1931.* London: John Lane, 1931.
McClelland, I.L. *Spanish Drama of Pathos 1750-1808.* 2 vols. Toronto: Toronto UP, 1970.
McKay, Douglas. *Carlos Arniches.* New York: Twayne, 1972.
Melcher, Edith. *Stage Realism in France between Diderot and Antoine.* Bryn Mawr: Bryn Mawr College, 1929.
Medina, Vicente. *Teatro.* Murcia: Academia Alfonso X El Sabio, 1987.
Montesinos, José F. *La corona merecida de Lope de Vega.* Madrid: Centro de Estudios Hispánicos, 1923. 136-146.
Montoto, José María. *Historia del reinado de don Pedro Primero de Castilla, llamado el cruel.* Seville: Santigosa, 1847.
Moore, Elise Provenchére. "Joaquín Dicenta, A Study of His Plays and Ideas." M.A. Thesis. Washington U, 1934.
Moore, John A. *Ramón de la Cruz.* New York: Twayne, 1972.
Mora, Francisco. *Historia del socialismo obrero español desde sus primeras manifestaciones hasta nuestros días.* Madrid: I. Calleja, 1902.
Morby, Edwin. "Notes on Dicenta Material and Method." *Hispanic Review* 9 (1941): 383-393.
Muñoz, Matilde. *Historia de la zarzuela y el género chico.* Madrid: Editorial Tesoro, 1946.
Myers, Judy Ann. "Social Drama of Joaquín Dicenta." M.A. Thesis. U of Georgia, 1972.
Núñez de Arce, Gaspar. "Raimundo Lulio." *Gritos del Combate.* Madrid: Fortanet, 1875. 151-184.
Paco, Mariano de. "Introducción." *Teatro.* By Vicente Medina. Murcia: Academia Alfonso X El Sabio, 1987. 11-54.
Paco de Moya, Mariano de. "María del Carmen, de Feliú y Codina." *Murgetana* 39 (1974): 65-75.
Palau, Melchor. "Juan José." *Revista Contemporánea* 10 December 30, 1895: 620-625.
Palomar, Fernando Castán. "Prólogo." *Los poetas.* Madrid: [no publisher], 1929. 5-12.

Payne, Stanley G. *A History of Spain and Portugal*. Vol. 2. Madison: Wisconsin UP, 1973.

Peak, J. Hunter. *Social Drama in Nineteenth-Century Spain*. Chapel Hill: North Carolina UP, 1964.

Pérez de Ayala, Ramón. "Juan José." *Obras completas*. Madrid: Aguilar, 1964. 455-58.

Pérez de la Dehesa, Rafael. *El grupo Germinal: una clave del 98*. Madrid: Taurus Ediciones, 1970. 17-105.

Ramos, Vicente. *Vida y teatro de Carlos Arniches*. Madrid: Alfguara, 1966.

Regidor Arribas, Ramón. *Aquellas zarzuelas...*. Madrid: Alianza Editorial, 1996.

Répide, Pedro de. "Prólogo." *Lorenza*. By Joaquín Dicenta. Madrid: R. Velasco, 1907. v-viii.

Rivas, Duque de. "Un solemne desengaño." *Romances II*. Madrid: Espasa-Calpe, 1965. 159-206.

Rubio Jiménez, Jesús. "El teatro en el siglo XIX (1845-1900)." *Historia del teatro en España*. Vol. 2. Ed. José María Díez Borque. Madrid: Taurus, 1988. 627-762.

———. *Ideología y teatro en España: 1890-1900*. Zaragoza: Libros Pórtico, 1982.

Ruiz Contreras, Luis. *Medio siglo de teatro infructuoso*. Madrid: CIAP, 1931. 121-129, 179-187.

Ruiz Ramón, Francisco. *Historia del teatro español*. Madrid: Alianza, 1967. 427-430.

Salaverría, José María. *La afirmación española; estudios sobre el pesimismo español y los nuevos tiempos*. Barcelona: Gustavo Gili, 1917. 330.

Salcedo, Angel S. *Ruperto Chapí, su vida y sus obras*. Córdoba: Hesperia, 1929.

Sánchez Portero, Antonio. *Noticia y antología de poetas bilbilitanos*. Calatayud: [no publisher], 1969. 139-149.

Sastre, Alfonso. *Drama y sociedad*. Madrid: Taurus, 1956.

Schinasi, Michael. "The Anarchy of Theatrical Genres in Mid-Nineteenth Century Spain." *Romance Languages Annual* 2 (1990): 534-38.

Schlegel, August Wilhelm. *Lectures on Dramatic Art and Literature*. Trans. John Black. London: Harrison and Co., 1846.

Sellés y Angel, Eugenio. *El nudo gordiano*. 2nd ed. Madrid: Tip de G. Estrada, 1878.

Shaw, Donald L. *A Literary History of Spain: The Nineteenth Century*. London: Ernest Benn, 1972.

Smith, W.F. "Contributions of Rodríguez Rubí to the Development of the *Alta Comedia*." *Hispanic Review* 10 (1942): 53-63.

Taylor, Florence Ivy. "Social Ideas in the Plays of Joaquín Dicenta." M.A. Thesis. U of Texas, 1930.

Tolstoy, Leo. *Resurrección*. Trans. Gonzalo Jover and Julio Ayuso. Barcelona: Casa editorial Maucci, 1903.

Toraño, Paulino García. *El rey don Pedro el cruel y su mundo*. Madrid: Ediciones Jurídicas y Sociales, 1996.

Torrente Ballester, Gonzalo. *Teatro español contemporáneo*. Madrid: Ediciones Guadarrama, 1957. 94-98.

Turner, Elizabeth Marie. "Joaquín Dicenta: (1863-1917) Un aspecto del teatro social." M.A. Thesis. Smith College, 1972.

Turrell, Charles Alfred. *Contemporary Spanish Dramatists*. Boston: Gorham, 1919.

Ugarte, Manuel. *Visiones de España: apuntes de un viajero argentino*. Valencia:

Prometeo, 1907. 117-119.
Unamuno, Miguel de. "La sociedad galdosiana." *Obras completas*. Vol. 5. Madrid: A Aguado, 1959. 466.
Weisler, Shawney Anderson. "Social Oprression and the Individual in the Theater of Joaquín Dicenta." M.A. Thesis. U of North Carolina at Chapel Hill, 1977.
Yxart, José. *El arte escénico en España*. Barcelona: La Vanguardia, 1894.
Zarzuela!. Ed. Christopher Webber. 9 Jan. 2000 <http://www.nashwan.demon.co.uk/zarzuela.htm>
Zorrilla y Moral, José. *El zapatero y el rey*. Madrid: Cuesta, 1901.
Zurita, Marciano. *Historia del género chico*. Madrid: Prensa Popular, 1920.

Printed in the United States
22818LVS00004BA/83